D1739161

CREATIVITY AND
MORAL VISION IN
PSYCHOLOGY

To my children
Anthony and Andrea

CREATIVITY AND
MORAL VISION IN
PSYCHOLOGY

Narratives on Identity and
Commitment in a Postmodern Age

Lisa Tsoi Hoshmand

SAGE Publications
International Educational and Professional Publisher
Thousand Oaks London New Delhi

For information:

SAGE Publications, Inc.
2455 Teller Road
Thousand Oaks, California 91320
E-mail@sagepub.com

SAGE Publications Ltd.
6 Bonhill Street
London EC2A 4PU
United Kingdom

SAGE Publications India Pvt. Ltd.
M-32 Market
Greater Kailash I
New Delhi 110048 India

Printed in the United States of America

Library of Congress Cataloging-in-Publication Data

Main entry under title:

  Creativity and moral vision in psychology: Narratives on identity and
  commitment in a postmodern age / by Lisa Tsoi Hoshmand.
      p. cm.
   Includes bibliographical references and index.
    ISBN 0-7619-0377-1 (cloth : acid-free paper). — ISBN
  0-7619-0378-X (pbk. : acid-free paper)
      1. Psychologists—Professional ethics—Case studies.
   I. Hoshmand, Lisa Tsoi, 1947-
   BF76.4.C74 1998
   150'.92'2—dc21
   [B]   97-45464

Acquiring Editor:	Jim Nageotte
Editorial Assistant:	Anna Howland
Production Editor:	Sanford Robinson
Production Assistant:	Denise Santoyo
Designer/Typesetter:	Danielle Dillahunt
Cover Designer:	Ravi Balasuriya
Print Buyer:	Anna Chin

Contents

Preface

This project began with an interest in the personal commitments that sustain uncommon professional contributions, and in what constitutes creativity in professional life. The inquiry took the form of biographical case studies, as I have learned that they can be illuminating and educational. Through David Lipsett's biography, for example, I have come to appreciate the rich intellectual context of the life and work of Gregory Bateson, anthropologist and pioneer thinker in cybernetic theory. From the autobiographical writings of Bruner and Sarason, contemporary psychologists who have made a significant impact on the field, I have derived academic insight and personal inspiration. These readings have convinced me of the value of such accounts, in which the personal opens the way into the social and the cultural. Autobiography is not mere subjectivity that serves its own ends, and biography is not simply voyeurism toward another's lived experience. It seems that we all create our own existential questions and search for answers in our encounters with other lives. Through reflection and mutual articulation, we seek a vision of moral, social coexistence.

In a previous project on applied epistemology, using naturalistic accounts of the thought processes and actions of researchers, I learned that the research activities of colleagues in therapeutic psychology are guided in many instances by "non-epistemic" factors. Differences in their approach to knowledge could not be explained completely by the heuristic reasoning used in problem solving during inquiry. I also learned that a person's worldview and knowledge interests derive not only from cognitive forms of rationality but also from deeply personal, social, and affective sources. The fact that normative considerations are involved in evaluating scientific and professional contributions poses questions of judg-ment. It became clear to me that to understand the transcendental goals of a person's work and its worth, we need to have a broader conception of knowledge and human rationality. We also need to move beyond the ordinary boundaries of science and the philosophy of science.

In the present project, I examine, from a cultural-developmental perspective, how one's participation in professional life represents identity achievement and moral functioning in particular contexts. My purpose is to develop and apply a conceptual framework that will link knowledge interests and creativity in professional life to identity development and existential choices. By focusing on the activities and practices of a group of professionals, I hope to illuminate the kinds of purposes and values that inform the life commitments of those in the professions. Some may consider this a project on descriptive ethics. Unlike traditional theoretical ethics, which mainly deals with meta principles of ethics, it aims to have more immediate relevance to moral living and, therefore, to restore the relationship between ethical theory and practice. To what extent this is achievable is of concern to those interested in understanding moral philosophy and identity development from a psychological and sociocultural point of view.

I have selected psychologists for this study because I am interested in how epistemic and moral issues are addressed by others in my profession in a postmodern age of relativism. In presenting the personal insights and moral vision of several contemporary psychologists who have made uncommon contributions, I hope to stimulate reflective dialogue that will have an impact on the professions. A narrative, hermeneutic approach is used in conjunction with the methodology of multiple-case study. To the extent possible, a social philosophical critique of the constructed text is attempted. Through this type of reflexive dialogical process, I propose that we can develop an expanded rationality as a community in dealing with issues of knowledge and in adopting moral stances.

This book has three parts. Part I provides the conceptual and methodological background for the project. In Chapter 1, I present ways of conceptualizing and studying moral identity in relation to issues of knowledge and creative living. I focus on how narrative, hermeneutic methods can be applied to biographical case study of professional identity and commitment, and what the methodologi-cal and conceptual justifications are for using such methods. Additional notes on methodology are included in the appendix for reference by students and other interested researchers.

Part II consists of facilitated autobiographical sketches contributed by a number of contemporary psychologists. These accounts of professional careers and lives illustrate the existential choices the individuals have made in terms of contributions to knowledge and society. They are presented with reference to the work of the psychologists and other documentation of their views.

Part III consists of a summative analysis of the accounts in Part II and further examination of the larger intellectual and professional context in which the emergent ideas and issues can be located. In Chapter 9, I explore the relationship between professional identity, creative projects, and moral vision, based on the biographical narratives in Part II and the interview data obtained from the participants. I focus on career patterns, gender issues, and social factors. I also summarize the perspectives of the participants on knowledge, the state of the profession, and issues of rationality and moral living. To contextualize the narrative construction of these texts of identity and the critical issues in their embedding societal context, I review in Chapter 10 the relevant philosophical discourse as a resource for readers who are interested in the proposed solutions to postmodern problems of relativism. I also discuss the implications for professional education and socialization. In concluding this project, I hope to have brought us full circle from ethical theory to practice, and back to ethical understanding.

I am indebted to the exceptional group of colleagues who have allowed their careers and lives to be examined here, and who have most generously shared their personal experience and insights with me. Without their contribution and trust in the dialogical process, this project would not have been possible. They will be a continuing source of inspiration for me, and, I hope, students and others who wish to be part of any reflective-generative profession. I am also thankful to Jim Nageotte and Sanford Robinson at Sage for their support and assistance in the production of this book. An additional note of gratitude is due to Donald Peterson and Roland Tharp, who not only contributed as authors but also offered very helpful suggestions in the final revision and organization of this manuscript. Finally, I wish to acknowledge my own family, who have provided me with grounding in values, and all who have given me hope for our common future.

LISA TSOI HOSHMAND

PART
I

CONCEPTUAL AND METHODOLOGICAL FRAMEWORK

CHAPTER 1

Knowledge, Creativity, and Moral Identity

LISA TSOI HOSHMAND

A ll of us, in moments of reflection, have questioned if we should be doing what we do and continue living the kinds of lives that we choose. My own questions concerning knowledge, creativity, and moral vision came from a growing desire to evaluate my own life, the knowledge and practices of my profession, and whether we are making significant contributions to the field and society at large. It is fitting that these questions should occur at midlife, but there are additional reasons for their timeliness. I have found issues of knowledge and judgments on the value of what we do as professionals (in this case, academic psychologists, researchers, and practitioners) to involve considerations that are highly complex and sometimes controversial. Having worked in university-based academic programs, a variety of mental health settings, and more recently a freestanding professional school, I feel that there are strengths and limitations as well as a range of values in these different cultures. Not only when confronted with critical incidents, but also in everyday professional life, I have had to negotiate my way through signals that are unclear, or contend with informal norms alien to my culture of origin. I attribute this ambiguity to the society and times that we inhabit.

It is intellectually and emotionally challenging to define oneself and a professional life of value in a climate of relativism that is accentuated by the

Postmodern age. Professional work inevitably involves conflict, both personally and socially, in the midst of diverse cultural forces with no common foundation of agreement. Dokecki (1995) describes the moral predicament of the contemporary professional as being faced with not only the postmodern lack of moral clarity but also tensions between the altruistic ideals of service and self-interested economic survival. He suggests that the answer to this predicament requires a creative response that can be likened to the improvisations of a jazz musician whose art comes not from convention, but from innovation. Hence, we may regard the resolution of moral conflicts and existential questions in a person's articulation of professional identity as a creative process in itself.

Clarity of existential stances presumably comes with moral commitment. I admire those in my profession who have led productive lives and acted with integrity and conviction. How these individuals make existential choices can be instructive for the rest of us. By studying their life circumstances and the problems to which they have responded in word and deed, I hope to come away with a better understanding of the creative drive in professional lives and identity development. To the extent that the actions of these individuals have addressed social issues from a value base, they may illuminate the nature of moral commitment and the reality context in which moral visions are actualized.

CREATIVITY AND EXISTENTIAL COMMITMENTS

Bruner (1962), writing about the conditions of creativity, commented that it is not sufficient to be merely useful, but that to be creative involves excellence and finding a dignity beyond the dominant value of practicality. Immediacy, passion, a freedom to be absorbed, and a paradoxical combination of detachment and commitment are some of the qualities he identified with being creative. Bruner derived his understanding of creativity from the arts and the humanities, viewing it as both a personal and a cultural phenomenon. As a cultural psychologist, he acknowledged the cultural sources of such powers as myth that shape our identity and participation in life. He suggested looking into the internal drama of each person for those instances of the "working out" of identity conflict that result in creative and surprising production.

Similarly, Runyun (1996) proposed that biographical studies can reveal the context of a person's creative work. He considered personal stories to be an important part of the analysis of cultural creativity, complementing economic, political, historical, and sociocultural analyses. One may gauge the level of creativity in a discipline or profession by the creative possibilities and constraints experienced by its members. My own view is that the personal and the social are co-constituted. Creativity is not just a cultural artifact, but is kept alive by the very process of articulating one's personal identity and social existence. In Oriental thought, the creative act is formative of self and the world, and purposeful, with life-giving vitality and power.

It would appear that notions of creativity are culturally rooted in the same way that our moral identities are culturally derived. Deutsch (1992) observed that theories of creativity are always closely related to a culture's cosmology. Judeo-Christian cultures emphasize purposive production of the new, like the creator's work. Thus, the term *creative* is applied not only to works of art but also to the productive work of scientists and others. In both Western and non-Western thought, creativity is associated with freedom and play, with rare form and grace that come with disciplined control of a medium. There is a communing aspect or subject-object unity in the creative process (Kelman, 1963). The end of creative activity is realized in the process itself, or the quality of the act, not in any uniform purpose.

This does not mean that purpose is irrelevant. Arasteh and Arasteh (1976) state that creativity in adulthood involves a vision and the purposeful actualization of that vision. They emphasize the transcending of cultural thresholds to follow one's creative tendencies. Sternberg and Lubart (1996) characterize creative people as being able to pursue novel ways of thinking in the face of resistance. Gruber (1988) and Wallace and Gruber (1989) apply an evolving-systems model to the study of creativity. They note developmental changes in a person's purpose, knowledge, and affect, concomitant with creative production. These recent researchers of creativity also favor multidimensional theories that consider a confluence of factors over unitary explanations.

In researching creativity in the life and work of professionals, one can adopt a multidimensional perspective and look for developmental shifts, examples of deviation from prevailing norms and ways of thought, and a sense of vision for alternative possibilities. When many intellectuals of our time have been drawn to the types of individual autonomy and expressivism spawned from the modern age (Bellah, Madsen, Sullivan, Swidler, & Tipton, 1985), one wonders to what extent social responsibility and commitment enter into creativity in professional life. The moral aspects of professional work deserve attention more than ever before, as we continue to assert the value of what we do and justify our ways of being in a postmodern age of shifting horizons.

▰▰▰▰▰▰ MORAL ONTOLOGY IN PROFESSIONAL DISCOURSE AND PROFESSIONAL LIVES

Although psychology is one of the disciplines that study human nature, moral nature is not a main focus of psychological science. Since academic psychology separated from its philosophical parent, we have reframed questions about moral ontology in quasi-scientific terms, for moral discourse is not supported by scientific ideology. Scientific methods of inquiry and the standards of objectivity associated with them tend to promote a psychology that does not give primacy to the intentions, values, and purposes of humans as morally aware agents of our own actions (Howard, 1985). Other than as issues of compliance with professional codes of conduct, moral concerns have not been at the center stage of psychology as a profession. Moral psychology as an area of inquiry has received attention mainly from developmental researchers, with its conceptual and substantive focus confined to cognitive and social development as precursors of mature moral functioning.

Theorists and researchers of moral development tend to separate the cognitive and social processes they study from the timeless questions about human virtues and visions of the good life and the good society. This relative neglect of the moral domain by my own and other science-based disciplines can be traced to the period of Enlightenment in Western history, when scientific rationality was adopted as the authoritative form of rationality. Empirical science, in replacing the moral precepts and authority of the Church, also favored material and efficient causes over final cause (Hoshmand, 1994). Philosophers of science in the modern period further emphasized the cognitive value of logical analysis, divorcing scientific reality from the realm of values. This has remained so in the Postmodern era, even though sociologists of knowledge have pointed to the value-ladenness of scientific theories. In the moral domain, the necessity of traditional metaphysics or transcendent beings is likewise called into question in conceiving of ethical systems. At the same time, contemporary philosophers have conceded that issues in moral discourse cannot be resolved by logical and linguistic analysis (see Jacobs, 1989), a problem to which we will return at the end of this book. It is against this historical background that the desire for new ways of thinking about our moral ontology has emerged, a desire that is felt across disciplines.

Professional life is one of the contexts for considering moral ways of being. In discussing professional identity in the Postmodern era, Newbrough (1993) proposed the concept of reflective and generative practice. A professional is one who engages in value-based work and continuously reflects on the merit and assumptions of such work. Science, which many professionals use to legitimize their social credibility, is not value-free. When applied in action, it invites evaluation of purpose and impact. Generativity comes in the potential creation of knowledge through practice, and in the engendering of care in a relationship. Dokecki (1995) further elaborated on the ethical implications of reflective-generative practice by exploring how professionals can give priority to goods internal, rather than external, to their practice. Moral purpose and intrinsic values in the search for knowledge and its application are relevant to the subject of this book.

Professionals may experience identity crises resulting from loss of faith toward our prevailing system of beliefs and practices. Referring to the growing disenchantment with the approaches to knowledge and living brought about by modern science, Heshusius (1994) proposed that we find re-enchantment in a "managed subjectivity." By this he meant a letting go of the preoccupation with self, and a move into a participatory mode of consciousness. He believed that such a state of consciousness, with its full somatic presence and deep empathy for the other, can render the act of knowing an ethical act. Unlike the alienation of total subjectivity and objectivity, a participatory mode of consciousness grants a basic kinship in social living. Dokecki (1995) similarly conceives of an ecologically situated, caring professional. The commonality in these proposed ways of dealing with intellectual problems of faith consists of one's connection with community.

When Sarason (1993) voiced his concern about psychologists' disinterest in religion and the human need for transcendence, he pointed to the separation between belief in divinity and belongingness to social community. Underscoring the acute need for a psychological sense of community in contemporary life, Sarason raised two empirical questions. The first concerns whether one can sustain a sense of community without a sense of transcendence or the sense that one's purposes are meaningful in terms of a commitment to the present and future purposes of a collectivity. The second concerns whether a secular base for transcendence can give sufficient meaning to how one lives. These are questions that we as psychologists must first confront for ourselves, then try to understand in others. When the need or desire for transcendence arises, and what the origins and contexts of community may be for a given individual during the course of professional life, as well as the nature of commitment to causes larger than ourselves, are some of the questions explored in the present project.

It is possible to address issues of moral existence in a naturalistic study because transcendental goals and moral systems have empirical realities that are reflected in personal histories and cultural traditions. Rather than dismiss transcendental questions and existential choices as belonging to the metaphysical realm (and therefore outside the interest of scientific psychology), I propose that we explore the relationship between the psychological and the moral. It seems to me that the conduit from the scientific to the moral involves understanding personal ways of knowing as an integral part of personal ways of being. Furthermore, we can locate the nexus between a person's existential stance and activities of knowing in the communities and practices of which the person is a part. These communities and practices engender norms and values, and, as I will argue, constitute the fabric of moral living.

In advocating a naturalistic study of the moral, I do not mean to promote psychologism. The "psychological" for me is inseparable from the social and the cultural. Human intentions and moral consciousness are revealed in personal as well as collective convictions, meanings, and actions in the communal context of living. We approach matters of knowledge within the symbolic and physical practices appropriated from our cultural and social environment. These practices that constitute modes of mutual action and social relationship enable collective agency and mutual accountability as we continue to interpret and respond to human realities. Rabinow and Sullivan (1987) explain that whereas objectivists and subjectivists, respectively, search for a reality before and behind our cultural world, one who uses an interpretive approach to human experience recognizes the irreducibility of intersubjective meanings. In granting intersubjectivity as the substance of cultural living, we may have a way of understanding diverse forms of knowing in relation to different ways of being.

An implicit assumption I hold about knowledge is that our intellectual interests and epistemic beliefs are inseparable from the cultural-psychological processes that shape our moral commitments and worldviews. Some consider all ontological beliefs (such as found in psychological theories of human nature) to be at root metaphysical, in which case psychologies and moralities are not dissimilar (Much & Harré, 1994). One may also regard science, with its powerful system of ideas and practices, as a special variety of metaphysics that modern cultures have endorsed. We can subject it to the same human understanding and social critique as other metaphysical systems that are symbolically constructed and communally shared. To the extent that the ideas and practices of psychologists and other professionals are culturally appropriated, they too can be subjected to critique and study.

My present ways of thinking and speaking about issues of knowledge and moral being place me within the discourse communities that consider human development, cognition, emotion, and epistemology as social (Cole, 1988;

Fuller, 1992; Harré, 1983; Rogoff, 1990). I resonate with a cultural conception of mind (Vygotsky, 1978; Wertsch, 1991), just as I find meaning and usefulness in the phenomenologist's approach to consciousness (Marx, 1992; Schutz, 1966). I tend to subscribe to a dialectical conception of development (Riegel, 1976) that is informed to some degree by constructionist ideas of selfhood (Markus & Nurius, 1986; Shotter & Gergen, 1989)—I believe that identity development results from the reciprocal interaction of personal and cultural factors in both their potentiating and constraining influences. How one's membership in such various discourse communities manifests itself in one's intellectual activities and professional life is of interest to me. This interest reflects the same valuing of reflexivity that I have emphasized in my previous writings (Hoshmand, 1994; Hoshmand & Martin, 1995; Hoshmand & Polkinghorne, 1992).

A reflexive question central to the present project concerns our own willingness (as social scientists and cultural observers, if not historians) to subject to judgment both ourselves and the communities in which we claim membership. Should we be evaluated (in our capacity for making sound intellectual and moral judgments) only by fellow experts, or by all who are competent in the natural language that is at the base of our academic and professional discourse? In whom do we place epistemic and moral confidence? How can we avoid ethnocentrism and professional myopia in applying standards of intelligibility? Above all, what may be the necessary conditions that would allow us to maintain the possibility of critical reflexivity and comparison? These questions provide the backdrop for this project.

In the remaining sections of this chapter, I review previous approaches to moral psychology and the psychological study of identity, leading to the need for a broadened conceptual and methodological framework for understanding moral identity.

▬▬▬ FROM ETHICAL THEORY TO MORAL PSYCHOLOGY

A central problem that ethical theory has to address is relativism, which is acute in the Postmodern age. Relativism implies for some an emotivist position that all judgments are merely a function of attitudes or feelings (Tierney, 1994). Yet, although people can choose to act or live a certain way by personal preference, not all actions and ways of living are justified in a given society. Objections to a subjective approach to issues of ethics have led to a polarizing tendency to stress objective standards of rationality (Trainer, 1991). These extremes of belief in human nature, based on an overconfidence in or mistrust of emotive and cognitive sources of judgment, call for a more realistic moral psychology.

The cognitive view of rationality reinforced by the scientific worldview had previously given way to a psychological conception of moral reasoning that presumes a developmental readiness in all people. Piaget's (1970) theory and research, on how cognitive processes show assimilative and accommodative changes with experience, provided a structural conception of epistemic development. Based on Piaget's genetic epistemology, Kohlberg (1984) theorized that moral development would proceed logically and sequentially in preparing an individual for rational decision making according to more or less universal ethical standards. Deriving support largely from a Kantian deontological or duty-based ethics, Kohlberg presumes in his model of moral development a universal standard of justice. His work reflects the universalist tradition of principle-based ethics premised on rational judgment. Although it opens the way for a developmental understanding of moral identity, it does not account as well for the divergent content of ethical systems or nonrational sources of moral choice. The concern is that cognitive theories of rationality may leave us with the prospect that individual and group economic self-interest might prevail as the "rational" choice.

Bandura (1991) tried to improve on cognitive theories of moral development with social learning theory, which emphasizes social and cultural influences on behavior. The concept of self-regulation he used implies human agency, as opposed to only factors of extrinsic determinism such as found in situational ethics. In acknowledging the role of the agent in human action, as well as the limits of self-regulation, we have the beginnings of a psychologically realistic model of moral action. From the perspective of human agency, Howard (1996) proposed that we return to a first-person psychology by attending to how holistic life stories as self-interpreted narratives serve to give coherence to a person's past and future actions. Thus, first-person narratives are used in this project as a source of information on the personal goals and intentions associated with moral ways of being.

Another line of research and theorizing that departs from the cognitive bias in the psychology of moral development came from Gilligan and her associates (Brown, Tappan, Gilligan, Miller, & Argyris, 1989; Gilligan, 1988, 1993). Partly in reaction to the gender bias in Kohlberg's research sample, this group highlighted the possibility of different moral voices and illustrated how people make sense of an actual moral conflict. The importance of context and the presence of relational motives such as care, which they demonstrated, added to the conception of moral psychology in situational ethics and justice-based principle ethics.

The morality of care is premised on the development of a virtuous self. Recent discussions of professional ethics in psychology have appropriately acknowledged the need to strike a better balance between principle ethics and virtue ethics (Bersoff, 1996; Kitchener, 1996; Meara, Schmidt, & Day, 1996). If professionals such as psychologists are to serve the common good, we have to be capable of ethical discernment and willingly choose to act in morally responsible ways beyond what is required by external regulation. On the other hand, the emphasis on individual character alone may increase the risk of idiosyncratic or unsound judgments. A psychologically realistic model of the development of moral identity must be able to account for the complex motivations of the moral self in total life context. Furthermore, it should help us understand how communities develop moral sense and justify their ways of living.

Giddens (1991) carried forth the notion of individual commitment to collective agency in instantiating social and moral goods. Personal choices enter into life politics and are given coherence by reflexive self-examination and dialogue. Little effort has been made, however, to study the very process by which professional communities (such as psychologists) evolve their ethical principles and standards, or to evaluate the moral goods constitutive of professional knowledge and practices. From a critical, hermeneutic perspective (Morrow & Brown, 1994), any interpretive analysis of communal efforts should include a deconstruction of ideas and practices in terms of their underlying assumptions and values. Critical theorists (Fox & Prilleltensky, 1997; Prilleltensky, 1994) have addressed the social ethics of psychology as a profession. In examining the political and social-ideological implications of our approaches to theory and practice, these authors criticized scientism and professionalization for maintaining the status quo and failing to share power with ordinary citizens. Psychologists and other professionals are faced with the challenge of demonstrating, through personal and collective agency in our work and professional commitments, a social ethic beyond individual self-interest and guild-interests.

As suggested previously, creative managing of inherent moral tensions in professional life would have to come from a reflective and generative professional self. It takes a socially responsible person to choose to set aside selfinterest to act with good intentions as depicted in virtue ethics. To conceive of human virtue and the good life as intertwined with our social nature and cultural-psychological being is not a new idea in moral philosophy. Aristotle (see *The Nicomachean Ethics,* 1980) was concerned with linking morality to human agency and personhood. Purpose and telos presume a human being capable of exercising logos and self-direction toward the good life. This moral sense, according to Aristotle, is supposed to be developed from practical living. We are able to understand human action and evaluate others as moral agents based on our practical knowledge and internalized norms of living (Jacobs, 1989). Developmentally, moral action and moral cognition seem to come with an increased ability to take responsibility for knowing and using the knowledge of what is right and true (Blasi, 1980; Lyons, 1983). This capacity is rooted in identity in the sense that the self becomes the source of moral compulsion, enacting one's intentionality.

MacIntyre's (1981) work on virtue ethics is an example of an attempt at grounding moral understanding in personal character and life history. Though more absorbed by issues of selfhood in relation to the particular conditions of modernity, the philosopher Taylor (1989) also attempted to find meaning in life history and the social nature of existence. The translation of such ethical theories into psychological and social terms, however, has yet to be realized. We need a type of discourse that includes a complex mix of conceptual, empirical, and philosophical dimensions. A conceptual framework that bridges the otherwise separate domains—those of the epistemic and the moral—may enable us to connect the psychology of knowing with moral reasoning and being.

To seek a broadened view of rationality, some have turned to phenomenological and interpretive theories of action (Packer, 1992; Tappan & Brown, 1992), and others to a socioanalytic perspective (Baumrind, 1992; Hogan, Johnson, & Emler, 1978). From a phenomenological point of view, ethical awareness is given in the experience of emotional attunement and the social nature of the life-world (Marx, 1992). Like practical wisdom derived from the experienced knowledge of practical living, such awareness is more often "prereflective" than the result of conscious deliberation of rules (such as implied in cognitive views of rationality). Compassion for others comes from the existential awareness of our mortality and our participation as members of interlinked life-worlds. Moral ways of being consist not of calculated reasoning but rather of self-interpretation in the concrete social contexts of living. Instead of an isolated self, a social self serves as the agent of moral action.

By invoking the concept of social phenomenology, we have a theoretical basis for using phenomenological accounts of life-world projects to understand a person's moral consciousness. If moral commitments are understood experientially over the course of professional life, identity development becomes the unifying focus. I comment next on the ways in which my own discipline has approached the study of identity and on how the limitations of our previous efforts have led to an interest in multidisciplinary contributions. I review in the following sections some of the conceptual and methodological developments that have paved the way for a broader understanding of identity.

━━━━━ BROADENING THE PSYCHOLOGICAL
STUDY OF IDENTITY

Psychological theories of personality have focused on identity formation in adolescence and young adulthood, with early concepts being informed by psychoanalytic thought. As Freud's theory was followed by the development of interpersonal concepts, ego psychology, object relations theory, and self psychology (Eagle & Wolitzky, 1995; Strozier, 1985), identity became associated with self structures and ego development. Although the unifying function of the ego implies a certain human capacity for rationality (Allport, 1968), its interaction with the collective or "non-self other" was not a primary focus in early theorizing. Rather, the lingering impact in the use of an individual's psychohistory or biography as an explanation of personality reflected an individualistic bias in Western concepts of selfhood. This is seen in Erikson's (1980) eight-stage theory of psychosocial development, in which valued developmental outcomes, such as individual autonomy, reflect culturally embedded beliefs.

An exception to the individualistic emphasis may be found in the work of Jung (1933, 1961), who was interested in non-Western ideas and conceived of a collective consciousness with metaphysical links to our cultural existence. Jung viewed the maturing adult as adapting to contrary tendencies in personality, thus introducing a dialectical dimension in development. Just as there was little questioning of the individualistic assumptions of personality theories in psychology, gender differences in development were generally neglected. Karen Horney (1950) was one of the first theorists to take issue with Freud's portrayal of women and his overvaluing of male sexuality. Concentrated efforts toward understanding gender differences in identity development did not capture the attention of the field until more recent years (see Gilligan, 1993).

Stage-theories of adult development such as Erikson's imply a more or less universal path of linear progression that does not account for individual differences in developmental process. Marcia (1966) modified Erikson's theory by proposing process variations that result in what he termed identity confusion, foreclosure, moratorium, or achievement. Josselson (1987) applied Marcia's concepts to research on adult development in women. Her research suggested that identity achievement can occur past the years of young adulthood, depending on the approach taken by the individual. Whereas some individuals may foreclose early in choosing their personal commitment or identity projects, others can remain in a moratorium state of identity search for an extended period until there is resolution. Her research lent support to the notion that there is intentionality or personal agency in identity development, and probably diverse paths and patterns as a function of person-environment interaction.

Another theoretical tradition in the study of identity follows from Murray's (1938) idiographic approach to personology. Murray's work had stimulated theorizing on psychological needs and research on personal motives. The framing of life motives continued to reflect a cultural emphasis on individual achievement (McClelland, 1961) as well as related motives such as power (McAdams, 1985; Winter, 1973), until individualistic concepts of self were challenged by cross-cultural theories and research. Contrasts between Asian and Western perspectives of the self have pointed to the strongly relational nature of selfhood in Asian psychology as well as philosophy (Markus & Kitayama, 1991; Marsella, DeVos, & Hsu, 1985). Comparison of concepts of selfhood across cultural traditions suggests that they can be traced to metaphysical assumptions about the nature of human existence and, at the same time, have manifestations in everyday consciousness and ways of living (Hoshmand & Ho, 1995). This allows us to evaluate the societal effects of particular forms of identity.

Ideological concerns with the realistic moral implications of the construction of identity in Western psychology (Cushman, 1990, 1993; Heller, Sosnia, & Wellber, 1987; Sampson, 1988, 1989, 1993) have also led to a new emphasis on the social dimension of selfhood. Because individualistic conceptions of self-hood and identity in Western psychology have been associated with reduction-istic research methodology in the practice of scientific psychology (Ho, 1993), however, conceptual advances in this area were constrained until alternative inquiry approaches became acceptable (see Appendix A for notes on methodo-logical developments). The postmodern questioning of methodological alle-giance to objectivist science has coincided for some with an interest in methods of inquiry that involve narrative and discursive modes that are more suited for the study of human intentions and meanings (Hoshmand, 1994). By using an interpretive approach to identify patterns of meaning in individual lives as narrated and enacted, these methods offer ways of understanding the complex interplay of personal agency in action with social and cultural factors for people in their life contexts.

We can find further support for a social and moral conception of selfhood and identity outside the discipline of psychology. Identity as portrayed in literature is almost always concerned with the self-consciousness of the actor's own intentions and actions and how they are perceived by others. The protago-nist's self-direction and expression of personal meanings offer opportunities for the molding of moral identity in a relational context, with social affirmation and disapproval. Possible stances are negotiated through interaction. Alternative ways of being are considered and internalized as reflexive talk. Not only will a character encounter many others in a given life space, but through our participation as readers who interact with the author's work or the narrating self as author, will undergo further interpretation and transformation. Although a certain protagonist may appear to represent the author's own voice, more than one voice often is associated with the development of a given character. Bakhtin (1973, 1981) applied this polyphonic nature of the novel, in particular, to the psychological understanding of identity. A person is at once his or her own author and multiply coauthored as a relational self.

This dynamic view of identity is supported by the recent interest in narrative psychology (Sarbin, 1986), which focuses on the self-interpretation of life stories. The multiple authoring of the self may be thought of as imagined internal dialogues of the relational self (Hermans & Kempen, 1993; Hermans, Rijks, & Kempen, 1993). Each voice conjures up a facet of one's history. It is in this sense that social constructionists regard identity as a product of human construction with symbolic processes and meanings that have social and cultural origins (Harré, 1983; Shotter, 1984; Shotter & Gergen, 1989). The idea that identity is achieved by story-form self-interpretation and social construction in the complex process of cultural living (Taylor, 1989) is consistent with the notion of the self as polyphonic, or multiauthored and multivoiced (Gergen, 1991).

A corollary of this is the conception of self or identity as a lifelong achievement (Coupland & Nussbaum, 1992). Life history and life story are intertwined in the process of self-interpretation. MacIntyre (1981) uses conversation or narrative as a core metaphor for human transactions such that human actions are "enacted narratives" (p. 211). Contrary to methodological behaviorism, which takes a detached observer's view of behavior, he argues that behavior is adequately characterized only when we know about the actor's intentions. To recount a person's actions, "we are involved in writing a narrative history" (p. 208). We shift from treating history as explanation to understanding history as a process. Ricoeur (1984) suggests that, from a phenomenological standpoint, narrative reflects the temporal sequence of life as lived. Narratives give life intelligibility by placing it on a meaningful continuum that connects past, present, and future, enabling people to chart the course of their lives.

The enactment of self narratives often corresponds to the performance of social roles. The previously cited research work by Gilligan and by Josselson suggests that there are gender differences in the developmental achievement of identity. How this is manifested in the simultaneous development of professional identity and career paths is of interest here. McMahon (1995) reports that women experience motherhood as an engendering process by which their identities are transformed. The cultural meanings of motherhood in this case provide the material for individual women to achieve gendered identities and gendered lives, even as they embark on varied paths under varied circumstances. The everyday living of a mother's role leads to perceived character changes and moral self-valuation, thus symbolically linked to female morality. This suggests that self-directed role enactment, such as in professional life, may be at once engendering and transformative of moral identity.

The self-directed aspects of life narrative also have to be understood in relation to the other-directed nature of identity achievement. MacIntyre (1981) argues that a person embodies and lives a narrative history that is uniquely his or her own, but is thoroughly grounded in the social: "the story of my life is always embedded in the story of those communities from which I derive my identity. . . . The possession of an historical identity and the possession of a social identity coincide" (p. 204). Levinas (1991) brings moral meaning to identity by speaking for "the other" that has been subjugated under "the self" in individualistic cultures. "My ethical relationship of love for the other stems from the fact that the self cannot survive by itself alone, cannot find meaning within its own being-in-the-world, within the ontology of sameness" (Levinas & Kearney, 1974/1986, p. 21).

This dialectic of self and otherness in identity achievement is reflected in social discourse and therapeutic notions of the human capacity for self-change (Hermans & Hermans-Jansen, 1995; Mair, 1988). Parry and Doan (1994) and other constructivists stress the revision and reconstruction of narratives. People have to deal with contingencies and constraints in life by changing direction, reformulating meanings, and re-envisioning the future. White and Epston (1989) consider these constraints to include the dominant discourse of a culture and the person's socialization. Following Foucault's view of power, White in particular has recommended that therapists assist clients in liberating themselves from the constraints of socially and culturally derived oppression, by externalizing the source of problems from the person to the dominant discourse and source of power. Revision of self involves not only taking authorship of one's life but also dealing critically with the larger social and cultural context. How this is manifested in professional lives is examined in this project.

To summarize, conceptual gains in the study of identity have come from a more dynamic and less linear view of the developmental process. Identity is now recognized as a lifelong achievement, motivated by personal agency in reciprocal interaction with ecological forces, and marked by signifiers that vary as a function of socially and culturally ascribed meanings. The narrative understanding of lives parallels the understanding of identity, both for the actor and for the other. Cross-discipline conceptions of identity development are beginning to follow a social-constructionist and cultural-historical approach to human ontology. The moral dimension of selfhood and identity consists of the accountability of the self to the social world and its co-constitution with the other as cultural beings. This merging of the psychosocial realm with the moral provides a new opportunity for addressing questions related to our moral ontology, in this case, by examining professional identity and commitment in a broad context.

THE DEVELOPMENT OF PROFESSIONAL IDENTITY IN CONTEXT

From a broadened conceptual standpoint, identity consists of personal ways of knowing and personal ways of being that are continuously evolved in the process of mutual action in our social world. I have argued from a multidisciplinary view that identity development is inherently moral in nature. It can be comprehended through narrative accounts and by placing the developmental process within its cultural-historical context. McMahon (1995) illustrates in her study of motherhood that both the historically situated self and the biographically narrated self are co-constituted by culture and society, including mythology and political realities that affect role enactment. It follows that professional identity can be gleaned from actual participation in one's discipline and profession, as well as self narratives on one's career and life, in the cultural and political realities of the time.

There is precedent in using narrative approaches in the study of moral commitment among productively involved people. Colby and Damon (1992) used the case study method and in-depth interviews to understand the qualities associated with persistent commitment to moral action among 23 people who had worked to address such issues as civil rights, poverty, and peace. They discovered a pattern of disregard for risks, certainty about matters of principle, faith and positivity, and a dynamic interplay between continuity and change. Of particular interest is what appeared to be a developmental transformation of goals through social influence, suggesting that unity of self and moral goals develops as a social process (Colby, 1994).

Concern with the moral implications of the work of psychologists has been voiced only periodically by a few (Albee, 1986; Prilleltensky, 1994; Prilleltensky & Walsh-Bowers, 1993; Sarason, 1986). Wallach and Wallach (1990) urge us to go beyond the minimalist ethic often associated with autonomy (a way of being priced by many) to rethink our beliefs about goodness. Because the work of psychologists and other professionals involves acting on particular knowledge interests with particular ways of knowing, it is important to understand epistemic commitments in relation to deeper existential commitments. The fact that activities pursued in the name of knowledge are embedded in a social context requires us to consider their social purpose and implications. When epistemic activities are intentional efforts at problem solving, personal goals for engaging in such activities may be considered transcendental in the sense that they motivate efforts that constitute larger identity projects in response to existential problems.

Cohen (1995) presents interview data on eminent colleagues in psychology in an attempt to link their ideas and their lives. In his review of previous work and recent analysis of such data, he is cautious about conclusive patterns; however, he makes a number of observations. One of his findings is the lack of interest in the psychology of the psychologist and the fact that many of the psychologists interviewed showed little interest in working directly with people. He detected a theme of status and power as manifested in a desire to be of influence and to have more defensible theoretical views than those of one's colleagues. At a descriptive level, Cohen's study and the study of highly committed persons by Colby (1994) suggest rather different motives by two groups of productive people. These differences may be due to the conceptual frames used, the informants sampled, and the extent to which the researcher had access to the total life context of the informants.

On issues of knowledge and scientific worldview, Cohen (1995) found that the psychologists he studied were comfortable with their own paradigms. In spite of an increasingly eclectic research practice, the traditional model of research held strong, as did the mistrust of intuition and idiographic methods. It seems that Cohen did not find the type of reflectiveness about the limitations of one's work and beliefs that he considered essential to the development of psychology. On the other hand, he noted that some of the psychologists had expressed the wish to be literary writers and even attempted to create novels and other literary works. Could this be a phenomenon of unfulfilled creativity in one's professional life? Without attempting a comprehensive biographical study, Cohen's project left unanswered questions about the relationship between professionals' work and their creative motives and life circumstances. To place the activities of an individual in total life context, the idiographical case study method can be used to augment the interview research of Cohen (1995).

In his case study approach to the sociology of knowledge, Campbell (1979) applied a "tribal" model to the academic success of two leading theorists in psychology, Tolman and Spence. In the case of Tolman, he pointed out that an open and undefensive sharing of his own creative process with students resulted in less institutionalization of his theoretical views by followers as compared with Spence's. Campbell's interpretation was that Tolman's skepticism and sophisticated perspective on the status of theory in psychology seem to have prevented him from acting in a manner that would have served careerist interests and provided a tribal leadership equal to his talents. A significant lesson was gleaned by Campbell from this case study of "default of leadership," in terms of the selfperpetuating role of authority, conformity, and loyalty mechanisms in scientific communities. Campbell's insight illustrates the generative potentials of descriptive case studies in contributing to theoretical understanding.

As stated at the outset, identity development is considered a creative process in itself. If culture provides opportunities for creativity as well as constrains such possibilities, the worldview and stage of development of psychology as a professional culture are relevant to the degree of creativity found in the lives of psychologists. Following Geertz's (1973) study of culture in terms of worldview and ethos, the professional commitments and careers of psychologists will be understood in relation to the collective worldview and ethos of the profession. Consistent with the view of knowledge as embodied (Campbell, 1979), we can assume that individual epistemic efforts reflect the social organization of knowledge in the discipline. Ochberg (1988) illustrates how the narrative construction of careers reflects cultural motifs and career cultures, as well as the individual's sense of community. The present conceptual framework includes the professionals' participation in the shared activities, cultural norms, and institutionalized practices of their professional communities and the knowledge enterprise (Shweder, Mahaputra, & Miller, 1987).

Surprisingly, the literature on the history of psychology seldom includes biographical and narrative studies of individual careers and lives. One of the few historical volumes on the academic careers of women in psychology, by O'Connell and Russo (1983), was supposed to be based on self-reflections. Unfortunately, it is not as revealing as one would have hoped. Autobiographical writing, such as by Bruner (1983) and Sarason (1988), has not been used for historical understanding of the discipline or as a source of hypotheses on the development of professional identity and the nature of our knowledge enterprise. Nor has such work been used to probe questions of moral ontology and creativity in professional lives. It is my hope that the historical and narrative development of professional identities in biographical accounts and enacted life texts will enable us to explore the relationship between knowledge, creativity, and moral vision.

▓▓▓▓▓▓▓ THE PRESENT METHODOLOGY

In this project, a narrative, cultural-historical, and hermeneutic mode of understanding was used to explore how a select number of psychologists find lived meanings of moral existence in enacting their epistemic and moral beliefs through their work as theorists, researchers, practitioners, and educators in their historical location and cultural context. In planning for this study, I searched for appropriate models and considered the relevant methodological literature (see Appendix A). George Howard was one of the few colleagues I know who crafted a parallel account of the personal and the professional (scientific) as an excursion into narrative psychology (Howard, 1989). The present project involves a similar combination of different types of discourse. I also read with interest the collection of autobiographical essays of psychologists edited by Lee (1994) but was disappointed with the lack of an overall frame of analysis and the absence of meta-level commentary. The interaction between the contributors and the editor in this case seemed minimal and thus not representative of a dialogical effort. My own desire was to engage colleagues in personal reflections and construct, at least partly through dialogue, the narratives of professional careers and lives.

Elms (1994) recommended that in using the biographical case study method, researchers should draw on diverse theoretical frameworks and methods of data gathering, use their methodological self-consciousness, and avoid single-factor reductionism in favor of complexity. The methods used in the present project include (a) the construction of a life line and the writing of an autobiographical sketch by the person whose career and life are being examined, (b) interviewing and dialogue, and (c) the collection and analysis of relevant documents such as career résumé, published works, presentations and other public statements, and prior interview transcripts (available in two cases) during the person's professional career. The data generated with these methods were used as convergent sources of information in this multiple-case study. Because of the interactive, dialogical mode of inquiry, the self-generated accounts can be regarded to some extent as assisted autobiographical sketches involving self-interpretation and facilitated construction.

I invited seven psychologists to be participants. The selection criteria were that the person has a mature career in professional psychology, is willing to examine his or her career and life in a reflective way, and is regarded by peers as having made uncommon contributions. Four of the participants are male and three female, with ages ranging from 45 to 77. The participants' ethnic backgrounds included Jewish, Chinese, English, German, Irish, Swedish, and part-

Native American descent. They come from both coasts, the Midwest, and the southwestern United States. Four of the participants may be considered to be in an active, midlife stage of their career. The other three are retired or near retirement. Three are clinical psychologists by training, two are counseling psychologists, and two are developmental psychologists. Altogether, the seven participants represent a range of interests in professional psychology, including clinical and counseling training and practice; special education; research in community psychology, health, and education; consultation to public and private institutions; and policy issues concerning all levels of education.

These participants have different histories of relationship with myself as the principal author and researcher. Roland Tharp has been a mentor and friend since I was a graduate student. I know Leo Goldman and Donald Peterson from prior professional interactions about my own work. Elizabeth Altmaier, Jill Reich, Barbara Keogh, and Derald Sue I have come to know as they participated in the project. I had not been previously acquainted with the three female psychologists, whose participation I solicited based on the recommendation of colleagues. It probably is not a matter of chance that I had some difficulty finding female colleagues with distinguished careers who were willing to participate in the project.

The interviewing questions (Appendix B) served both as a tool for direct data gathering and as catalysts for reflection. They included questions about faith in the prevalent orientation to knowledge in the discipline, the participants' goals and rationale for the courses of action taken, their personal perceptions of the culture and ethos of the profession and its social contributions, and the symbolic communities in which they hold membership. During the interviews, I encouraged the participants to elaborate on issues and controversies in psychology that they have encountered in their professional lives. I used converging information in the interview data, the autobiographical accounts, and the archival data to discern patterns and themes, which were then verified with the participants.

It was my intention to utilize a dialogical process as much as possible. Constraints of time and distance, however, made it difficult at times to achieve the degree of reciprocal exchange with the participants that I had hoped for. As the project proceeded, I became concerned about my own ability to exercise reflexivity in bringing social and philosophical critique to this collaborative effort. I felt the need for a project consultant who could provide critical review of my interpretations of the contributed accounts and biographical information. After consulting the participants, I decided otherwise, knowing that I was never completely alone.

The main concern with the project was whether I would do justice to the autobiographical accounts in the interpretive summary. Realizing that any life, even if confined to the scope of academic life and professional career, is multidetermined and perhaps overdetermined, I felt that there should be no shortage of interpretive possibilities. To some extent, decisions about what meanings and significance to draw from the participants' present rendition of their professional lives already have been made by them as they wrote their own chapters. There is probably an element of invention that goes beyond factual reconstruction (Bateson, 1989; Renza, 1980). As depicted by Hare-Mustin (1994) in her reflexive essay, the autobiographical account and its interpretation involve an ongoing process of uncovering clues, detecting themes, and discovering change in one's life. The logic of interpretation should be more akin to a part-to-whole narrative logic (Bruner, 1990) and be in search of formal cause (pattern) and final cause (intentionality) as opposed to reductive linear causes.

Consistent with the multidisciplinary perspective discussed, both personal and social meanings were interpreted in cultural and historical context. In recognition of the embeddedness of these narrative accounts and the potential variability of life paths, especially between genders, an "aleatoric mode" of construction was considered (Gergen, 1990), whereby individual careers and lives are not expected to follow any given linear path or yield to identical causal forces. Following a conversational metaphor, I used the dialogical process to search for both questions and answers, and to present different voices of experience. From these multiperspectival accounts, I tried to deduce not only personal visions of moral existence but also possible implications for collective agency. To the extent that the authors and I are embedded in the ideology of the profession and the times, the interpretive accounts need to be deconstructed for their cultural and value assumptions, and held up for critical questioning and juxtapositioning against other, broader horizons. The dialectical process of construction will not end with the summary and interpretations offered in Chapter 9. I expect readers to apply other perspectives to critique and expand what is dialogically constructed and interpreted here.

In a sense, the narrative accounts in Part II of this book are as much stories of individual professional lives as statements on the state of the profession and our society during the historical period in which the participants' careers have taken shape. The series of interviews also can be likened to a group conversation with colleagues about contemporary psychology, society, and our collective future. In asking what can be learned, I hope that readers will glean from the following chapters a historical and cultural understanding that is more poignant and intimate than is possible from extraspective accounts. The different types of voices and themes that emerge can be viewed as offering dialogic possibilities, whether in contrast or in consonance.

APPENDIX A

Notes on Methodology

The use of psychohistory and psychobiography in the study of identity (Erikson, 1975; Lawton, 1988), such as the cases of Martin Luther and Mohammed Gandhi (Erikson, 1962, 1969), reflected early psychoanalytic influences. Critics consider this approach to be vague as far as providing methodological guidance for researchers. The imposition of theory on data has been objectionable to those who are not sympathetic with psychoanalytic ideas. Part of the objection comes from objectivist assumptions about the nature of scholarship and the fear of subjectivity (Pletsch, 1985). Whether interpretive methods, considered by some to be more clinical than scientific, can be a legitimate means of generating theoretical knowledge is an issue (Carlson, 1988).

The biographical case method has not been widely practiced as an approach to theorizing in the social sciences because of its questioned status as a tool for scientific knowledge. While expressing concerns about the fallibility of conclusions from case studies, Campbell (1975) conceded that they can be valuable in probing tentative hypotheses. Psychologists, however, have been too restrictive in the choice of research methods to see biographical evidence as useful to theory development (Howe, 1982). A well-developed rationale for the use of case study methods did not become available until the work of Bromley (1986), who stated that a biographical case study approach can be justified if it is demonstrated to be better than common sense and is open to critical questioning. Under these conditions, the study of lives as multiple-case research that integrates personality and social psychology (Rosenwald, 1988), or the use of biography to uncover the reciprocal relationship between social structures and human actions (Lemert, 1986), can reveal social facts and psychological realities as potential general truths.

As researchers extend personological inquiry with the use of idiographic methods and biographical accounts (McAdams & Ochberg, 1988; Runyun, 1983, 1988), the study of personal motives and identity becomes a search for narrative patterns. This interest is reflected in McAdams's (1985) work in the study of identity with life story. His focus on power and intimacy as core motives reflects the conceptual influence of Murray (1938). The narrative study of personal identity derives support from the root metaphor of contextualism that Sarbin (1986) credited to Pepper's

(1942) world hypotheses. Contextualism is one of the fundamental ways by which we order the world and make sense of human experience. The historical event takes on significance in time and space through our narrative structuring and organization of motives and actions. Recent interests in narratology (Polkinghorne, 1988) and interpretive research methods (Hoshmand, 1994) have given impetus to the narrative study of identity in life context. The dual influence of personality (motivation) research, in the tradition of Murray, and of narrative methodology, as proposed by Sarbin, is seen in the work of Hermans and his associates (Hermans, 1988; Hermans & Van Gilst, 1991). This group has derived psychological motives, such as heroism and love, from collective stories by individuals. The person is regarded as a motivated storyteller (Hermans & Hermans-Jansen, 1995), whereby the manner of telling could be as informative as the substance of the story told.

Although there is a growing interest among researchers and practitioners in following a narrative conception of identity, it should be noted that this conceptual shift does not necessarily mean a corresponding shift to a constructivist philosophy and methodological paradigm (as explained in Hoshmand, 1994). Researchers differ in the degree to which they treat personal stories as revealing actual motives and personality structures as opposed to representing a process of self-interpretation and identity construction. In other words, they differ on how strongly they draw a distinction between historical truth and narrative truth (Spence, 1982). For the purposes of the present inquiry, both historical truth and narrative truth are considered to be relevant.

Further methodological developments in the human sciences have provided means of studying identity in ways that are consistent with recent conceptions. Interest in narrative knowing has linked the social sciences with the narrative tradition and methods of the humanities (Polkinghorne, 1988). New paradigms of research (including the ethnographic, phenomenological, and hermeneutic) that are more contextual and interpretive in nature offer alternatives to methodological behaviorism and methodological individualism (Hoshmand, 1994). The narrative study of lives has been presented in Josselson and Lieblich (1993) from a variety of perspectives (including, for example, Collingwood's theory of reenactment, Gadamer's theory of dialogue, and Derrida's theory of deconstruction) as well as methodological approaches (such as life history interview, diaries, and case studies). Although more work in this area is expected, many questions continue to be raised by researchers about the nature and justifiable use of narratives. Lieblich and Josselson (1994) state in the second volume of their series on the narrative study of lives that we do not have a well-developed theory of the narrative in the social sciences, and that the state of the art is at a stage of creative ambiguity.

The developments in narrative methodology have been accompanied by a renewed interest in psychobiography and case study in personality research. Runyun (1983) had placed both within the idiographic tradition, arguing against the criticisms of idiographic approaches in mainstream psychology. He describes a number of methods developed previously by Allport and other researchers of varied theoretical persuasion. In his subsequent review of progress in psychobiography in relation to theoretical developments in personality psychology (Runyun, 1988), he identifies several conceptual and methodological issues that need to be addressed. They are concerned with relating the individual to his or her social-historical context, accounting for the relationship of the author to the subject, and evaluating the relative plausibility of alternative biographical interpretations. Similarly, questions are raised about ethical, conceptual, and methodological issues in the narrative study of lives (Josselson, 1996; Josselson & Lieblich, 1995). These issues will be addressed further in Part III of this book.

In the same special issue on psychobiography and life narratives where Runyun's review appeared, both measurement-oriented and narrative approaches were featured (McAdams & Ochberg, 1988). Other contributions to narrative methodology have come from qualitative researchers, personal construct theorists, and social constructionists (Mair, 1988; Neimeyer, 1993; Neimeyer & Mahoney, 1995; Shotter & Gergen, 1989). Of particular interest here is the empirical research on the validity of autobiographical life stories reported by Howard, Maerlender, Myers, and Curtin (1992). These researchers argued in support of the use of the autobiographical method based on demonstrated construct validity comparable to standard research instruments,.

Previous studies of academic careers and lives have varied in substantive focus and methodological approach. Some have stressed demographic and historical factors for a given cohort (e.g., Lawrence & Blackburn, 1985). Others have attended to developmental and discipline-specific aspects of faculty careers (Baldwin & Blackburn, 1981; Becher, 1989; Clark, 1987). The purpose may be more descriptive than analytical, as in Keller's (1994) presentation of the career decisions and experiences of 13 academic psychologists that convey a sense of freedom in following personal dreams and passions. Ethnography has been used with narrative biographical study in illuminating how the local culture and organizational context interact with personal disposition in shaping careers and the intellectual journey of the individual (Gubrium & Holstein, 1995; Weiland,

1994, 1995). These methodological developments and examples of recent work provide the background for a narrative biographical case study of professional identity and commitment.

APPENDIX B

Interview Questions

1a. What are the formative experiences and significant life events that have shaped your life goals and professional identity?

1b. By reference to your life line, identify the critical choice points and explain how they have been critical.

2. When did you begin to have a clear sense of your place
   a. in the profession, and
   b. in society?

3a. Who are the people you now identify with or consider to be your reference group?

3b. What other memberships, professional and civic, do you hold?

4a. What are the goals, purposes, and intentions in what you have been doing professionally?

4b. How have they evolved?

5. Which institutional and cultural practices do you
   a. promote, and
   b. try to change?

6. What do you feel most strongly about in your current commitments? Why?

7a. What are your views of the psychology profession, psychological science, and our models of knowledge?

7b. How do you see your work as fitting in with this picture and addressing the issues involved?

8a. Which orientation, professionally and socially, do you have faith in or lack faith toward?

8b. What have you done about such faith issues?

9a. What does being creative mean to you?

9b. When have you felt most creative and why?

10a. What is the relationship between the personal, the social, and the professional for you?

10b. How should it be for all of us?

PART II

NARRATIVES OF CAREERS AND LIVES IN PSYCHOLOGY

CHAPTER 2

The Professional Psychologist as a Moral Agent

DONALD R. PETERSON

A t one level or another, I have understood from the beginning of my career that the fundamental mission of psychology is not only to seek truth but also to do good. I have not previously written anything about that, partly to avoid seeming mawkish but more fundamentally because I am reflexly suspicious of anyone, including myself, who openly declares that he or she has a passion for "doing good" unto others. The wisdom of two of my guiding spirits lurks ever in my mind. Henry David Thoreau once said that if anyone came toward him with the avowed intention of "helping" him, he would run as fast as he could in the opposite direction. Karl Raimund Popper claimed that the deliberate effort to make others happy—to create a heaven on Earth, as heaven is envisioned by the helpers—can only lead to hell.

The belief that psychology is inherently a moral enterprise, however—that we are obliged not only to advance knowledge but to improve the human condition—is more than platitude. The validity of the belief is most patently obvious in the professional activities that psychologists undertake. As professional psychologists, either we are effective or we are not. If we are not effective, we had better close the shop. If we are effective, our work changes the human condition in some way, and every change moves those to whom we minister in some direction, for better or for worse. Like it or not, professional psychologists are moral agents. It is not enough to attend rigorously to the technical efficacy of our procedures, though we must discriminate critically in choosing techniques. It is not enough to examine the empirical credibility and heuristic power of our theories, though we must attend closely to the way we appraise, reject, sustain, and amend our theoretical constructions. It is not enough to probe and ultimately to vindicate the epistemic foundations of our scientific and professional inquiries, though we must examine deeply and comprehensively the ways of knowing upon which our formulations and actions are based. Beyond techniques, theory, and epistemology, we must be profoundly concerned about the moral basis of our work as professional psychologists.

My appreciation of this truth has deepened gradually over the years, though not in a continuous and orderly way. As I look back now, it seems to me that any "moral vision" I have gained is less a product of deliberate search on my part than of situations I entered more by chance than by choice, and of relationships with other people who either were in my world before I got there or came into my life almost accidentally later on and helped me, not by design but in the natural course of our lives together, to see my world in progressively different ways.

EARLY DEVELOPMENTAL EXPERIENCE

I grew up in the tiny village of Pillager, Minnesota, which was founded by my grandfather and other settlers less than 25 years before I was born. My father built the house in which we lived. Except for crumpled newspapers stuffed between the wall studs, the house was not insulated. Heat through the frigid Minnesota winters was provided by wood-burning stoves. For the first 10 years of my life, water came from a handpump in the kitchen. Our toilet was an outdoor privy. In the winter, we bathed in a washtub near the cookstove in the kitchen. In the summer, we swam in the Crow Wing River. And yes, I walked to school through snow, in temperatures of 40 degrees below zero and colder, often into bitter wind, uphill going to school and downhill coming home.

I thought it was the best world anybody could possibly want. I had chores to do, but plenty of time and freedom to master and enjoy a tough physical environment, swimming the river where one of my friends had drowned, skating for miles on a winding creek, and skiing in the wild hills north of town. Pillager had its share of ruffians and rascals and was far from free of petty animosities, but it was a self-contained, self-sufficient town, where self-reliance in personal belief and action, and honesty and civility in the treatment of others, were generally assumed. Our house was never locked, and neither were the houses of most of my friends. The "law" in town was represented by one elected constable, whose main job was to control anybody who got drunk and disorderly in the local saloon. This our lawman sometimes managed by waiting until the drinker passed out and could be hauled off to the one-cell jail in a wheelbarrow. There were no observant Jews or practicing Catholics in town, and the Lutherans, Baptists, Methodists, and nonsectarians pretty well left one another to their own beliefs.

My parents were not churchgoing people. They scorned as hypocrites those who paraded their own virtues and preached their versions of morality to others. My mother sent me to Lutheran Sunday school, but I decided very early that the talk of brimstone I heard in my lessons was nonsense. I could not believe that God, whom I imagined to look like my father, only larger, bearded, and wearing a white robe, would roast me in eternal hellfire for anything I could conceive of doing. I started to skip Sunday school just often enough to avoid detection, and I spent the nickels I had been given for the collection plate on ice cream cones and candy bars. When I reached the teen years, my parents allowed me to choose whether or not to go to church, and I chose not to go.

From my mother, a rural schoolteacher, I got the idea that I might get a college education and "make something of myself," though it was not at all clear what I might take up for a career or how we could pay the bill. From my father, whom I helped build houses from foundation to chimney cap, I learned the importance of using the right tool for the job, of keeping my tools sharp, and of making sure that the foundation of any building we were putting up was perfectly squared and leveled before a single sill was put in place. Otherwise, we would have to make adjustments at every stage of the following construction.

My father also taught me something about responsibility and redemption. As a 10-year-old boy with a new slingshot, out for adventure on a sunny Sunday afternoon, I broke all the windows in the west wall of a public building. To me, the windows were irresistible targets in a shooting gallery. With some excitement over awareness that my behavior was forbidden but mindless of effects, I fired carefully selected pebbles from the cover of a clump of bushes nearly 50 yards from the base of the building. With growing pride in my skill, I systematically plinked out 96 panes of glass. A few days before, after I had finished making the slingshot, I proudly showed it to my father. He examined my workmanship critically, nodded basic approval, and showed me how to improve the binding of rubber to the pouch. When word of the window breakage got around, my father asked me if I was the one who did it. I would not have dreamed of lying to him. I confessed in tears and heard a brief, somber lecture on the consequences of behavior. Together, up and down ladders, over 3 sun-baked days, with contributions that depended on our skills, my father and I reglazed the window-panes I had broken. I was allowed to keep the slingshot but confined future fire to tin cans on fenceposts and an occasional unsuccessful shot at a rabbit.

From my brother, 5 years older than me, adventurous and athletically gifted, I learned that we could change our world when it needed improvement. At the time, there were no organized sports in our school, and there was no football field in town. For our sandlot games through the long, crisp, Minnesota autumns, my brother and I laid out our own field, complete with pine pole goalposts, in a pasture at the edge of town. The best hills for skiing were heavily overgrown with trees and brush, so we spent much of one summer chopping out our own trails to enjoy the following winter.

Growing up in that world, I came to expect most people to tell the truth and to feel some mixture of scorn and pity for anybody who didn't. Most of the people I knew thought the best way to get anything done was to dig in and do it. There was next to no talk of morality in my home, but most of the people I knew and all the ones I admired were honest and caring. In later years, I read a fair amount of ethical philosophy, and in fact developed a considerable interest in comparative religion, but I was never drawn to any theistic belief and never felt any need for one.

When World War II came upon us, I enlisted in the Army and entered a world I had not known before. For the first time, I saw raw racism and anti-Semitic hatred close at hand. I saw grossly stupid, brutishly ignorant, boorish, dishonest, cruel people in action. Those were just in my own platoon. Among other comrades in arms, I saw intelligence, racial and religious understanding, gentil-ity, compassion, courage, and ways of looking at the world different from any I had conceived. In Germany with the medical battalion of an armored division, I saw grisly death and gained some sense of the evil that caused it. All of this broadened my awareness of the world we live in but did not change my religious beliefs. I remained a silent atheist both in and out of foxholes. Whatever had formed in me early by way of moral outlook was basically unchanged by my wartime experience. I cannot say that I came back from the Army resolved to build a better world, but I had seen what could happen when people listened to the wrong leaders and let their prejudicial hatreds run away with them. I was ready to come in on the good side if I could find a way to make a living at it.

GRADUATE SCHOOL AND EARLY CAREER

The GI Bill offered me a chance I would not otherwise have had for a good college education. With hope of earning a livelihood by some kind of writing, I signed up as an English major at the University of Minnesota. Of all my courses, however, those in psychology interested me most. A graduate student who taught an introductory course in experimental psychology suggested that I consider psychology as a career, so I went one day to the psychology department to consider changing my undergraduate major. "I'd like to talk to someone about going into psychology," I said to the secretary. "Clinical?" she asked. I wasn't sure what clinical psychology was. I said "Yes." She sent me to see Paul Meehl, then an associate professor, who spent an hour telling me about the field, what was involved in graduate study, how to support myself financially, and options for a career after I got my PhD. I could not imagine a better match with my inclinations. I decided then and there to become a clinical psychologist.

Throughout my time as a graduate student, I assumed that everything I could conceive of doing as a psychologist was good. As a scientist, I would seek knowledge. The primary wrongs in my purview were erroneous beliefs, and the way to do good was to replace invalid propositions with valid ones, by thinking rationally and doing careful, well-designed research. Logical empiricism, as taught by Paul Meehl and Herbert Feigl, formed the core of my belief system. Philosophy of science was as close as I came to a religion in those times. The good and the true were one and the same.

In my professional work, I assumed that the tests I gave and the psychotherapy I did were good for my clients. When I gave the Stanford-Binet to a little girl, found a low IQ, and recommended placement in a special class for the "educable mentally handicapped," I did not doubt that my recommendation would work to the benefit of the child and everyone around her. When I was assigned a young homosexual man as a patient for psychotherapy, I did not question the assumption that I should try to cure his psychosexual disorder, or at least turn him toward a healthy sexual interest in women. When my efforts failed, as they inevitably did, I attributed the outcome to his "pregenital fixation" and the well-known therapeutic recalcitrance of the "narcissistic personality." I never questioned the assumption that homosexuality was a psychological disorder, nor did I doubt the direction that healthy change should take.

I do not recall any talk about the axiological foundations of psychology during my years of graduate study. Psychology was science, free of superstition and unconcerned about metaphysical mysteries. We thought of ourselves as logical empiricists, critical realists, and functional pragmatists, but not as moralists. Integrity in all our studies and in all our reports was silently assumed. Violations on our part were unthinkable. When we learned of dishonesty on the part of others—faked data, fudged reports, and the like—we considered the culprits more pathetic than sinful. If there was any cheating among my classmates, I did not know about it. I believed the intellectual and professional integrity of the Minnesota faculty to be uniform and absolute. To the limited extent that I knew about the personal lives of the faculty, I also saw nothing but decency and social responsibility there. No special thought was given to the morality of the psychological enterprise. If it was anything other than perfectly honest, there seemed no point in doing it. Implicitly, I considered clarity and truth not only necessary but sufficient guides to an informative science and a socially valuable profession.

In my first job at the University of Illinois, teaching undergraduate courses in personality and human development, working at the psychological clinic, and starting my research with Raymond Cattell on personality structure in children and with Herbert Quay on personality factors in juvenile delinquency, I maintained my implicit faith that rational thought and empirical knowledge were sufficient guides to a morally sound psychology. The first hint of conflict arose when some results from my research on children's behavior disorders failed to jibe with some of the conclusions Cattell and I had reached in our work with preschool children. Ray and I had published a series of articles describing the multifactorial complexities that appeared to emerge from factor analyses of the questionnaires, life records, and objective tests we had used in our investigations. The structures we reported were defined by 16-20 factors that appeared to represent early developmental forms of the factors that Cattell had previously educed from his many studies of adults. In my independent research on children's behavior disorders, however, the procedures I had learned from Cattell did not seem to work dependably. In replicated studies, I could not get the same structure twice. On a hunch, I tried taking out only a few strong factors rather than the large number that Cattell characteristically retained for rotation, and I found that this produced far more stable, replicable solutions. My discovery was one of several that ultimately led to the "big five" factor systems that have become commonplace in personality description today.

I was apprehensive about publishing the report, however. My results were consistent with the conceptions of one of Cattell's ideological adversaries, Hans Eysenck, and I feared that they might offend Cattell, who had taught me everything I knew about factor analysis and had befriended me in a warmly personal way. If published, the article might advance my reputation at the expense of a mentor I liked and admired. I sent a preprint of the paper to Ray, with a letter asking for any suggestions he could offer in reconciling the differences between our findings and the differing conceptions of personality the findings appeared to require. I waited a month for a reply but received none, so I sent the manuscript off to the editor of the *Psychological Review*, where it was published in 1965.

Some time later, Ray called me in distress. He had just given a colloquium at another university, and some people in the audience had asked him what he had to say about the discrepancy between his results and "Peterson's findings." What had *I* found, he wanted to know. I reminded him about the report I had sent him long before, but it turned out that he had not read it. I recalled a smiling conversation early in our acquaintance when Ray had said he rarely read the works of others in his own area of expertise: Too much to keep up with, he said, and most of it not worth reading. I suppose I might have guessed that he would ignore my report too, but I had surmised otherwise, and by now the deed was done. Our differences were on public display. Still, I felt no misgivings about the rectitude of my behavior. Facts were facts. If reputations had to suffer when the truth was told, so much the worse for reputations.

I also took some comfort in the belief that Cattell was big enough to absorb any blow I could land on him. His contributions to personality measurement and theory were monumental, and he was very sure about the validity of his ideas. My confidence was justified a few months later, when Ray sent me an article that included a conceptual rejoinder to my argument and some evidence supporting Cattell's position on the issue that divided us. Penciled in above the heading was a sketch of a man thumbing his nose, followed by words of friendly regard. The whole experience improved my faith in open, good-natured scholarly dialectic.

PSYCHOLOGY AND MORALITY

The first severe jolt to my simplistic identification of truth and virtue came through my relationship with O. Hobart Mowrer. Mowrer had earned a lofty stature in psychology primarily through his contributions to learning theory and his pioneering conceptions of personality, psychotherapy, and other "clinical" phenomena in scientifically accessible terms. In his middle years, his thinking took a new turn. At first through clinical and personal experience, though later with substantial empirical support, he came to the view that the prototypic human neurosis was not, as Freud had claimed, a distorted expression of natural impulses, repressed and otherwise constrained by an irrational, tyrannical superego. Instead, Mowrer argued, the root cause of neurosis, of psychological "dis-ease," was to be found in the *under*development of social conscience, in lack of restraint, in an all too facile readiness to express selfish impulses, in the well-deserved guilt that followed, and in the self-deception and social hypocrisy that disguised and justified continuing irresponsible behavior.

Mowrer[1] published his views in several journal articles, of which the most widely read and controversial appeared in 1960 in *American Psychologist* under the title " 'Sin,' the Lesser of Two Evils." He also wrote a book, *The Crisis in Psychiatry and Religion,* that advanced his conception, and developed a novel form of therapy, *The New Group Therapy,* that was consistent with his moral and theoretical views. Far from the "let it all hang out" license of many encounter groups of the time, Mowrer's "integrity groups" ran according to strict rules of behavior and followed the clear guiding principles that Mowrer considered keys to personal salvation and social survival. The moral imperatives were *involvement* (no "copping out"—like it or not, we must all stay in this together), radical *integrity* (no lying, no cheating of any kind), and social *responsibility* (no unkept promises, no looking to others to solve our problems). This sounds harshly puritanical, but Mowrer himself was a deeply compassionate man. Although his system of morality was firm in its principles, human lapses were assumed and the road to redemption was clearly marked. When the dark depressions that ultimately ended his life were not soaking through his soul, every meeting with him would bring out his sharp wit, the twinkle in his eye, and his ready laughter.

I did not attend Mowrer's group sessions, but his office was across the hall from mine, we talked often, and his views of morality added substance to my own. When he published a collection of essays and empirical reports under the title *Morality and Mental Health,* he included a study I had done that corroborated his theory of neurosis.

Mowrer was passionately devoted to the integration of psychology and religion. To him, the "sickness of the soul" that pervaded modern society lay in the loss of honest communion among all of us partners in the human enterprise, and the cure was to be found in establishing personal integrity through responsible, caring relationships with one another. He often noted that the word *religion* literally means "re-ligation," a re-tying of the bonds that hold human beings together. With financial support from the Eli Lilly Foundation, he brought clerics of several persuasions into summer residence at the University of Illinois, and among other activities in his program held weekly seminars in which Jesuit priests, Protestant ministers, Jewish rabbis, and secular psychologists might consider together the issues that concerned them all and find, if they could, some common ground. The seminars were open to the university faculty. Among psychologists, Perry London, Lloyd Humphreys, and I attended the meetings with fair regularity. To my knowledge, no earthshaking revelations emerged from the Lilly program, though several participants wrote books based in part on the experience. For me, the chance to discuss both psychological and metaphysical matters with intelligent, broadly representative, deeply literate colleagues opened intellectual vistas and spiritual possibilities I had not known before. I did not undergo any epiphanies, but the mysteries of the eternal and the infinite took on new meaning for me, when once I would have dismissed any talk about subjects of that kind as superstitious nonsense.

Through those years, Perry London was thinking through the ideas that eventually took shape in his book *The Modes and Morals of Psychotherapy.*[2] Then and after, I was working through the ideas that formed my book *The Clinical Study of Social Behavior*. Perry and I spent many hours together, raising questions, sharing information, leading one another to out-of-the-way sources we had run across, trying out new thoughts, rejecting many, and molding a few of our conceptions into communicable form. Our technical emphases differed; his were on treatment, mine on assessment. The scope of our considerations varied, but we shared a common understanding that the professional ministrations of psychologists were inherently and unavoidably moral actions, that moral decisions were required at every turn.

What, then, were the principled foundations of our work? Obviously, we could not find them in our science. The objective analysis and interpretation of data requires freedom from metaphysics and moral constraint. Where else? Just as obviously, in a moral philosophy of some kind. I cannot presume to speculate on the full complexity of Perry London's beliefs, but he expressed many of them eloquently in *Modes and Morals* and made it clear to anyone who asked that a deeper foundation lay in his Judaic faith. Perry had studied for the rabbinate before he came into psychology, and he continued his search as an observant Jew to the end of his days.

I sometimes envied the clarity, the sense of boundaries, and the traditional continuities that a coherent religious faith offered to London and some other psychologists I knew. My early atheistic rejections had rid me of confining dogma and some harmful superstitions but also had limited the scope and threatened the solidity of my affirmative beliefs. The homely values that were almost in the air I breathed in my early years, along with the principled inspirations of Meehl, Mowrer, and others who affected me so profoundly later on, offered a reasonably satisfying basis for most of the choices I had to make, but I also felt a need for deeper moral understanding.

I read a great deal on my own and through all my years in Illinois was a member of the Unitarian church. More recently, I have joined another religious community known simply as Unity. In both, I have found a freedom from dogma that allows me to preserve my intellectual integrity, an absence of the symbolic ritual that is important to many but which I find distracting, and a practical, humane moral philosophy that I find both comforting and uplifting. Beyond those guides, I still am searching.

▬▬▬ EDUCATING PROFESSIONAL PSYCHOLOGISTS

In my career as a psychologist, the most severe test of my convictions has come from my advocacy of the Doctor of Psychology (PsyD) degree, professional schools, and the principle of direct education for the practice of psychology. In my position on these matters, I have often been at odds with prevailing cultural norms. Some critics have regarded my stand as antiscientific, damaging to the discipline, and a danger to the public. If I believed any of those claims were valid, of course, I would never have taken the stand in the first place. In maintaining my position, enacting its full implications through most of my career, and living with the consequences, I have often found myself in the front rank of a beleaguered minority, and sometimes very nearly alone.

I consider the work I do as an educator as clearly a professional job as anything I have ever done in clinical practice. My educational policies and practices must therefore be as securely grounded in moral principles as any other professional action. An obvious principle, one to which every director of clinical training I have ever known would surely assent, is that we owe our students, and the public the students will later serve, the best education we can possibly provide. Wide differences prevail across our individual definitions of excellence, however, and even more across our beliefs about ways to attain excellence. I have offered my own views on these matters in many statements over the past 30 years. The main ideas and the experiences that influenced them are described in my 1997 book, *Educating Professional Psychologists: History and Guiding Conception.* Here, I can only summarize some of the conditions that led me on the path I took and some of the moral issues I met along the way.

In 1964, Lloyd Humphreys, then head of the psychology department at the University of Illinois, asked me to direct the department's PhD program in clinical psychology. By many counts, the program was a successful scientist-practitioner program of the kind that developed in most American universities after World War II. Humphreys and his predecessor, Lyle Lanier, had recruited a distinguished faculty. The educational program had been carefully designed and was closely monitored. Our federal training grants were routinely renewed after reviews that often described our program as outstanding. Our accreditation by the American Psychological Association (APA) was never in doubt. Large numbers of highly qualified applicants sought admission to the program. Stringent standards were maintained in evaluating student performance. All of our graduates obtained good jobs, and many of them went on to become distinguished scholars in their own right.

That was admirable, as far as it went. I advocated then, and still do, maintaining the kind of clinical research program that ours exemplified, but I was troubled by some other features of our educational system, both locally and nationally. At the time I began to direct the clinical program at the university, I also was working as a consultant at a state psychiatric hospital in Kankakee, Illinois. Anybody who saw the movies *Snake Pit* or *One Flew Over the Cuckoo's Nest* would have recognized comparable conditions at Kankakee. Not one of the psychiatrists had been trained in the United States. Most of them spoke very poor English. Listening to a conversation between an MD who had recently come into the United States from Rumania and a black schizophrenic adolescent who had just come into the hospital from South Side Chicago was a weird experience for me as an observer. I could only imagine how it felt to the frightened, confused young man. The psychologists on the staff were well intentioned, but they didn't know what to do. The chief psychologist had a PhD from a reputable university but spent most of his time giving projective tests to newly admitted patients. The rest of the psychologists had master's degrees, did a lot of testing, saw a few relatively articulate, attractive patients in whatever kind of individual psychotherapy they had been taught to do, and sometimes ran group sessions with some of the more lucid patients on the wards.

The hospital was mainly a human warehouse, but I did not believe it had to remain so. By this time, behavioral methods had been used with good effect in residential treatment of psychiatric patients by Atthowe and Krasner in California and by Allyon and Azrin in Illinois. I knew about the work, and I organized a comparable but appropriately modified program for children and adolescents at Kankakee. With willing help and sustained management of the program by psychology staff, the program became measurably successful. I knew, however, that my work was only a drop in the bucket. We needed to do much more, and we needed competent, well-trained psychologists to take the necessary initiatives. Nearly every time he saw me, the hospital superintendent, a recent immigrant from Lithuania, said, "Why don't you send me more Ph's?"

I would have been glad to do so, but our Ph's *(sic)* were not inclined, nor in my view as well prepared as they might be, to work in places like the Kankakee State Hospital, though that was clearly one of the situations where public needs were greatest. During the years of my administration, some 85% of the graduates of our clinical PhD program went into academic positions in other psychology departments. Our record was a point of pride to many faculty members, but I could not imagine that the taxpayers of the state of Illinois who paid my salary, or the taxpayers of the United States who provided funds for the stipends and fellowships that supported our students, would approve of our use of their money to train college professors while the needs for competent professional service in the public agencies of the state were so grossly undermet. To whom were we accountable?

The 15% of our graduates who did not take academic jobs went into practice of some kind and were variously esteemed by faculty. The hierarchy of values was implicit but crystal clear. At the top were those of our graduates who joined the faculties at Michigan State, Northwestern, Stony Brook, Vanderbilt, Waterloo, and other universities, where the Illinois version of empirically grounded, broadly behavioral clinical psychology was welcome, and where the young blood we sent into their programs created some energizing effects. Next in value were graduates who went off to teaching positions in other schools but did not contribute conspicuously to the conceptual and technical advances we wanted to encourage. Then came a long drop in professorial esteem for anybody who went into practice, though a distinction was maintained between graduates who took jobs in the public sector and those who went into private practice. Graduates who became chief psychologists in the community mental health centers of the time were seen to be doing decent, respectable work. Anybody who went into private practice, however, was derided as a "hand-holder," abominated as an academic mistake, an educational failure, a waste of money and other resources, and above all a waste of faculty time that might otherwise have gone to the hugely important research of the professors.

How did those *psychotherapists* ever get into our program? Our catalogs and brochures made it clear that the clinical psychology program at the University of Illinois was not intended to train mere practitioners. The only people we wanted in our program were those who would devote their lives to research. How did the others sneak through our screen? I advised many students in those days. Some confessed to me that they had simply lied to gain admission to the program, pretended an interest in research that they did not possess, kept up the pretense throughout their studies, and then, PhD in hand and license in sight, gone off to the life of practice they had intended to enter from the very start. This they told me in confidence, and I kept their secrets. I advised some of them to rig a precise little conditioning experiment for dissertation research instead of the practically important but scientifically uncertain field studies many wanted to do but that would never have passed the gimlet-eyed inspections of our thesis committees. Then I sent them on their way with my personal blessing, but with serious discomfort over the deception our value system had encouraged in them, and in which I was a silent accomplice.

As near as I could tell, the situation that prevailed at Illinois was common nationwide, and in some ways the national picture was even more muddled. For all the scientific preaching that went on in graduate programs across the land, the modal number of publications from PhD clinical psychologists remained at zero. Only one program in the country, at Adelphi University, publicly declared its program open to psychologists who wanted to devote their lives to professional service. Yet already, by 1964, the number of practitioners in the APA exceeded the number primarily involved in the academic pursuits of teaching and research. As many critical clinicians made violently clear by their protests, the training they had received in their research-oriented graduate programs did not prepare them well for the demands of practice. I believed that we could do better. As a professional educator, I felt a moral obligation to try.

Among other advantages, the recommendations of the APA Committee on the Scientific and Professional Aims of Psychology[3] offered a way to free ourselves of our hypocrisies and to keep the promises to society that support of our programs implicitly entailed. The chair of the committee, Kenneth E. Clark, had been my undergraduate adviser at the University of Minnesota. My graduate school mentor, Paul Meehl, and the head of my department at Illinois, Lloyd Humphreys, were among the most influential members of the committee. From long personal acquaintance, I had perfect confidence in the integrity and high respect for the wisdom of all three. By reputation, I had equal confidence in the integrity and wisdom of Jerome Bruner, Carl Rogers, Kenneth Spence, Robert Harper, and the other members of that illustrious group. When the committee recommended the creation of programs designed to prepare psychologists, directly and thoroughly, for careers of professional service, and at the same time to strengthen and clarify the purpose of our research programs, their conception meshed exactly with my own views and values, and it offered the encouragement and support I needed to act on my beliefs.

Lloyd Humphreys and I presented our proposal for a practitioner program leading to the PsyD degree for deliberation at the Chicago conference on the professional training of clinical psychologists.[4] The proposal was vigorously criticized and sometimes angrily attacked by several participants, and it was opposed by the majority in the final resolutions. I respected my adversaries, some more than others, but did not believe that issues of this kind could be settled by popular vote. I studied the critical arguments of my adversaries carefully, and I weighed their merits as judiciously as my predilections allowed, but once the direction of responsible professional action was clear in my own mind, I saw no alternative but to advance it. I developed the proposal in more thorough detail and presented it as persuasively as I could to my colleagues in the psychology department at Illinois. Lloyd Humphreys advocated the proposal with equal vigor. In that situation, affirmative faculty consensus was essential. To go ahead with the plan without the firm support of colleagues would have been foolhardy, however deep our personal convictions. Lengthy, often passionate, but consistently open and respectful discussion followed. After a formal debate, the faculty voted decisively to proceed. Three years and countless hours of planning later, the program went into effect.

Since then, I have had many misgivings about the professional school movement and the PsyD degree. For various reasons, proposals to develop PsyD programs at the University of Minnesota, New York University, and other strong research universities failed. The program at Illinois was discontinued. Practitioner programs and professional schools flourished instead in small universities and freestanding professional schools, where resources often are limited and traditions of research often are weak. I had conceived of practitioner programs as complements to research programs, not as replacements, but the educational pattern that places PsyD and PhD programs in affiliative partnership was rarely established. Better tests than my perceptions are needed, but the levels of quality among practitioner programs that I have seen in my work on the APA accreditation committee and through other observations often fall sadly short of the levels I once envisioned.

What are my responsibilities in this situation? My causal responsibility in advocating direct professional education and the PsyD degree is clear and well known to the community of educators concerned with these matters. My deliberate actions as an administrator were instrumental in creating the first PsyD program in the United States. I abjure responsibility, however, for other practitioner programs that developed outside my purview. The psychologists who developed the first freestanding professional schools in California, for example, did not ask my opinion before they went ahead with their plans. I had serious reservations about those plans from the beginning, and have since questioned the general prospects for sustained quality in freestanding professional schools openly and publicly, in situations where my views could not escape the attention of educators in charge of the schools.[5] At this stage in the professional school movement, I consider my responsibilities to consist primarily of advancing standards and encouraging critical self-studies through such agencies as the National Council of Schools and Programs of Professional Psychology,[6] continued public clarification of my views about professional education in psychology, and sustained effort to reach the highest attainable level of quality in any program in which I hold a position of influence and authority.

From my perspective, the 30-year history of the professional school movement is too brief, the forces of governing societal change too uncertain, and the course of development of our discipline too unstable to allow very confident predictions about the way our field will look even 30 more years from now. It is clear that we face immediate challenges of considerable peril as well as opportunities for public benefits that we are scarcely beginning to realize. I can imagine no other course for responsible professional action than to continue critical analysis and respectful dialogue,[7] and to sustain our quest for quality with all the ingenuity and dogged persistence we can find within ourselves and seek to inspire among others.

═══════ **FURTHER REFLECTIONS**

After the Vail conference on levels and patterns of training in professional psychology[8] and before I came to Rutgers University as dean of the Graduate School of Applied and Professional Psychology, I withdrew from administrative duties for a time and turned my attention toward research and conceptualization in close interpersonal relationships. The research was concerned primarily with the assessment of interpersonal process, and conceptual inquiries were conducted primarily in collaboration with others. In the summer of 1978, Harold Kelley assembled a group of nine social psychologists to examine the still largely unexplored field of close relationships. Throughout that summer, we met daily in the conference rooms and sculpture gardens of the University of California, Los Angeles (UCLA) to consider the theoretical, methodological, and factual intricacies of relationships between husbands and wives, parents and children, and other people living their lives in close interdependent relationships with one another. Among other products, our deliberations led to the 1983 book *Close Relationships*. In our several ways, each of us has continued to pursue the topic throughout our careers to date.

In my research and theoretical inquiries as a social psychologist, moral issues were never salient, though of course we were never free of social responsibility. If, like Timothy Leary, we had concluded that the road to personal enlightenment and a free society was to "tune in, turn on, and drop out," our declarations would have carried the imprimatur of our scholarly credentials and probably would have had a greater impact, at least in the short term, than any of our scholarly works have had. We would likely be better known to the general public than we are today, and some of us might be richer. I did not know anybody in our little circle at UCLA, however, who aimed for wealth or fame or sought to perpetrate a social revolution. Our primary values were clarity and coherence in our conceptions of human relationships, and sound methodology in our research. In our collaborative quest, I recall hearty disputation about the ways we might shape our theoretical formulations and lengthy arguments about ways to conduct our investigations, but I do not recall any serious differences over moral issues. Truth and clarity were sufficient guides for the scholarly search.

For me, moral issues rose to prominence only in the professional side of my work. In my own clinical practice with married couples, and in the supervision of students in clinical work with families, the complexities of meshing the morality of the practitioner with that of the client were unavoidable. As practitioners, my students and I inevitably exerted moral influence on our clients, but we did not become on that account moral arbiters, imposing our own morality on those whom we were hired to serve and whose values might differ from our own. Our superordinate obligation in all cases was to help our clients live their lives in more effective, satisfying ways, not on our terms but on theirs. This required us, first of all, to understand the moral positions of our clients, which often were implicit and poorly articulated, and then to work out interpersonal resolutions in which our own values played a part but the long-range welfare of each client overrode all other concerns. No principles comparable with the values of truth and clarity that governed our scientific pursuits stood forth to guide our professional choices. Decisions about divorce, for example, almost always involve painful consequences not only for the couple but also for others in their lives, no matter which way the decision goes. I do not personally hold the moral position that defines divorce as a sin or, in all cases, a psychological mistake. In my own practice and in the cases I supervised with student therapists, decisions about divorce fell about as often in one direction as the other, depending on the particulars of each case.

Every professional action I have ever taken ultimately has led to moral questions. Sometimes the choices are clear, but often they are not, and the search for moral foundations can try the soul. About 10 years ago, the late president of Rutgers University, Edward J. Bloustein, asked me to help him organize efforts to deal with a rash of racist, sexist, and homophobic offenses that had erupted on our campus. With the help of many others, we organized teams of students, faculty, and administrators to revise curricula; recruit minorities; educate faculty, staff, and students about cultures other than their own; set up a grant program to encourage constructive intercultural activities; and in general do whatever we could to create a safe, nurturant environment for people of all colors, creeds, and sexual orientations in our large, diverse, and contentious community. I have described this work in other reports[9] and cannot even summarize it here, except to say that we found the political subtleties of community assessment to be even more complex than we had imagined, and the intercultural animosities and discriminatory abuses that appeared on our campus to be worse than they were when we first began our studies.

The main effect of all this work on me has been to trouble me more than ever about the dreadful fix our society is in. For me, the most vexing questions have not been matters of psychological theory or technique: The most difficult questions and the areas where I still find most of us wandering and often at odds are matters of value and moral direction. When I take a stand on affirmative action or multicultural education, what is the right thing to do? What visions of our university and of our society are we working to realize? Answers to these questions do not come from psychological science. For me, the most useful ideas have come from history, philosophy, and biography. As a white man, I have learned more about the experiences of black people by reading Frederick Douglass, W. E. B. Du Bois, Richard Wright, Claude Brown, James Baldwin, Ralph Ellison, Eldridge Cleaver, Malcolm X, Alice Walker, Maya Angelou, and the Delaney sisters than from anything I have seen so far in our scholarly journals. The histories of human slavery, colonial conquest, and the waves of immigration that have crossed our shores over the past three centuries are essential to understanding the development of American society as we see it, in all its turbulence, today. We cannot survive without moral direction, and that must come from a philosophical understanding of social justice.

In my own thinking, the concepts of pluralistic integration that found cogent expression in the early writings of William James,[10] W. E. B. Du Bois,[11] and Horace Kallen,[12] and were brought into contemporary context by historian John Higham,[13] have been most helpful. I have summarized some of those views, and suggested implications for psychology, in a recent paper,[14] but the search goes on. As soon as I finish writing this chapter, I shall return to some inquiries into the lives of other white, male, Protestants who have faced, each in his own time and place, some of the moral dilemmas I am trying to resolve. I cannot say where the inquiries will lead. For me, the immediate goal is the search itself.

For psychology as a whole, the proximate goal is also search rather than outcome. As scientists, psychologists have always understood that their fundamental aim is advancement of knowledge through systematic investigation, whatever practical uses may eventually derive from any knowledge they obtain. This is true not only for basic science but for applied research as well. Although applied research is instigated in hopeful prospect of practical utility, the investigations themselves are not conducted as stimulants to change. They are defined as research. Uncertainties of outcome are assumed, and neither the authors of the studies nor those who pay for them suffer any confusion about the purpose of the work.

As professionals, however, psychologists have all too often perpetuated the illusion that they are the bearers of an arcane wisdom who already possess the answers to complex questions about the human condition and know from the start how to cure the ailments of their clients. They set themselves up as experts who know, going in, what is wrong with people and how to fix them. In doing so, they offer promises that cannot be kept. With every failure comes a loss of credibility and public confidence.

The ultimate aim of professional work is favorable change in the condition of the client, but the precipitous leap to treatment and corrective intervention, without careful study of each client, not only risks failure but also often creates new, even more serious problems. The immediate aim of professional action in psychology is assessment before treatment, diagnosis before therapy, understanding the condition of the client before attempting to change it, seeing things right before trying to set them right. When professional psychology is conceived as the *study* of behavior, as disciplined *inquiry,* research and practice are seen to hold a common core. The central task for both is not to provide immediate answers to complex questions, but to seek answers to those questions by the different means that our science and profession provide. In the primacy of inquiry as a defining function, the science and profession of psychology share a common mission.

APPENDIX

Abbreviated Professional History

1948	BS, University of Minnesota (Psychology)
1950	MA, University of Minnesota (Psychology)
1952	PhD, University of Minnesota (Clinical Psychology)
1952-1974	Instructor to Professor, University of Illinois
1963-1972	Director, University of Illinois Psychological Clinic
1964-1972	Director of Clinical Training, University of Illinois
1965	Participated in Chicago Conference on Training in Clinical Psychology; admitted first class of PsyD candidates in 1968
1970-1972	Editor, *Journal of Abnormal Psychology*
1973	Participated in the Vail Conference on Training in Professional Psychology
1975-1989	Dean, Graduate School of Applied and Professional Psychology, Rutgers University
1978-1980	Served on Committee on Accreditation, American Psychological Association
1980	Served on Executive Committee of Council on Postsecondary Education
1981	President, National Council of Schools of Professional Psychology
1986	Participated in Utah Conference on Graduate Training in Psychology
1987	Organized Committee to Advance Our Common Purposes, Rutgers University
1996	Began project on the course of bigotry in America

═══════ **NOTES**

1. O. H. Mowrer, " 'Sin,' the Lesser of Two Evils," *American Psychologist, 15* (1960): 301-304; *The Crisis in Psychiatry and Religion* (Princeton, NJ: Van Nostrand, 1961); *The New Group Therapy* (Princeton, NJ: Van Nostrand, 1964); and *Morality and Mental Health* (Chicago: Rand McNally, 1967).

2. P. London, *The Modes and Morals of Psychotherapy* (New York: Holt, Rinehart, and Winston, 1964).

3. American Psychological Association, Committee on Scientific and Professional Aims of Psychology, "The Scientific and Professional Aims of Psychology," *American Psychologist, 22* (1967): 49-76.

4. E. L. Hoch, A. E. Ross, and C. L. Winder, eds., *Professional Preparation of Clinical Psychologists* (Washington, DC: American Psychological Association, 1966).

5. D. R. Peterson, "Organizational Dilemmas in the Education of Professional Psychologists," in *Quality in Professional Psychology Training: A National Conference and Self-Study,* ed. J. E. Callan, D. R. Peterson, and G. Stricker (Norman, OK: Transcript Press, 1986); and "Essentials of Quality in the Education of Professional Psychologists" (keynote address for conference on clinical training in psychology, National Council of Schools and Programs of Professional Psychology, La Jolla, California, January, 1993).

6. D. R. Peterson, R. L. Peterson, J. C. Abrams, and G. Stricker, "The National Council of Schools and Programs of Professional Psychology Educational Model," *Professional Psychology: Research and Practice 28* (1997): 373-386; and D. R. Peterson, R. L. Peterson, and J. C. Abrams, *Standards for Education in Professional Psychology* (in preparation).

7. Compare R. M. McFall, "Making Psychology Incorruptible," *Applied and Preventive Psychology, 5* (1996): 9-16; and D. R. Peterson, "Making Conversation Possible," *Applied and Preventive Psychology, 5* (1996): 17-18.

8. M. Korman, ed., "National Conference on Levels and Patterns of Professional Training in Psychology," *American Psychologist, 29* (1974): 441-449.

9. D. R. Peterson, *Students Speak on Prejudice: A Survey of Intergroup Attitudes and Ethnoviolence Among Undergraduate Students at Rutgers University* (New Brunswick, NJ: Rutgers University, 1990); and "Working Against Prejudice in a Large State University," in *Toward Ethnic Diversification in Psychological Education and Training,* ed. G. Stricker, E. Davis-Russell, E. Bourg, E. Duran, R. Hammond, J. McHolland, K. Polite, and B. Vaughn (Washington, DC: American Psychological Association, 1990).

10. W. James, *A Pluralistic Universe: Hibbert Lectures at Manchester College on the Present Situation in Philosophy* (New York: Longmans, Green, 1909; reissued with additional commentary, Cambridge, MA: Harvard University Press, 1977).

11. W. E. B. Du Bois, "The Conservation of Races" (1897), cited in J. Higham, *Send These to Me: Jews and Other Immigrants in Urban America* (New York: Atheneum, 1975).

12. H. M. Kallen, *Culture and Democracy in the United States: Studies in the Group Psychology of the American Peoples* (New York: Boni and Liveright, 1924).

13. Higham, *Send These to Me.*

14. D. R. Peterson, "The Gift of Diversity: Second Annual Rosalee G. Weiss Lecture" (presented at 103rd annual convention of the American Psychological Association, New York, 1995).

SELECT BIBLIOGRAPHY

Behavior problems of middle childhood. *Journal of Consulting Psychology, 25* (1961): 205-209.

Scope and generality of verbally defined personality factors. *Psychological Review, 72* (1965): 48-58.

The clinical study of social behavior. New York: Appleton-Century-Crofts, 1968.

Is psychology a profession? *American Psychologist, 31* (1976): 572-581.

Need for the Doctor of Psychology degree in professional psychology. *American Psychologist, 31* (1976): 792-798.

With H. Kelley, E. Berscheid, A. Christensen, J. Harvey, T. Huston, G. Levinger, E. McClintock, and A. Peplau. *Close relationships.* San Francisco: Freeman, 1983.

Twenty years of practitioner training in psychology. *American Psychologist, 40* (1985): 441-451.

With J. E. Callan and G. Stricker (Eds.). *Quality in professional psychology training: A national conference and self-study.* Norman, OK: Transcript Press, 1986.

With D. B. Fishman (Eds.). *Assessment for decision.* New Brunswick, NJ: Rutgers University Press, 1987.

Connection and disconnection of research and practice in the education of professional psychologists. *American Psychologist, 46* (1991): 422-429.

Education and training in psychotherapy: An overview. In D. K. Freedheim (Ed.), *History of psychotherapy: A century of change.* Washington, DC: American Psychological Association, 1992.

Patterns of prejudice: Continuing studies of intercultural animosity and abuse at Rutgers University. New Brunswick, NJ: Rutgers University, 1995.

The reflective educator. *American Psychologist, 50* (1995): 975-983.

Making psychology indispensable. *Applied and Preventive Psychology, 5* (1996): 1-8.

Educating professional psychologists: History and guiding conception. Washington, DC: American Psychological Association, 1997.

With R. L. Peterson, J. C. Abrams, and G. Stricker. The National Council of Schools and Programs of Professional Psychology educational model. *Professional Psychology: Research and Practice* 28 (1997): 373-386.

With R. L. Peterson and J. C. Abrams. *Standards for education in professional psychology* (forthcoming).

CHAPTER 3

On Becoming a Psychologist/Educator

JILL N. REICH

The opportunity to reflect on one's knowledge, one's choices, and the values underlying them is a special opportunity. Through it, one stumbles on to patterns and identifies themes, one wonders about choices and paths not taken, and one seeks to make sense of the events experienced—at the very least to form a story that makes some sense to me and to you. This exercise has not been easy to put on paper although a great delight to discuss (one pattern of my behavior I cannot deny); perhaps this is a dramatic statement of the role that discussion plays in my approach to knowledge.

First, I must clarify that from my perspective it is central to the role of psychologist to be an educator, whether one's chosen area of functioning is teaching, research, service, application, consultation, administration, or some combination thereof. I have found that although the content of my work is unique to the discipline, my efforts as an educator are common across many areas. Taking this perspective emphasizes that education occurs not only in the classroom, in seminars, and in teaching programs, but also in research and application, in supervision of others, in consultation to organizations and industry, and in presentations to other professionals, legislators, policymakers, special interest groups, and the general public.

To look at where this path leads in terms of what I do as a psychologist and how I arrived at these ideas, let me turn to some work I did several years ago when thinking about graduate education and faculty roles. From a variety of measures of faculty workload, preferences, and values, I identified four basic functions that serve as the basis of what I do as a psychologist and what others (e.g., E. Boyer) have posited as the foundation of the educator/scholar—namely, synthesizing knowledge, creating knowledge, communicating knowledge, and applying knowledge. Although throughout my career, my various roles and responsibilities may focus more or less on any of these functions at a particular point in time, there is little I can do as a psychologist that does not fit into this overall paradigm. This means that as I look across my career lifeline, I can focus on those aspects that differentiate my various work roles (as teacher, researcher, and consultant or administrator), or I can recognize and attend to those areas of similarity and grow enormously from the opportunities gained by their integration. I believe that the time has come—in fact, it is long overdue—that we as a discipline come together, recognizing our common interests, functions, values, and contributions. Neither psychology nor psychologists can tolerate the divisions that have characterized our recent past. Not only have we much in common, but the challenges we face, as psychologists and as citizens, also demand that we come together.

In my present position as Executive Director of Education for the American Psychological Association, I have the honor and opportunity to view education's and psychology's place in the academy from the broadest view possible. Working always toward our two goals of enhancing quality education and training in psychology and of advancing the application of psychology to education, I am part leader for education; part teacher, especially for those disenfranchised from education and/or psychology; and part cheerleader for the discipline across all perspectives in education and across all levels of educational programming. What I have learned in my 18 months on the job is that quality education demands integration, complex tasks, collaboration, teamwork, and continued outreach to new ideas and other disciplines. I have found ever more evidence that psychology has much to contribute to this changing world, and once again I must learn that change is the only absolute, an insight I first remember noticing many years ago in college.

THE BEGINNING

As I reflect on the past, what stands out in dazzling focus is the sinuous pattern of the paths taken, the importance of role models, and the need for a bit of good old-fashioned luck. Looking back to my family history, it is readily apparent that teachers and education played an inordinately powerful role, especially for the women of the clan. Ranging in areas from ballet to business, my mother, her sisters, and my father's sisters (we are a family of mostly women) were all teachers, and many of their aunts were teachers too—a feat that became extraordinary only when I realized as an adult how unlikely education of women must have been back these many generations. Schools and their teachers were places of authority that demanded excellence. Unfortunately, I cannot say that they provided a welcoming environment; in fact, throughout my grammar and secondary school years, schools were more a place of authority and fear than delight or joy. Still, I knew that learning was important; books were a constant friend, and academic success was recognized and valued.

Other facets of my present life too were firmly set forth during my childhood. These patterns, ideas, and values that I can see have served as guideposts and challenges throughout my life are fundamental in their persistence although manifest in different forms and situations. For example, although authoritarian and firm, my family was loving and supportive; the firmness I am only now beginning to appreciate, the loving I never doubted. Both parents encouraged me to excel, to compete but to keep a sense of balance and fun in so doing. I probably have taken lessons in most sports known to man (or woman), including swimming, diving, golf, tennis, and skiing, as well as piano, singing, and always, always—from the age of 2—ballet. Yet, in the midst of this constant activity, there remained a sense that it must be fun and never take the place of intellectual endeavors. I remember becoming absolutely committed to diving and even becoming quite good at it. One summer, my coach suggested that I take the plunge (so to speak) and become involved in a level of competition that would demand singular focus and extensive practice throughout the year. I was eager but not allowed to do so by my parents. They protected my childhood and demanded obedience. Ironically, on my part, I think that this led to a persistent rebellion, a firm grounding in valuing the search for excellence, and a struggle to maintain balance amid a tendency toward intense and passionate involvement in areas of interest.

It was not until my college days at Regis College in Weston, Massachusetts, when I serendipitously began to work as a research assistant for a cognitive psychologist that I truly experienced the real fun of learning—of synthesizing, creating, communicating, and applying knowledge. It was a first, and I was hooked. My mentor was a psychologist, so I wanted to be one too. Of course I shall never know for sure, but I believe that it was the excitement of learning that turned me into a psychologist. Although the range probably was not infinite,

I suspect that I would have followed whatever discipline provided this experience. Ray Nickerson, an applied cognitive psychologist, introduced me to the excitement of learning. He let that excitement lead the way and support the necessary hard work rather than demanding excellence as an external standard of success. He cared about me as a person and let me know that. And, he included me in the intellectual challenges he faced, letting me see him struggle and sometimes lose that battle to understand, rather than maintaining the facade of absolute authority and expertise.

A further important lesson learned through this experience was that I was responsible for my own learning. Mentors and teachers are important guides, as sources for what is relevant and how to do things, but only you, the learner, can be responsible for the learning. I'm not sure just how I came to this conclusion, but I remember quite clearly arriving there. Perhaps it was wanting to take some credit for the fun I had discovered; perhaps it was that I attended a small, liberal arts college limited in its offerings; or maybe it was just luck. Of course, one never knows for sure at which of the many points in one's life are the true critical choices. As one of my graduate school friends liked to remind us all, "the problem with life is that there is no control group." I am convinced, however, that this psychologist at this time in my life provided one of those experiences.

Looking back, I am chagrined to report that after I completed my baccalaureate degree and worked for a short time as a research assistant to a group of psychologists investigating early infant development, I then promptly left the United States to spend almost 3 years in Switzerland—mostly skiing, if the truth be known, although I worked as an English teacher to keep head and hearth together. This is not the most obvious step to take in convincing you of my newfound delight in learning and enthusiasm for psychology, but it was important to my development nevertheless. It was a time to mature emotionally, to learn just how much I wanted to pursue the life of a scholar, and, for reasons still unknown to me, to become confident in my ability to learn. During my Swiss sojourn, once again I was learning by being outside the relevant context; perhaps it is the opportunity to compare and contrast that is important to the growth that seems to come as a result.

Returning to graduate school was a joy. Certainly, I don't mean to romanticize the hard work, anxiety, challenges, and grief that we all experienced then and throughout our professional lives, but those years served to focus my interests, motivation, and goals.

My graduate experience came at another lucky time, I believe. It was a time in developmental psychology when we were just beginning to apply an information processing model to our study of cognitive development—we thought we had found "truth." I write this with the unease that results from having to admit my naivete and arrogance, yet I also include this part of my story as I realize that the time and the confidence it provided was a lucky turn for my learning to be a developmental psychologist. At a time when I was just beginning to learn this vast knowledge base of ours (before beginning graduate school I had only one course in psychology, one which I did not like, and my learning had been idiosyncratic and sporadic), I was able to believe that the context within which I learned and worked was "it." I did not have to question my ability to find answers to my questions, nor did I have to deal with the multilayered complexities of "what ifs." I have often speculated what it must be like to be a student today in a time when we are sure only that whatever we think about a phenomenon is likely to change. In this stage in the development of my thinking, change is a concept that is exciting and challenging. I fear that when I was just starting out on this path, it may well have been more overwhelming than I could have handled. There is a cohort effect to the learning trajectory I am trying to describe. Being a student 20 years ago was different from today in ways that have direct effects on what I learned and how I learned it.

As a graduate student then, I mastered the rudiments of what would serve as my foundation for being a teacher, a researcher, and a member of a professional community that included my department, my institution, my discipline, and my community. How did I learn all these roles? I'm not really sure, but I think it was by watching those around me and seeing them in these roles as well as building on the experiences of my family, their values, and their expectations.

FROM GRADUATE SCHOOL TO NOW: STARTS, STOPS, AND INTEGRATION

Although my graduate education and training assumed an academic career, as the days ticked away toward completion I found that personal factors drove me to want to stay in Hanover, New Hampshire, making career opportunities quite restricted. In this process, I learned many lessons, among the most important being that it was far easier for women than men to insert personal factors into career choices. This is evidence of gender stereotypes, certainly, but it made it easier for me nevertheless. Perhaps more central to my career, however, I learned how very important it is to view your knowledge and skills in terms of what others need and are looking for; to place your expertise in their context, their language, and their needs. It is so unnecessarily limiting to take the stance and identity that I am a psychologist and as such work in X settings doing Y things. Rather, if you look at your expertise more conceptually (i.e., you ask yourself who needs your expertise rather than asking what are the career paths of psychologists), you open new vistas for yourself and those to whom you can make significant contributions. Taking this approach led me to a research associate position with the New Hampshire/Vermont Regional Perinatal Program at Dartmouth Medical School. I was brought on to evaluate an education program for physicians and nurses caring for high-risk infants. Over a few years' time, this experience led me to a faculty position in the Department of Maternal and Child Health at Dartmouth Medical School and a focus for my own research and career. I completed graduate school with extensive knowledge of and research skills in the cognitive development of infants and young children. At the medical school, I learned that I could apply this expertise to an investigation of the long-term outcomes of premature and sick newborns.

I was beginning to see that interests and desires could merge. I could take my intellectual expertise and apply it to issues of great meaning to me; I could turn personal boundaries of geography into real opportunities. Had I not wanted to remain in Hanover, I doubt that I would have made the effort to chart a different terrain for my newly minted degree. Moreover, I quite unexpectedly (at least on any conscious level) managed to bring together early cognitive development and high-risk infants, an area of very deep and personal concern. I had grown up with an older sister who was severely compromised by cerebral palsy; in her life of 24 years she never reached beyond about a year in developmental age. I raise this aspect of my life here as this is when it became relevant to me—and to my story. The reason for this is, I believe, a tribute to my parents, for they raised all of us together, at home, in the belief that nothing was abnormal about our situation. Some of that, no doubt, was denial, and some of the results were likely negative; yet, after many years of reflection and observation, I continue to praise and appreciate their decision—it has given me admiration for the demands of parenting, sensitivity to individual differences, interest in cognitive development, and a need to take my adult place in society by contributing to the common good. In all, I believe that my experiences growing up with a sister who experienced severe handicaps made me realize the dialectic of life, the capriciousness of success and the constant of change.

Not long after I established my place within the medical school, the opportunity to join a traditional faculty in the Psychology Department at Loyola

University of Chicago, came my way. I cannot say that I sought the position, but I cannot say that I ran from it. Once again, personal circumstances seemed to open new vistas while intellectual and career interests carried the torch to new places. The Loyola position was particularly appealing as it combined the advantages of a traditional academic position in the College of Arts and Sciences with the challenge of bringing my applied research agenda to this setting. So began what would become an 18-year career in Chicago that moved me through the faculty ranks from assistant to full professor, along the way taking consulting positions, directing our graduate program in developmental psychology, beginning the Center for Children and Families, and serving as department chairperson and associate dean of the graduate school.

The lessons of these many years were varied and rich. In retrospect, a pattern to my growth as a professional is that I develop new areas and then integrate them into existing interests and expertise. In this case, as a new faculty member, I first had to learn to teach psychology. Until then, my psychology knowledge was quite idiosyncratic, mostly directed by my research interests. I had to learn both content and how to make it real and understandable to the learner. I had to learn to meet many demands—of a diverse student body, of the balance between teaching and research, and of what it meant to be a citizen of my department and institution.

During this time, I continued my research by establishing the Infant Development Project with a close colleague and friend, Deborah L. Holmes. Through this project, which sought to describe and explain the long-term developmental outcomes of prematurity, illness, and hospitalization on newborns, we built a research team of faculty, graduate students, and undergraduates who were engaged in the excitement and fun of learning, and able to contribute to the knowledge base that served sick infants and their families. I had now incorporated teaching into my earlier research agenda. The years were moving along, and I was learning and contributing in ways that brought patterns of earlier experiences into new forms and functions.

In retrospect, I have learned that about every 4 to 5 years, my attention starts to wander. More immediate goals have been reached, and although I've not always been aware of so doing, retrospectively I can see that I must have begun to look about for new adventures and new challenges. About the time of settling into my role of Associate Professor of Psychology, one that required becoming a successful teacher and researcher, I began to become interested in administrative positions—areas through which I could take my knowledge and expertise to more programmatic structures, extending what I could do as an individual by developing environments in which others could excel in implementing common goals. I made this move in the obvious ways, first as director of our doctoral program in Developmental Psychology, then as the founder of the Center for Children and Families, and finally as an academic administrator, as associate dean of the graduate school and then as department chairperson.

A common theme in all these administrative endeavors is the push to integrate the many roles and functions of the academy—to find the intersect between teaching and research and to do so in ways that serve the community and contribute to the common good. In looking back, it seems that I began this process more specifically and then moved it into ever extending concentric circles. For example, our doctoral program in developmental psychology, my first administrative responsibility, focused on the psychology graduate students and developmental content areas. Next, I moved into developing the Center for Children and Families, a multidisciplinary endeavor bringing together faculty and graduate students/residents in psychology, education, and pediatrics in projects to serve the community's families through interventions that also provided opportunities for research and teaching. Perhaps the most rewarding endeavor I have ever had the honor to serve, the center's work also taught me the vagaries of politics. Ultimately, we lost our funding because the low-cost, Head Start-type program utilizing student staff and parent contributions served a community of low-income, multiethnic families whom the state decided were not "needy" enough to warrant continued funding.

New horizons for developing linkages across the teaching, research, and service roles and responsibilities of faculty were provided me as associate dean of the graduate school, where I was able to develop a Teaching Fellows program to support advanced graduate students becoming junior faculty, learning to balance and integrate their teaching and research roles. This is a theme that pervaded my work as department chairperson, in which the focus expanded to include undergraduate and graduate students and faculty. While there, I was able to apply my planning work heretofore done outside the university to the needs of the department. In particular was the development of a strategic plan for the department that then served as the motivating factor in establishing a department identity, a road map for present and future projects and a means against which to measure progress, realign new initiatives, and report to ourselves and others what we accomplished. For example, it served as a means of identifying a gap in our efforts to advance diversity through our education programs, leading to the establishment of the Social Science Research Opportunity Program (SSROP) with our colleagues in sociology and political science. This program supported minority undergraduate students in a year-long research project designed to introduce them to the challenges of the discipline, of research, and of a future academic career. Noble goals all, but what was most creative about this program (since other institutions had already established similar programs) was that this effort was tied to the faculty mentor broadening his or her research to include a factor of diversity. This tack was taken to expand the faculty's interest in and understanding of diversity, and the result would serve to enhance that person's teaching of diversity in the future. In this way, the project served to support a group of minority undergraduate students and to enhance faculty learning in ways that would live on in their teaching and research for years to come.

This approach to academic administration, one that seeks to find the intersect of teaching, research, and service in ways that enhance, support, and advance the discipline and the community we serve, has become the foundation of all that I do. It served me well in my position as Dean of the Faculty at Trinity College, a small, elite liberal arts undergraduate college in the midst of Hartford, Connecticut, whose stated mission is to "foster critical thinking, free the mind of parochialism and prejudice, and prepare students to lead examined lives that are personally satisfying, civically responsible and socially useful." Here, I was able to extend my educational philosophy and approach across all disciplines.

So my story returns full circle to my current position, placing me in the midst, once again, of psychology, now within the discipline again but extending across all levels of education and training and involved with students and faculty from every type of academic institution. The view is spectacular, the possibilities are endless, and there is much to learn and contribute.

WHY A JOB CAN'T ENCOMPASS IT ALL

Still, there is a bit more to the story of how I got here. One's workplace cannot provide all the grist for this mill we call life—not even professional life. I have found that opportunities for learning and contributing available through volunteer service and consulting work are essential to one's development. In these arenas, I learned new ways of thinking, further refinement of ideas as well as an expansion of possibilities. I learned that psychology is part of a system and that we, as psychologists, must work in teams and must be knowledgeable about the need to collaborate with other disciplines. I also learned that we, as psychologists, have unique and important contributions to make to the overall task being shaped.

Once again, my reflections point out to me that I began this work within focused areas linked directly to psychology, then moved into broader fields. My first such encounter was with the APA Accreditation Committee. At the time, I really didn't know much about accreditation; in fact, I knew very little before being asked to join a site visit team. It was my good fortune to join a team of two outstanding psychologists and mentors—Jim Hurst and Roger Myers—whose introduction to accreditation served to extend over many years even to this day. I also benefited from working with Paul Nelson, Deputy Director of the Education Directorate, perhaps the person most knowledgeable about our accreditation history, process, and values. All took me under their proverbial wings, not only patiently explaining our task but also, and more important, showing me the philosophical underpinning of the process, why it is important to psychology, and how such a system serves to both ensure quality and advance program development. I am deeply indebted to each of them, as this was my first step in thinking about the process of education, thinking about its measurement and wondering how to affect the system beyond my own involvement in it. This was another central moment in my eventual development as an administrator.

A second major impact on my career was the work I have done as a consultant to the architectural firm of Walter H. Sobel, FAIA. This too began somewhat serendipitously through a social conversation about what architects and psychologists do, a conversation that became a 20-year professional consultantship that lasts to this day. Through this work, I learned the varied ways that a research psychologist can contribute to the questions, answers, and implementation issues an architect faces in designing a building and working with clients. Quite unexpectedly, I also learned the value of time, for there is little in the academician's life that causes her to think about time in 15-minute units of productivity, but in an architect's office, one's time is charged to the client in that way. I was forced to ask myself if my work product deserved that charge. Moreover, it was through this work that I learned over and over the need to listen and to find answers to meet the needs expressed—not answers you want to impose. These are all strategies and lessons that have served me well in so many situations in and out of the academy.

These lessons were more directly placed in the service of child development through work in social policy, assisting one of our Illinois legislators and working with the Chicago area United Way. The particulars are not important to the story; rather, what is important is that one finds opportunities to utilize expertise and knowledge in ways that have direct contributions to the community and learns from these experiences in ways that expand professional development. It not only is more efficient to combine one's professional and volunteer efforts, but clearly one also can be more effective when these kinds of bridges are built.

THE PSYCHOLOGIST/EDUCATOR I HAVE BECOME

The themes that have emerged from my story are central to what I do and how I do it. These themes serve as signposts for how I see the work of education and psychology's role in it. They are part of the psychologist/educator I have become.

The first theme is change. Throughout my life's story is a recognition of change and the need to embrace it. Whether in the form of knowledge or process, outcome or beginning, integrating or measuring, change is a constant. For example, new knowledge and new skills affect all that we do: what we teach and how we impart information, the questions we research and the way we seek answers, how we practice, and the skills we bring to our interventions. Yet, whatever the source and the results, our expanding knowledge and skill base in psychology, while good and necessary, carries conflicting pressures—most notably for increased generalization *and* increased specialization, for advancement but within circumscribed time periods, for creative and novel but quickly measurable results, and for the production of new jobs and careers while at the same time old ones are rendered obsolete.

An area of dramatic change for the remainder of our professional lives will be technology. As the newest wave of technology permeates our environment, the next wave already spans the horizon. We have virtual reality, telecommunications, computer-assisted instruction, interactive media, electronic mail, bulletin boards, chat rooms, group work systems, and telemedicine. These and other electronic technologies offer powerful new tools for synthesizing information, creating new knowledge, and communicating and applying what we learn.

Further, the changing profile of our national demographics affects all that we do: what we communicate, to whom, and how. Psychology builds and tests its knowledge base against the experiences of a multicultural population, throughout the life span and under a variety of conditions associated with age, gender, race, ethnicity, and socioeconomic groups. We must incorporate demographic factors into our questions, content, methods, understanding, and application. Without such relevance and applicability, psychology will be unable to ensure the validity of our science, the meaningfulness of our interventions, or the understanding of our teaching.

Today, most psychologists and educators are convinced that the demographics of the student population have changed. The challenge now is to take the next step of integration, that is, to truly recognize and understand that as psychologists we *must* incorporate diversity into all that we do. We cannot understand human behavior if we do not include factors of diversity in our research; we cannot teach about psychology if we do not master the implications of demographic factors on our theories, models, and research results. Further, it is the responsibility of all of us, regardless of our background.

To look at our history just over the past 20 years in which I have been a psychologist is to realize anew the absolute of change. Psychologists are engaged in careers and contributions that didn't exist even that short time ago. What does that tell us about the next 20 years ahead? A common theme in my presentations to faculty, students, and practitioners around the country has been the importance of learning from the past and from our discipline. In particular, if you think about any theory or model of developmental psychology, you will realize that systematic change (i.e., development) comes about because of some kind of negative factor, whether that be thought of as disequilibrium, uncertainty, frustration, or the like. I have never known anyone to propose that we sit around, consider that our lives are going well, and so decide to change. Rather, we are faced with some challenge, some crisis, or some imbalance, something that no longer fits into our regular way of doing things.

These past few years, ones in which I have focused almost exclusively on administration, have taught me that I truly am a developmental psychologist. I see the world from this perspective, I think about questions from this vantage point, and I find answers within this context.

Contribution to societal needs is another central theme. The identification and press of societal needs must and does influence all that we do as psychologists—as educators. Our society is rapidly moving toward being one consisting of those who have and those who have not; there is an increasingly larger percentage of elderly left uncared for, an increasing incidence of violence and child abuse, a national health care system in crisis, and an education system in disarray. Welfare reform is a political football rather than a system of caring. Our discipline and our expertise has much to contribute to these areas. Moreover, these same areas influence what we do and how we do it. Societal needs and national policies have influenced the content of our work and the methods we use to go about our business. Over the last decade, because of these areas, psychology has seen the growth of behavioral medicine, chronic illness interventions, and life-span developmental theories and applications. We have contributed to ways of addressing substance abuse, violence prevention, and AIDS. We have studied and advanced human-computer interactions, human factors, workplace productivity, and public health. Not only have we expanded our expertise into these areas, but these areas, with their unique questions, challenges, and needs, also have forced us to re-evaluate our questions, our methods, our theories, and our understanding of psychology and what it means to be a psychologist. With each new territory into which we tread, we continue to learn, to expand our knowledge, to communicate our findings, and to apply our results.

PUTTING THESE THEMES TO WORK

First, these themes mean that the academy no longer lives in an ivory tower; it's time to join the real world. For those who have not yet tried it, be assured that once you start focusing on what folks want from higher education, you realize that everyone (psychologists and policymakers) has the same goal: We all want to enhance learning, advance knowledge, and contribute to the nation's good. I have often found that, at least for our discipline of psychology, the problem is not that we cannot meet the demands our publics seek from higher education but that we are not very good at explaining what we do in terms that our constituents understand and want. For example, a recent note from Curt Burgess, a Presidential Faculty Fellow from the Psychology Department at UC-Riverside, proposes that we must move away from arguing about the relative importance of teaching versus research—an argument, by the way, that reflects a no-win situation because higher education demands both if we are to be viable and strong. Rather, he proposes that we move to the more relevant concept of faculty impact on student education, a concept that encompasses the many roles of faculty and focuses this work on our students. This approach provides an important response to a major concern of the American public—that education needs to focus on students' learning. It is a theme recognized not only by educators but also by researchers and their major funding agencies, public and private. We must realize that many of our publics view the role of educator as one of arrogance, privilege, and isolation. They think that teaching occurs only in the classroom; they hear that faculty "teach" one, two, or three courses a semester and conclude that faculty are loafers, and even worse, loafers with tenure. This is all salt in the wounds of a public fearing for its own job security. The ill feelings are further exacerbated by the continuing rise in tuition costs.

The good news is that most of us psychologists need not change what we do but instead, rather as Curt did, learn how to explain what we do in ways that the public can understand and support. Surveys and conversations alike suggest that the American public wants its graduates to be able to write, to be able to think critically, to have a work ethic, and to be able to move easily in a world of change; America wants graduates who value lifelong learning and who can contribute to the public good. These goals apply to our graduates, whether from precollege or graduate programs. To achieve these goals, faculty with their students must be involved in teaching, research, and service/practice, all familiar roles to each of us. The difference the world now demands is that we learn to explain these activities in terms of our role as educators—in terms of how these activities affect student learning.

AFTERTHOUGHT

There is much to be done, and enough work and enough glory for everyone to shine. There are great successes on which psychologists can build, but we cannot succeed in isolation. Psychologists are educators, and as educators, we must lead the way. To be effective, we must ask ourselves what are we doing and why. It may not happen every 5 years or so, as has been my experience, but it must occur in the growth of a psychologist/educator. The results of this reflection must be implemented, dynamically translated into new forms and functions that in turn will change our tasks and thinking.

We must extend our work in ways that apply our expertise. We must educate the public (not just our students) about what we do and how to use our expertise for the common good. We must be willing to think about how our research relates to societal needs and act to implement it in this way. Although this occurs for some through their work, most often, as in my case, it comes from volunteer efforts. If we do not contribute to these questions, they will be answered without our expertise. Our choice is not whether or not the questions will be asked or the needs be identified; rather, our only choice is whether or not to bring our knowledge and expertise to bear on the response. This is no easy task. Some would say that it diverts necessary time and attention from our real work of creating knowledge. This is true: It does take considerable time, effort, and expertise. But what is the alternative?

We can and must educate the future in all of its forms.

APPENDIX

Abbreviated Professional History

1966	BA (English), Regis College
1976	PhD (Experimental/Developmental Psychology), Dartmouth College
1975-1977	Research Associate, Regional Perinatal Program, Department of Maternal and Child Health, Dartmouth Medical School; Assistant Professor, 1977
1976-1977	Research Consultant: Women in Science, Dartmouth College and National Science Foundation
1977-1994	Assistant Professor (1977-1984), Associate Professor (1984-1990), and Professor (1990-1994), Loyola University of Chicago; Director, doctoral program in Developmental Psychology, 1984-1986; Associate Dean, the graduate school, 1986-1990; Chairperson, Department of Psychology, 1990-1994
1978-present	Consultant, Walter H. Sobel & Associates Architects and Planners, Chicago; Committee on Planning and Urban Affairs, American Institute of Architects
1979-1982	Committee on Accreditation, American Psychological Association; Chairperson, 1981-1982
1984-1987	Consultant, Representative Lee Preston, Third Representative District, Illinois General Assembly; Governor's Task Force on the Child Witness, State of Illinois
1985-1990	Director (1985-1987) and Codirector (1988-1990), Center for Children and Families, Loyola University of Chicago
1985-1990	Task Force on the Scope and Criteria of Accreditation, American Psychological Association; Chairperson, 1987-1990
1985-1994	Visiting Scientist, Museum of Science and Industry, Chicago

APPENDIX

Abbreviated Professional History *(continued)*

1986	Cochair, International Association of Infant Mental Health Annual Convention
1988-1990	Consultant, American Academy of Pediatrics
1988-1994	Board of Directors, Ox-Bow School of Art Institute, Chicago
1990	Group Leader, National Conference on the Scientist-Practitioner Model for the Education and Training of Professional Practice of Psychology
1991	Invited participant, National Conference on Enhancing Undergraduate Education in Psychology
1991-1992	Needs Assessment Committee on Children and Families, United Way of Chicago
1992	Consultant, Education Directorate, American Psychological Association
1992-1994	Cochairperson and Convener, Steering Committee for National Conference on Post-doctoral Education, American Psychological Association
1993-1994	Senior Policy Fellow for Education, American Psychological Association
1994-1995	Dean of the Faculty and Professor of Psychology, Trinity College
1995	Executive Director, Education Directorate, American Psychological Association

SELECT BIBLIOGRAPHY

With S. Friedman and G. C. Carpenter. New born attention: Differential response decrement to visual stimuli. *Journal of Experimental Child Psychology, 10* (1970): 44-50.

With J. D. Baird. Children as environmental planners. In *Advances in environmental psychology* (Vol. 3), ed. J. Wohlwill and I. Altman. New York: Plenum, 1978.

With D. L. Holmes and J. F. Pasternak. *The psychology of infants at risk.* Hillsdale, NJ: Lawrence Erlbaum, 1984.

With W. H. Sobel, D. H. Mahan, and E. L. Deam. Involving the public and serving the public. *Justice System Journal, 10* (1985): 339-352.

With J. A. Durlak. Preventive interventions in the environment: Examples and issues. In *Prevention: Towards a multidisciplinary approach,* ed. L. Jason, R. Hess, R. Felner, and J. Moritsugu. New York: Haworth Press, 1988.

With D. L. Holmes and M. L. Reiff. Kindergarten performance of children born at risk. *Canadian Journal of Psychology, 42* (1988): 189-200.

With D. L. Holmes and J. S. Gyurke. The development of high risk infants in low risk families. In *Applied developmental psychology* (Vol. 3), ed. F. J. Morrison, C. Lord, and D. Keating. New York: Plenum, 1989.

With J. C. Kaspar, M. S. Puczynski, et al. Effect of a hypoglycemic episode on neuropsychological functioning in diabetic children. *Journal of Clinical and Experimental Neuropsychology, 12* (1990): 613-626.

With B. F. Fretz et al. The complete scholar: Faculty development for those who teach psychology. In *Handbook for enhancing undergraduate education in psychology*, ed. T. V. McGovern. Washington, DC: American Psychological Association, 1993.

CHAPTER 4

Still the Serendipitous Maverick

LEO GOLDMAN

In an article in the April 1985 issue of the *Journal of Counseling and Development*, I was the subject of a "Life Line" interview with Wayne Anderson. The title given to the article pretty well reflects the essence of my professional life: "Leo Goldman, Serendipitous Maverick." Most of my career changes and other professional activities came to me rather than being sought out, yet, especially during the past 25 years, I have been in disagreement with and critical of the traditional thinking and writing of the field in much of my writing and teaching. Essentially, I believe that all of that reflects values that occasionally have conflicted with each other: on one hand, a value on education and achievement within the existing structure, and on the other hand, a value on changing existing structures and professional practice—a nontraditional, even antitraditional, stance. What follows is an attempt to trace the sources of my values and behaviors.

FAMILY AND EARLY DEVELOPMENT

I suppose that much of my professional history can be traced back to my early life—family, setting, and the times. My parents were immigrants—

father from Poland, mother from Russia—each having migrated alone around the age of 20 to a country whose language they knew not at all, and with just enough money to live on for a month or so. They left anti-Semitism, lack of political and religious freedom, and very limited opportunity for education and career. Although both were raised in Orthodox Judaism, each soon became a "free thinker," and they lived the rest of their lives without any religious identification or activity. I had no religious education of any kind, but my mother taught me to read and write Yiddish. They were, and remained, "ethnic Jews," as I have.

Although both had only the equivalent of perhaps elementary education, they were intelligent and eager to learn. They went to night school to learn English; attended lectures on science, medicine, political theories, and other topics; and had a small but good library of Yiddish books of fiction and nonfiction. They worked hard—my father as a carpenter in millwork shops, my mother as a seamstress until I was born, and from then on as a full-time homemaker. "Full-time" in those years meant 6-day weeks and short vacations, and of course no unemployment insurance, old age benefits, Medicaid, or Medicare, and no one-stop supermarket, washing machine, dryer, electric refrigerator, elevator, or automobile. In fact, we did not have a telephone until I was about 18, but that had to do with the Depression rather than its unavailability.

Another important fact of my home and family was my parents' socialistic idealism. They were active members of a Jewish socialistic fraternal organization and read a Yiddish newspaper that was socialistic in orientation. Their belief was that in a gradual, democratic way, this country would move toward what I suppose we would now call a welfare state. Their socialism also dreamed of a world free of racism and other "isms" that deny opportunity to people. I must add that, after my own lifetime of observing socialistic experiments in various countries, I no longer share my parents' beliefs; my perceptions of human instincts, needs, and behaviors lead me to conclude that economic and political socialism will not lead to any utopia, and that the kinds of better living they dreamed of will not come from socialism.

Although I wish it were different, I believe that people are motivated primarily, at least in initial reactions, by what is good for themselves and that the best economic/political system we have so far developed is one in which individuals and organized groups have freedom to produce, sell, and buy what they wish, but within a framework that monitors and limits any harm they may do to other people or their society and environment. It also is necessary to educate people constantly about their responsibilities to their community and society, especially to the weak and powerless. The dream of a socialistic society, on the other hand, hinges on the belief that people are, or can be, motivated primarily by what is good for the society. I don't think that our knowledge of people and of socialistic experiments supports that belief.

We moved five times until I was about 20, first, when I was an infant, from Kingston, New York, to Brooklyn, New York, then within Brooklyn, first upscale as income increased during the 1920s, and then down in 1929, when the Depression began, and up again when things improved in the late 1930s. My father lost his job in 1929 and, after unsuccessful efforts to get another, opened a little storefront millwork shop, where he struggled for years, gradually earning enough to live on, and eventually taking on a partner who was primarily a salesman and who brought in much business, enough so that my father could retire at 65 without Social Security coverage. He was disappointed when I told him, on my discharge from the Air Force, that I was going to graduate school; he had held on to the business in the expectation that I would take it over. But I had no liking for the business world and would have been a dismal failure.

Although we never went hungry and always lived in decent tenements (though always four of us in small one-bedroom apartments), I must have felt that we were on the brink of complete poverty. For example, when I graduated from high school at $15\frac{1}{2}$, having been accelerated several times, I expected to go to work (shows how naive I was!), but my mother insisted that I go to college. Fortunately, the four city colleges of New York were completely tuition-free and even lent textbooks for the required courses of the first 2 years. I also later learned that all the salary I earned in summers during my college years, and gave to my mother to help out, went into a savings account in my name.

I worked for my father after school and summers, starting when I was about 12 and continuing all the way through college; I helped move lumber and finished products and did the small amount of bookkeeping and typing needed. Somewhere around then, I did my first writing, using his typewriter to hunt-and-peck a little neighborhood gossip sheet and making as many carbon copies as I could at one time. It was many decades before I recognized that writing was something I enjoy very much and do well and relatively easily. Only during the past weeks, at this writing, I was asked to write a page for the magazine of an environmental organization telling about my experiences as a volunteer there. I received a rave reaction from the editor, who said that it was the best such piece she had ever received, and that I had a "voice" and came through as a person. I was delighted—this is the kind of feedback one does not receive from professional journals in psychology and was very welcome indeed, since I so value good writing and good communication in general.

My home was a protective and caring place for my sister (6 years younger) and me. We always had dinner together, listened to the radio together in the evenings and on Sundays, and a few times each summer went to parks and beaches. My father took pictures with his Kodak bellows camera during some of these excursions, and I can follow my increasing height and my promotion from knickers to "longees" in the annual summer visits to Prospect Park. But I do not remember any hugs or kisses; my father was more emotionally expressive than my mother, but there was no touching, and no verbal expressions of love, or compliments. I think they would both have been uncomfortable with such actions.

Socially, I was very limited, pretty much a loner through late childhood, adolescence, and even through my 20s. It was only in my 60s and 70s, after having left my marriage and begun to develop my own relationships with both men and women, that I realized that I had passively given in to my mother's controlling behavior. I think that she had difficulty in physical intimacy and subtly controlled my early efforts to do things that involved that and even any kind of risk.

Without being aware of it, I suppose I have always valued education and high achievement in activities that advance truth and beauty and human life in general—a reflection of the values of my parents and of Jewishness in general. Money has never been much of a motivating force in my life; my choices and efforts, and most of my professional activities, have been selected and continued on the basis of what would be intrinsically interesting and fulfilling and seemed worth doing.

For the past 20 years or so, my path has been one of espousing nontraditional causes professionally. Partly this has to be related to my social isolation during so many of my developmental years, but that is only what makes it feel comfortable. More substantive is the orientation toward change, toward progressivism, even radicalism, in scientific and professional thinking and functioning. My two "crusades"—critical of standardized tests starting in the early 1970s, and of quantitative research methods starting in the mid-1970s—have placed me outside the "establishment" and the "networks." Not only do I feel apart from many of the prevailing beliefs and practices, but indeed I feel alienated from the people who are the writers and editors.

It also occurs to me, as I write this, that my New York socialistic Jewishness, which I realized only in recent years was more apparent to other people than to me, does not harmonize well with what I see as the dominant middle America, which seems to be midwestern, of northern European ancestry, religious, and conservative. My awareness of this fact came to strong realization only some 6 or 7 years ago, during my term as President of the Division of Counseling Psychology of APA. I go into detail on that later.

Another thought that occurs to me as I write is that almost every new professional opportunity aroused in me a mix of anxiety and enthusiasm. Whether it was a new job, an invited piece of writing, candidacy for office in professional organizations, or an invitation to lecture or teach a new course, almost always my first reaction was to look for reasons not to do it—seeing the offer as a threat, I think, and expecting that I would not be able to do it well or would not like it. Yet almost always the positive pull won out, and almost always I accomplished the task well and enjoyed the acknowledgment and reactions that followed. My story is a familiar one: well-meaning parents who took high achievement in school for granted, were disappointed at anything less, and rarely complimented.

COLLEGE AND EARLY CAREER EXPLORATION

As mentioned previously, I helped out in my father's millwork shop after school and summers through high school and college. I majored in sociology at City College of New York (a 1-hour subway trip from home) and thought of going to a school of social work for a master's degree, but I believe that the age minimum was 21, and I was not yet 20. So I took the easy way and went to work for my father and his partner, doing estimating from architects' blueprints and specifications, preparing detailed shop drawings, and visiting construction sites to get exact measurements for kitchen cabinets and other items of millwork that needed to be individually fitted.

In fact, I should back up a step: My first year in college was in the School of Engineering, which was the closest major at any of the city colleges to architecture, the area that my father thought I should go into. Even though I have long thought that architects are in one of the most fascinating fields, and I enjoy reading about and seeing good buildings, it really was not the field for me. I realized that when I dismally failed the entrance exams for Cooper Union, a top-notch, tuition-free technical college in New York City. My father had thought that it would be a good choice, that he could help me get started because he had contacts with general contractors and architects. So, with architecture out (it had to be a free college or nothing), the next closest field was civil engineering. It took very few months in my freshman year for me to realize that this was not for me. I managed to pass courses in analytic geometry and calculus without any idea as to what they were about and for. I sought counseling at the college but got no real help. On my own resources, I went through the college bulletin and found that the sociology courses were the most appealing, and some of the psychology courses as well. I became a sociology major, which, some 35 years later, must have contributed to my criticism of the quantitative research methods that rule the counseling psychology literature and my rediscovery of some of the qualitative methods that were the major research approaches in sociology and anthropology when I was an undergraduate.

Another small piece of the jigsaw puzzle: During my senior year, I became editor of the *Sociolog*, a mimeographed little magazine produced by sociology majors. At this point, I cannot understand how I had the self-confidence and managerial abilities to do that, but it appears that I did—another indication that for me writing and editing stimulate creativeness and bring forth abilities as few other activities do.

I really was drifting on graduation, with no sense of long-term career direction—a dominating theme in my life, with never more than the next step in my thinking. Being drafted into the Air Force in 1942 gave me 3 more years to mature and also introduced me to personnel work and occupational classification, which, when I was discharged in 1946, led me to think of vocational counseling as a possible occupation. I sought counseling at a VA Guidance Center. That was not much help either, because it was an assembly-line operation: preliminary interview with an assistant, a uniform battery of standardized tests, and one brief interview with a counselor, who quickly looked over all the papers and said something like "We'd be glad to welcome you into the profession." That experience has stayed with me and influenced my own approach to career counseling, which is a flexible and dynamic one in the use of tests and interviews, more like what is done in good personal counseling or psychotherapy.

My master's program at Teachers College, Columbia University, was uneventful. Because classes were large, I rarely spoke and was hardly known to any of the faculty. One component, however, merits mention: my fieldwork, 1 day a week as I recall, took place at the VA Regional Office in New York City, in a special unit that provided counseling—vocational and personal—for severely disabled veterans of World War II. That began an involvement with the field of rehabilitation counseling that was to recur several times in later years.

Upon graduation with an MS in vocational guidance, I obtained a job at the Veterans Counseling Center at Stevens Institute of Technology in Hoboken, New Jersey. This center, however, was much less an assembly-line operation than the one I had experienced as a client and had brought together an unusual group of imaginative counselors, from whom I learned some creative test interpretation approaches, none of which have ever appeared in the professional literature, which does not welcome such reports if they lack quantitative research evaluation. My job was titled psychometrist and consisted of administering stand-ardized tests to clients, and scoring them, as prescribed by their counselors. Each morning, there were several clients who could not see their counselors for an hour or more, so I would administer an interest inventory and then, if the counselor was not yet ready to see them, would guess from the inventory results what further tests the counselor would want, and administer one or two. This was a great way to sharpen my assessment skills.

This bit of serendipity deserves a paragraph because, along with further experiences to be mentioned, I was beginning to develop an area of expertise far beyond what most students and counselors at that level had, which later led to a specialization, articles, a book, speaking engagements, and visibility that in turn led to committees, boards, and elective offices in several professional organizations. The area was vocational assessment; the book, *Using Tests in Counseling,* became a standard text on using tests, although years later I became a major critic of the use of tests. The book reflected my value on high achieve-ment but in a traditional mode; the critical articles some 20 years later reflected my value on questioning and changing the established traditions when they no longer seemed valid. The latter could not have happened until I myself was established and had matured quite a bit more.

I stayed on this job for only a year; upon passing a federal civil service test, I was appointed to the VA Regional Office where I had done my fieldwork. My title was vocational counselor, but again my role was that of full-time psy-chometrist, now working only with severely disabled veterans—amputees, blind, deaf, brain-injured, and others. It was a rich experience for me, because I spent a half day or more doing individual assessment with each client, at the end of which I wrote an interpretive report for the counselor.

During these 2 years, I continued to take courses at Columbia and gradually realized that I would not be satisfied being either a psychometrist or a counselor at this level. I did not have any idea what I did want, but I knew what I did not. During the year at the VA, I applied for admission to the doctoral program and was interviewed by Donald Super, the head of the program, who was very impressed by my test scores and, from then on, knew me as an individual and became my adviser and mentor.

Super's own specialization in vocational assessment now completed the series of experiences that led to my making a place for myself as a contributor to the literature. My dissertation examined the relationship between aptitude profiles and Rorschach scores. Although the results were unimpressive, the study bridged these two areas and reflected something of a breadth of interests. Related is the fact that, over the years, I have often been called on to teach testing courses in counselor education programs because I was one of the few people with interest and some expertise both in testing, with its emphasis on precision, and the counseling process, which is more subjective and imprecise.

I had good reason to want to complete all the PhD requirements: I was engaged in 1949 and married in 1950, and, on referral by Donald Super, had an assistant professorship waiting for me at the University of Buffalo, effective on the day the PhD requirements were completed. I was to become the first full-time faculty member, and coordinator, of the graduate program in counselor education. I pressed everyone to speed the dissertation process and finished in record time. We moved to Buffalo in December 1950, weeks before my final oral exam, so that I could begin the spring semester a month or so later.

A related incident tells something about my limited self-awareness and lack of long-term career thinking. Approaching completion of my dissertation, I asked Super for assistance in finding my first postdoctoral job. My thought was that I would do counseling, supervision, and research in a community agency or perhaps a college counseling center. Super referred me to a highly regarded community counseling agency in Cleveland that had just such a position open. I arranged a visit, thinking that, among other pluses, this would be close to my wife's hometown. At the end of the visit, the very wise director said something to this effect: "We'd love to have you, but you wouldn't stay for long. You'll soon want to be a professor." To the best of my recollection, that was the first time that thought had ever entered my consciousness. She was, of course, absolutely right (and a great career counselor!): I was not enough of an active doer to remain satisfied with that kind of applied job. I needed the ivy.

What I did indeed realize, many years later, after having taught in several different graduate programs, is that my best role is that of a bridge between theory and research, on one hand, and practice, on the other. I was not outstanding in either role, but I was oriented enough to both that I could play a productive and very happy role as a bridge. I could teach practitioners what they needed to understand and know about research and theory, and I could write and speak to researchers about the kinds of studies that I thought would be meaningful and helpful to practitioners. One factor in the development of this bridge role was that at Buffalo, while the director of the university's Vocational Counseling Center was on leave, I served as acting director for a year, and remained on the staff on a part-time basis for my remaining 5 or 6 years at the University of Buffalo. This provided good opportunity to develop my own approach to vocational counseling (very different from the traditional "test 'em and tell 'em" approach that still prevails). Also, because the center was under the aegis of the

Psychology Department of the College of Arts and Sciences, from then on I held a joint appointment there and in the School of Education—another bridge role.

The years at Buffalo were happy; as contrasted with the situation in the 1990s, and indeed since the mid-1970s, there were lots of students and money was available, both from university funds and from government programs such as the NDEA Institutes, to bring in new faculty, develop practicum facilities, and purchase audio and video equipment. Also, during these years, our two daughters were born, and we bought a house—a big step for someone who had lived all his life in small apartments.

In 1954, halfway through my 8 years at the University of Buffalo, national legislation provided, for the first time, funding for training rehabilitation counselors. At the initiative and with the active collaboration of two rehabilitation counselors from the Buffalo area, we submitted an application and received a grant to begin a rehabilitation counselor graduate program as a specialty area within our counselor education program. I served as coordinator for a semester, until we could bring in a specialist in the area. That person, over a period of perhaps 5 to 10 years, developed it into a major program in itself. For me, it was a revisit to a specialty area in which I had done fieldwork during my master's degree, which I visited subsequently in my job at the VA Regional Office, and which I would visit again some 20 years later as a staff member in an educational research center.

I wrote my first journal article while at the University of Buffalo. A former fellow graduate student at Columbia published an article describing a method of teaching a career development course. My reaction was this: I'm doing something equally original and significant; why am I not publishing it? I did, and this bit of serendipity led to many more publications. Of course, today's graduate students are much more aware than I was, and more is expected of them; beginning academic jobs often expect at least a small publication record.

As I look back now, I wonder why I went for ABPP board certification as a diplomate. I was doing only very part-time counseling and had no thought of beginning a private practice. Why then? Maybe because, like a mountain for a climber, it was there, and by now I had caught the bug: If there is another kind of professional credential, go for it. The public rationale, of course, is that one who educates professionals should possess the highest certification available as a sign of competence for oneself and one's students. Both the article and the ABPP experience also reflect my value on achievement at a high qualitative level.

Another event during those years played an important part in my professional development. In 1954, the national convention of the American Personnel and

Guidance Association (APGA; later the American Association for Counseling and Development, and at this writing the American Counseling Association) was held in Buffalo. Donald Super was the incoming president and selected me to be program coordinator for the convention. This suddenly brought me into contact not only with the program coordinators of the then five divisions, but also with the Executive Council of APGA. It was my task to edit and publish the convention program, as well as to plan and schedule the all-APGA general sessions. I enjoyed this kind of work and was good at both the details and the aesthetics of it, but I must add that once again serendipity was at work in that I was responding to an external invitation. Certainly this and other initiatives that have come to me would not have come had I not demonstrated that I did these things responsibly and well. Indeed, new jobs and new extracurricular activities frequently came to me, and I never had a chance to get very bored.

There were, however, two exceptions where I clearly took a major initiative. The first was almost 30 years later, when I felt ready for a job change and spelled out for myself what I would like to do next; a short time later, I received an announcement from Fordham University of a position vacancy, for which I immediately applied. The second occurred soon afterward, when I reached out to colleagues to let them know that I wanted to become active again in association governance and editorial positions that I felt would be helpful as we prepared to develop a doctoral program in counseling psychology at Fordham. These are discussed in detail later in this chapter.

The final event to be noted during my University of Buffalo years was my first sabbatical leave. I was in my 7th year at the university when a colleague who had arrived the same year as I did asked if I was going to apply for a sabbatical for the next year. I had not thought about it until then, but his urging was this: If you are eligible for a leave, try to get it—very good advice indeed, which I have passed along to others. But I had to have a plan, an activity, to justify the leave. Then I remembered that in the advanced course in testing for counselors, I had had to develop all my own materials: counseling cases, a framework for test interpretation, and syntheses of material in the journal literature. There was no textbook, so I proposed to write one. I got the leave for the spring semester of 1958, spent much of the semester in the library searching the literature, and wrote a draft of what later turned out to be the first four chapters of *Using Tests in Counseling*. Probably no single thing I ever did played so vital a part in my professional reputation and later advancement in various roles. Lady Luck has visited me on a number of occasions, and fortunately I had the good sense to accept her overtures.

▨▨▨▨▨▨ AS COUNSELOR EDUCATOR

During the sabbatical semester, I received a letter from Robert H. Mathewson, Coordinator of Counselor Education for a program that was offered at four of the city colleges of New York, asking if I wanted to be a candidate for the position of coordinator of the program at Brooklyn College, one of the four. I had met Mathewson at state conferences, knew his writing, and had the highest regard for him as a thinker, a leader, and a humanist. Although the thought of returning to New York City was not especially attractive, my regard for him led me to apply. By the time I was offered the job, I realized that I could now live in a suburban house rather than the kind of small city apartment I had grown up in, and I accepted the offer.

Moving back to the New York City area was a mixed blessing. One plus was being close to my parents, who still lived in Brooklyn, sharing a two-family house with my sister and her family. My daughters, then 6 months and 4 years, could now see their grandparents, aunt, uncle, and cousins much more frequently. On the other side of the ledger, life in Buffalo had been relatively easier—commuting to work, getting together with friends, visiting museums, attending concerts, and the less stressful pace of life in general. In a short time, however, I realized that I was getting bored with the social life, which was limited to a small group of colleagues, and that I missed the New York pace. I also realized how much it meant to me to be at the ocean. I had a truly moving experience when we visited my aunt in Long Beach and I stood on the boardwalk, entranced by the sea and surf.

I believe that my main reason for the move was the quality of the graduate program I was joining. Under the leadership of Robert Mathewson, beginning in 1950, four of the city colleges formed a kind of federation to offer a common master's program in counseling. At first, most of the courses were offered at a central location in Manhattan, but gradually each college offered most of the courses on its own campus. One of the basic principles observed by all was that the number of students should be limited—at first 20 and later 25 per year were admitted at each college. Because up to 100 applications were received at each college, this provided an opportunity to do some real selection, something few master's programs could do at that time. After a review of records, we used leaderless groups and individual interviews, and could fill our classes with highly motivated students who had good cognitive and relationship abilities.

The college community had a very different character from that at Buffalo. The faculty at Brooklyn and the other city colleges lived all over a tri-state commuting area and traveled typically an hour or more, most by public transportation. Many were native New Yorkers and had family and old friends in the area. At the University of Buffalo, by contrast, most of the faculty were "out-of-towners," so most of our social life was with each other, which was easy to arrange, because most of us lived minutes from each other and from the campus. In retrospect, I found that the much more limited involvement with the college and with colleagues suited me better—it was the big city atmosphere I had grown up in, and it felt right. My family immediately made good friends in the immediate neighborhood, and later the children broadened their friendships through school.

My task in leading the program at first was similar in one way to that at the University of Buffalo: In both cases, I needed to gradually replace a group of people who had limited credentials to teach in this program with others whose doctorates were in counseling. This incurred some wrath among some of the "old-timers" who felt that they owned the courses they taught (at that time, Brooklyn and the other city colleges were almost entirely undergraduate liberal arts and sciences institutions, and it was considered a privilege to teach a graduate course). In addition, my predecessor as coordinator had selected students whom I, and the new colleagues we brought in, did not regard as suitable candidates for counseling positions. In my 3rd year, in fact, a group of students, encouraged by my predecessor (who had continued as faculty adviser to the student association), met with the chair of the department, asking that I not be granted tenure because I was harming the program by making unreasonable demands and setting excessive standards. The department chair supported me fully, I did get tenure, and within another year or so most of the students in the program had been selected by the "new" faculty and me, and there was a very different tone in the program.

This 3-year experience reflects moral and value conflicts: On one hand, I value harmony and amicable relationships and was most uncomfortable in the hostile scene that prevailed. Not only is this something I value in general, but I regard it as essential in a program that prepares students to help others to live harmonious and amicable lives. On the other hand, my commitment to preparing the most qualified and highest quality professional counselors made the existing situation untenable. I was concerned that we would be providing the graduate credential to some of the "old" students who lacked the qualities needed for effective counseling. As long as they met academic requirements, however, there was nothing we could do except hope that they would find the new climate uncomfortable and drop out of the program.

During these first years at Brooklyn College, I completed work on *Using Tests in Counseling,* which appeared in 1961 (later revised for a 1971 edition) and received one rave review and a few good reviews in various professional journals. It turned out to be just the book that many professors had been waiting for, though they did not all know that until they saw it; no one else has written a book with just that content ever since. This was the first book in the counseling field that focused on the counselor's use of tests—selection, interpretation, and reporting to the client, with extensive case studies—rather than the technical characteristics of the tests themselves, which were included but were not the focus. The book led to my appointment to the editorial board of the *Personnel and Guidance Journal* (now the *Journal of Counseling and Development*), and, in the next few years, to the Presidency of the Association for Measurement and Evaluation in Guidance, the Board of Trustees of ABPP, and other organizational roles, none of which I sought in any way, but all of which I welcomed.

In my 6th year at Brooklyn College, Robert Mathewson decided to retire, and, at his recommendation, I was appointed to succeed him as CUNY Coordinator of Programs in Counselor Education. (In 1961, the loosely confederated city colleges became The City University of New York in order to offer doctoral programs, which was done through the central Graduate School.) This would mean for me a much longer commute, but with the job came a support staff, who made it possible for me to write and to travel to conferences, governance meetings of organizations, and speaking engagements. I also taught a course or two each semester, but I gradually decreased the teaching, finding that I could not do justice to it. That convinced me of what I had felt all along, that professorial tasks, not administration, are what I enjoy the most, put the most energy into, and do the best. There were, however, to be more jobs ahead that involved administration, that I was asked to undertake and felt I could not refuse.

One more bit of serendipity—this a wonderful experience—occurred during my 5 years in this position. Mathewson had enjoyed a Fulbright year in The Netherlands previously and wanted to return, but for only a half year. He suggested, and I happily agreed, that we apply for a shared year, he to go in the fall, I in the spring. Accordingly, in August 1965, my family and I sailed to Europe, then toured England, Norway, Sweden, and Denmark for 3 weeks before arriving in Amsterdam, where I lectured at the municipal university and developed a consulting relationship with the school psychology department of the Amsterdam public schools. During my last weeks of the Fulbright, I attended an international counseling conference in Switzerland, where I met the director of a major vocational guidance institute in Jerusalem. This led, 8 years later, to a 2-month consultantship there, setting up a closed-circuit television system for counselor supervision.

During my stay in Amsterdam, I was nominated for the Presidency of the Association for Measurement and Evaluation in Guidance (AMEG) and for the post of Secretary of the Division of Counseling Psychology of APA. I was elected to both, mainly on the basis, I suppose, of the visibility resulting mostly from the book and a few journal articles.

A job opportunity arose in 1969, when CUNY was ready to begin its first doctorates in the field of education; the very first program would be educational psychology, which was to be followed by programs in administration, curriculum, counseling, school psychology, and others. The CUNY Dean of Teacher Education prevailed on me to become the first Executive Officer, with the rationale that I was enough of a generalist to help build and oversee that diverse group of programs. I was reluctant to take on that much of an administrative job, but the Dean, a younger man and a close personal friend since our years together at Buffalo, was very persuasive, and I accepted. Soon, however, the New York State Regents decided to place a freeze on all new doctoral programs because of the lack of jobs for PhDs; therefore, the educational psychology program has remained to this date as the only one in education. Happily, I was able to return to a combination of teaching and the journal editorship that I had begun in 1969.

THE JOURNAL

By the late 1960s, I had formed a pretty well-defined idea of what a professional journal for counseling practitioners should be like. In 1968, during a break at a meeting of the Executive Council of the American Personnel and Guidance Association, on which I served as President of AMEG, the APGA president mentioned in an informal conversation that my name had come up a number of times as a possible editor of the *Personnel and Guidance Journal*. He asked if I was interested. Was I ever! I prepared for the Council a brief statement of my conception of what that journal should be, and I was soon appointed Editor-Elect, to assume the editorship a year thence.

This activity was the creative highlight of my professional life. It was what I could get the most excited about—using the printed word to communicate, stimulate, inform, and persuade practitioners, and to do it in an interesting and well-written manner. With the strong support of the Editorial Board and the publication staff at the Washington headquarters of the Association, we redesigned the journal, in both contents and appearance. I immediately introduced special theme issues and special sections and published an average of three per year, all on timely topics and each one guest-edited by a person identified with and well regarded in the topical area. Some were about the special counseling needs of Blacks, Women, Asian Americans, and other populations that were not being well served by our field. Other issues focused on areas within counseling practice, such as technology, groups, careers, and the role of paraprofessionals in counseling settings. All the articles in those issues were planned by the guest editors, and almost all the articles were written by members of the particular group or experts in the theme area. I will also take credit for directing, in the early 1970s, that no sexist pronouns or occupational titles were to be used. The publication manager said that was contrary to Association policy; I replied that it was mine and that I would not send the package of articles for the next issue unless he agreed. He agreed.

I estimated that I spent about 20 hours a week on this task. I had no associate or assistant editors, and I personally conducted all correspondence with authors, examined every book sent in for review, selected the reviewers, and edited every review. I also wrote an editorial for each issue, encouraged letters from readers, and placed both up front. I gradually increased the number of Editorial Board members, to the point that we had appropriate numbers of women, minority group members, and younger people—a development that was welcomed by members of those excluded groups.

I angered some readers by reducing drastically the number of traditional quantitative research articles. My announced policy from the start was that we would publish only research that had something to say to master's level practitioners; very few such manuscripts were ever received. My inclusion of poems raised a few more hackles, but I think that most readers welcomed the changes.

By 1970, my year as Executive Officer ended, and I found a niche for myself in the CUNY central Guidance Laboratory, where students from several colleges came for their practicum. The flexibility and secretarial support enabled me to handle the journal work, including about a thousand letters we sent out each year. In 1971, I was elected to a second 3-year term as editor.

MY TWO CRUSADES

In 1970, I was invited to speak at the Minnesota State Testing Conference, on any topic of my choosing. To help me choose, I asked who the other speakers were going to be; learning that they were mostly test authors and publishers who were going to speak about their tests, favorably I was sure, I decided for the first time to take a different tack: What are the *negatives* about tests? I reviewed the literature with a critical eye and concluded that, for counseling purposes, the reliabilities and validities that had demonstrable value for *selection* purposes could offer clients only the grossest estimates of success in a particular college or occupation, such as "There are two chances in three that someone with your test scores would end up between the 40th and 80th percentiles in grades during your freshman year." Making matters worse, few master's level counselors, in my experience, knew enough about tests to use them with true professional competence and to use those "predictions" properly. I concluded that counselors should make very limited use of standardized tests.

Months later, I received an urgent call from the AMEG Convention Program Coordinator: The luncheon speaker for the convention had suddenly been taken very ill, and could I, as a Past President, be prevailed on to fill in on such short notice? I could, if I used the Minnesota speech; they agreed, I did, and someone in the audience asked if it could be published in the AMEG journal. A revised version of the paper was published in 1972 as "Tests and Counseling: The Marriage That Failed." It had quite an impact. Several test publishers put together program sessions for the next two conventions, where they disagreed with my conclusions; I was invited to participate, and did, but saw no reason to change my position. Ten years later, someone organized a convention session to revisit my article; other speakers said they had observed some improvement both in the tests and in the sophistication of test users, but I concluded again that standardized tests had little to offer in counseling applications, especially in the hands of master's level counselors.

By 1990, I had reached the point of offering a positive proposal: use *qualitative* methods of assessment instead of, or at least in addition to, standardized tests. I have been almost the only voice on this point in print, but I have heard occasionally from practitioners who found these methods productive and valuable—work samples, simulations, in-baskets, and games and exercises of various kinds, some of them homemade. Unfortunately, it is academics who do almost all the publishing, almost never practitioners, so the latter are rarely heard from. In any case, this series of incidents illustrates again a typical pattern in my professional history: an innocent request for a traditional contribution led instead to very nontraditional outcomes, certainly antiestablishment in nature, and what I regard as one of my most creative productions.

My other crusade began in a similar manner. During the 1975 APGA convention, I was invited to participate in a major session that addressed itself to the question, How well are we responding to the needs of the neediest—the poor, incarcerated, minorities, women, and others? My task was to see what published research had been doing to help our field meet those needs. As with tests, my search of decades of journals found almost nothing that offered any real help. During that same semester, I was teaching a research methods course for counselors; each week, we examined two research articles that I thought were among the better ones, and each week we found so many flaws in these quantitative studies that we concluded that they had little or nothing to offer to practitioners.

From this emerged the 1976 article "A Revolution in Counseling Research," the 1978 edited book *Research Methods for Counselors,* and several brief articles. Not much changed in the literature until people like Lisa Hoshmand[1] provided theoretical frameworks for qualitative research approaches and also produced good research studies. The *Journal of Counseling Psychology* finally published its first few qualitative research articles in the 1990s. My "Revolution" article was the first critique of traditional research methods published in that journal; I was surprised it was accepted.

As I see it, quantitative research in the counseling literature has contributed little to either practice or theory. Few journal editors or reviewers agree with that and are instead committed to the research paradigm they learned and have themselves followed, which places major value on measurable hypotheses drawn from previous research and theory, precision of measurement and statistics, and what they regard as objectivity. Qualitative research, by contrast, begins with phenomena as observed and then teases out interpretations and hypotheses, acknowledging the subjectivity of the process but making explicit the thinking and behavior of the researcher, so that the reader can judge the validity of the findings. There is a vast gap between these two approaches; my hope is that younger psychologists will gradually shape a paradigm change, but this may require new journals and even perhaps new organizations.

Although I myself have done little research, but instead have functioned more as a bridge between research and practice, and a critic of both, my teaching methods are very harmonious with qualitative assessment and qualitative research. I use inductive, experiential methods whenever possible and try to engage students in an active search, having them experience something—an observation, a visit to a place of work, a simulation in class, a role play or actual interview with a client—before I do any lecturing, and then my lecturing relates to those experiences as far as possible.

MORE CAREER MOVES

By 1974, New York City was in great distress financially and made major cuts in CUNY, including closing down the central Guidance Laboratory. Randy Tarrier, the director of the lab, and I used the opportunity to run a three-semester master's program for a dozen students, collected from the six participating colleges, who were ready to be full-time students. It was a glorious experience; we could apply what we both believed in—team teaching, placing students in field experiences from the first month on, integrating experiential and academic components, and asking for a full-time commitment by students. It was the only such experience I ever had, except for some of the NDEA Institutes years earlier, and it confirmed my belief in this kind of professional education.

This happened only once, because by 1975 the New York City financial situation was so bad that the state of New York took over most of the financing of CUNY. I spent my remaining years at CUNY in two half-time jobs at the Graduate Center—developing and directing a small program of continuing education, and participating in applied research projects in an R&D center—the Center for Advanced Study in Education (CASE). In the first, I developed a program for people in middle- and upper-level positions in the publishing field, and a couple of other smaller programs. At CASE, I returned to my interest in career aspects of disability, because most of our grants were for program development and evaluation in relation to career development of students with disabilities in school and college, some of which involved training counselors to work with these students through internships and workshops.

For the next 7 years, I learned much from these new kinds of activities, especially because the CASE projects often took me into the field to visit schools, colleges, and agencies. There was, however, no teaching and no real academic contact, and I had left the mainstream of counseling and counseling psychology. Much as I enjoyed the excellent colleagueship in CASE and the many learning experiences, I was ready to return to academe. I listed on a sheet of paper what I would like to do in my next job; Lady Luck was with me again.

When I received an announcement in 1982 from Fordham University of a vacancy for a senior professor in counseling psychology, I immediately wrote of my interest, because the credentials called for, and the job description, could have been written with me in mind. The 5-year, non-tenure, nonrenewable contract we negotiated was followed, by mutual agreement, by four 1-year contracts until I reached mandatory retirement age; actually, they extended this to age 71 because the APA site visit would occur the next year. During this time,

I worked with doctoral students for the first time since leaving Buffalo in 1958, enjoyed it immensely, and tried to persuade them to use qualitative research designs in their dissertations, despite much opposition from the traditional faculty. Those few who successfully did such studies had to add quantitative data—like wearing both a belt and suspenders—to satisfy the traditionalists.

LEADERSHIP IN THE DIVISION OF COUNSELING PSYCHOLOGY

While at Fordham, I let people around the country know that I was back in academe and would like to become active in national association activities. Within a year or so, I was appointed to the editorial board of *The Counseling Psychologist* and later of *Professional Psychology.* I was nominated and elected to the Executive Board of the Division of Counseling Psychology, first for a 3-year term as Council Representative, and then as President. The latter was in no way serendipitous; a valued professional friend offered to serve as campaign manager, and we went for it. All these activities were rich experiences, but they confirmed again that ideas and words are my forte, not political leadership. I had good ideas for the growth of the Division, but I could not persuade my colleagues on the Board to raise the dues (which were far below those of comparable divisions), expand the newsletter, and provide the funds for our committees to function more actively—I was not in the network, which consisted predominantly of faculty at midwestern universities. In fact, one of my major commitments as President-Elect was to bring people from both coasts into active work on committees.

As it turned out, my Presidential Address[2] was a one-shot crusade on that point that broadened to become a critique of the governance and editorial leadership of the Division. When I was seeking an interesting and significant topic for the address, I received in the mail (serendipitously!) copies of convention presentations and articles that highlighted the dominance of four universities in counseling psychology (referred to as the "MOMM[3] schools")—three of them midwestern state universities, the fourth an East Coast university with a faculty almost all of midwestern origin. I did a little quantitative research going back several years and used my swan song speech to report that indeed the faculties and PhDs from these four constituted about half to three-fourths of the members of committees, editorial boards, and elective offices in counseling psychology over a period of several years. This was at a time when there were more than 60 APA-approved counseling psychology programs. I went on to note that there was also an underrepresentation of younger people, minorities, and people who worked anyplace but in universities.

In all fairness, my observation is that some of the underrepresented—those from the East and West coasts, for example, and non-university people—do not reach out for organizational activities to the extent that the dominant groups do. These roles, to be attained and done well, require active and frequent effort, reaching out to people by phone and mail (these days e-mail and fax), and time commitment. They also thrive on networking, which is something those mid-western folks seem to do exceedingly well. I did not do that, and my impression is that very few people in, for example, New York City, Boston, or Philadelphia do. Perhaps this is a phenomenon of large cities, in addition to geographic location. In any case, I think that there was some effort to broaden the base of leadership and involvement, and the term I heard from people who heard and read my address is "inclusion."

AFTER RETIREMENT

I did not want to retire, even at 71, and, even though I had started extensive travel 7 years before then, and visited both my daughters every week, I found that I did not have enough to do, as I anticipated. Fortunately, I have usually taught one course a semester as an adjunct faculty member at various universities in New York City most years since then, a situation that brought with it the welcome opportunity for colleagueship. Also, most years I have been involved with one or another R&D project at CASE, where again I continued enjoyable contact with valued colleagues. This was still not enough, so for the past 2 years I have worked as a volunteer at an environmental organization, where I answer inquiries from members about various environmental issues, developments, and problems. I came to this with some knowledge of conserva-tion, having joined several such organizations after my first safari in Africa. This fund of knowledge has grown with the use of resource files and consultation with the experts at the organization.

My need for a sense of community could not be met satisfactorily within professional associations, because I disagree so strongly with the establishment on many issues. There are, however, several colleagues from past and present work settings with whom I have remained close friends. I enjoy the col-leagueship with people at current work and volunteer settings, of which there are several at any one time. Fortunately, my two daughters live in the New York

City area; each has two children, and I visit both families every week. All these relationships provide me with a good feeling of my place in the world.

━━━━━ **REFRAIN**

I am of my era and place on the globe, of my family and ethnic history, and of my own personality—itself the product of a lifetime of interaction between all of those and my genetic and constitutional makeup. I never dreamed in childhood, adolescence, and even young adulthood of the professional place I would reach, the achievements, acknowledgment, and the prominence—doctorate, professor, psychologist, author, editor, and holder of national office. Indeed, even after I began my professional career, and at each step along the way, I still did not think or plan far ahead. Yet, at each step, when an opportunity appeared, something moved me to take it, without envisaging where it would lead, and often with some concern as to how well I would do it. I have not written nearly as many books or articles or been as active in leadership posts as others with whom I sometimes compare myself, yet I know that I have attained a place that is a mountain-top above where I grew up and how I ever viewed myself and my expectations.

I remind myself occasionally, usually when feeling uncomfortable in a situation, that there has to be considerable stress from the distance between where I began life and where I am now. Essentially an introvert and somewhat shy, I have been happiest in roles that involved writing, editing, and relating individually or in small groups with colleagues, students, and others. I do get turned on by large audiences, but I am ready to leave when my speech is ended.

Never a network player, I have in fact particularly enjoyed and perhaps been the most creative when taking a different road and trying to persuade others to join me. I am similar to my parents in these respects; they were good role models.

Although religion has played no role in my life, I believe that I operate out of a fundamental set of moral and ethical principles. I do not have the support that members of organized religions do, but I have no problem in maintaining my beliefs and basing my actions on them—truth, beauty, freedom, a responsible concern for the world I inhabit and all its constituents, and a recognition that none of these is fixed for all time but must change. Resistance to change is human but must be opposed by the recognition that, in all of time, change is a basic theme. True, change does not necessarily mean progress or betterment, but without change there cannot be progress or betterment.

Finally, as I look back, I consider myself very fortunate to have spent most of my life in work that is intrinsically satisfying and in institutions where there is the optimal combination of independence, freedom to be as creative as one wishes to be and can be, and security. Although some compromises with values needed to be made from time to time, they are insignificant compared to the fact that I could base daily decisions and choices primarily on what I have believed to be best as a teacher, writer, and participant in a university community. Many people leave their moral beliefs at home when they go to work; they may be well paid for that, or at least can hold on to their jobs, but I am grateful that I have not had to do that. Having a family who were happy to live on a professor's salary has been a great help.

LOOKING TOWARD THE FUTURE

Our entire world is in a difficult transition period, with major economic, social, and political changes. Communication via satellite has brought to underdeveloped nations and areas increased awareness of life in the technologically advanced countries. Air transportation has made it possible for manufacturers to have work done where labor is cheapest. The computer and the Internet have further speeded communication, distribution, and financial transactions on a global scale. All of this, though helping to raise standards of living for the less developed areas, has added a great deal of stress in all parts of the world. As the differences between the wealthy and the poor increase, unemployment, migration both within and between countries, and hostility between ethnic and socioeconomic groups also have increased. Political changes—many violent—complicate matters. Ethnic, religious, and other subgroups want independence either within their countries or as separate political entities; this centrifugal force seems universal and is accelerated by the fundamentalists in all groups.

Psychologists and counselors should be at the forefront in the study of these stress-inducing events, applying their developmental understandings and their growth and wellness professional skills. We should contribute to dealing in particular with the worldwide trend toward separatism among ethnic, religious, and other groups. This is frontier work and requires open-ended methods of research that will help us understand complex problems and design effective interventions for large numbers of people and countries. We will need to move from our emulation of the physical sciences and traditional long-term, one-to-one remedial activities, and create a psychological science and practice that grow out of human realities.

APPENDIX
Abbreviated Professional History

1940	BS, City College of New York (major: Sociology, minor: Psychology)
1947	MA, Teachers College, Columbia University (Vocational Counseling)
1950	PhD, Columbia University (Counseling Psychology)
1950-1958	Assistant to Associate Professor, University of Buffalo
1956	Diplomate, American Board of Professional Psychology
1958-1964	Associate Professor and Coordinator of Graduate Program in Guidance, Brooklyn College
1963-1964	Executive Council, Association for Counselor Education and Supervision
1963-1965	Chair, Commission on Testing, American College Personnel Association
1964-1965	Chair, Association of Counselor Educators of New York State
1964-1969	Coordinator, Counselor Education Programs, City University of New York
1965-1966	Fulbright Lecturer, University of Amsterdam, The Netherlands
1965-1968	Committee on Scientific and Professional Ethics and Conduct, APA
1966-1968	Executive Council, American Personnel and Guidance Association
1966-1971	Trustee, American Board of Professional Psychology (Vice President, 1969-1971)
1967	President, Association for Measurement and Evaluation in Guidance
1969-1975	Editor, *Personnel and Guidance Journal*
1970-1975	Professor, Guidance Laboratory, CUNY Graduate School
1975-1982	Director of Special Programs and Project Director, Center for Advanced Study in Education, CUNY

APPENDIX
Abbreviated Professional History *(continued)*

1982-1991	Professor, Graduate School of Education, Fordham University
1983-1986	Editorial Board, *The Counseling Psychologist*
1984-1987	Representative (Division of Counseling Psychology), APA Council
1986-1991	Director of Training, Doctoral Program in Counseling Psychology, Fordham University
1989-1990	President, Division of Counseling Psychology, APA
1989-1994	Editorial Board, *Professional Psychology*

NOTES

1. L. T. Hoshmand, "Alternative Research Paradigms: A Review and Teaching Proposal," *The Counseling Psychologist, 17* (1989): 3-79.

2. L. Goldman, "Participants and Gatekeepers" (Division 17 Presidential Address), *The Counseling Psychologist, 18* (1991): 117-132.

3. Minnesota, Ohio State, Missouri, and Maryland.

SELECT BIBLIOGRAPHY

Using tests in counseling. New York: Appleton-Century-Crofts, 1961; rev. ed., 1971.

Tests should make a difference. *Measurement and Evaluation in Guidance, 3* (1969): 53-59.

Psychological secrecy and openness in public schools. *Professional Psychology, 4* (1972): 370-374.

Tests and counseling: The marriage that failed. *Measurement and Evaluation in Guidance, 4* (1972): 213-220.

Test information in counseling: A critical view. In *Proceedings of the 1973 Invitational Conference on Testing Problems.* Princeton, NJ: Educational Testing Service, 1973.

A revolution in counseling research. *Journal of Counseling Psychology, 23* (1976): 543-552.

Research methods for counselors. (Ed.). New York: John Wiley, 1978.

Research is more than technology. *The Counseling Psychologist, 8* (1979): 41-44.

Moving counseling research into the 21st century. *The Counseling Psychologist, 17* (1989): 81-85.

Qualitative assessment. *The Counseling Psychologist, 18* (1990): 205-213.

Participants and gatekeepers (Division 17 Presidential Address). *The Counseling Psychologist, 19* (1991): 117-132.

Reaction: A broader scientific base for professional psychology. *Professional Psychology, 24* (1993): 252-253.

CHAPTER 5

Reflections on Choices

The Road Not Taken

ELIZABETH M. ALTMAIER

My fifth-grade teacher, Miss Albertis, was convinced of the value of memorizing poetry for building character as well as an early appreciation of literature. Because Robert Frost was her favorite poet, I had an early encounter with his work. I was, and remain, especially struck by the visual images and the metaphor of "The Road Not Taken."

One of the appealing aspects of writing a chapter such as this one is the opportunity, forced as it is, to think back over events and to develop a structure for them. It is akin to therapy in that this perspective taking results in alternate views of history and of the future. Jack Martin's[1] theory on the nature of psychotherapeutic change postulates that the events of one's life, captured in memories, are woven into a theory that we have about ourselves. This personal theory then assumes an agentic role as we encounter life. Martin identifies conversations, within ourselves or with others, as the means by which we construct, modify, and carry out this theory.

This chapter is a conversation I had with myself. In reconstructing now why I made the choices I made, I think of Robert Frost's image of two roads diverging in a yellow wood. It seems that choices I made, in retrospect, appear to have been less traveled roads. I wonder now why they seemed more appealing at the time, and that is one of the harder aspects of this conversation: to determine and describe their appeal. I also consider whether I am making comparable choices now, and am likely to in the future. This is a theme I will return to at the end of the chapter.

MAKING MY CAREER CHOICE

I recently participated in an interview conducted by a graduate student studying the role of chance in career choice. I began the interview by relating to her that I had chosen psychology as a college major literally by chance: I deleted a few majors that seemed completely undesirable from the list of possible majors available at Wheaton College (Illinois), then used a childhood counting rhyme to successively strike majors from consideration. I remember being left with sociology and psychology, and psychology was the eventual winner.

In spite of this unorthodox approach to selecting my major, I enjoyed my coursework tremendously and appreciated the investment that Wheaton's faculty made in my professional development. Although it is difficult, and indeed unfair, to separate out one person from a group of caring and competent faculty, from the perspective of looking back now, Onas Scandrette had a strong influence on my subsequent choices. He accomplished this in two ways. First, he was the faculty member I was assigned to assist in my senior year when I was serving as a departmental assistant, and he strongly encouraged me to continue with graduate study in psychology. At that time, I wasn't sure what a doctoral program involved, but it sounded like a lot of time spent with *Psychological Abstracts,* and I wasn't sure I wanted any more of that kind of time, having put in a good many hours already in tedious citation search. (Today's graduate students are surely shortchanged in their character development by not having to search *Psychological Abstracts* by hand.) He convinced me, however, that my enjoyment of psychology would only deepen with more exposure, and I decided to pursue graduate study. I had to be convinced that I had the ability to complete a doctoral program. Once convinced, I was able to make a choice that did not conform to the directions that I had originally thought I would pursue, having entered Wheaton with the somewhat conventional career choice (at that time) of elementary education.

Thinking about my pursuing graduate study, I am struck by the contrast in what I had thought my choices were at the time I made them versus the choices I now can define. Related to my life's direction, my mother noted in a family Christmas letter during my junior year of high school that I was volunteering in a local hospital to assist me in deciding between a career in nursing versus one in teaching. Indeed, those two career choices were the only ones I considered, growing up in a middle-class conventional family: father working in New York City, mother at home in suburban New Jersey, two older brothers on whom career expectations were placed, and me, for whom marriage and motherhood was the preferred option. Thankfully, we have experienced a significant difference in how women view their possible career choices, and I am excited over the range of options that my teenage daughter is considering.

Besides encouraging me to pursue graduate studies in psychology, Dr. Scandrette's influence consisted of his interest in studying the tolerance of ambiguity. I had been raised in a religious home to believe that ambiguity existed only to be erased or resolved. That tolerating, and indeed embracing, ambiguities seen in persons, situations, and ourselves was desirable was a provocative thought. Further, that one could choose to tolerate ambiguity, even practice it as a new skill, was a choice that I had not previously thought possible. Dr. Scandrette was full of stories about people who had found tolerance of ambiguity to be a resource for coping with difficult life circumstances (wording I would use today, but he did not use then, being psychoanalytic in orientation), and it appeared to be a choice worth considering.

Graduate study at Ohio State University was a difficult but rewarding 4 years. I remember being challenged, supported, encouraged, and discouraged in equal amounts, occasionally by the same people. I was presented with an early choice that was not then typical for students at Ohio State, namely an opportunity to choose an adviser after my initial adviser left the faculty. I chose Ted Kaul as my adviser, a selection he tells me was because I was sure I would work harder for him than for anyone else. That may have been true, and Ted's reputation among students was such that this assertion is likely. While faculty, in general, never provide as much emotional support as needy graduate students prefer, Ted was unfailingly direct in his assessments, treated me with great respect, and did, indeed, expect a lot of hard work from me. It is conventional to say that one "owes a great deal" to a person who was a doctoral adviser; I must say that I do, in fact, owe Ted a lot.

One particular contribution is his influence on my choice of research topics in graduate study. Ted encouraged me to "follow my nose" in choosing research topics for my MA thesis and PhD dissertation. At the time, I found the typical Ohio State counseling psychology topics (career psychology, social influence model) rather uninteresting. I had a strong liking for social psychology; therefore, I proposed a master's thesis on the utility of role-playing as an alternative to deception in research that necessitated misleading of the subject. My thesis investigated whether informed subjects could faithfully represent the results of deceived subjects (the answer was "sometimes"). For my dissertation, I continued this line of thought but focused on how researchers might assess subjects' propensity to present themselves for research (subject roles). Although the results were quite mixed, the process of "following my nose" in defining a topic and in developing experimental procedures was invigorating. Ted encouraged me to pursue my own interests in spite of some opposition from faculty who felt that these topics weren't "counseling psychology." I guess that they aren't, but I developed, in these unconventional research choices, an abiding sense of the thrill in being an independent investigator, and that has been a lifelong reward.

What did I gain from graduate study? One question to be addressed here is the source of the goals, purposes, and intentions of our professional lives. As a graduate educator myself, I have a strong commitment to graduate training as a time for forming ideals and principles that underlie one's professional life. Although the content of what we know today will change, commitment to the integration of science with practice, to the value of professional service as a means of giving back to the community, and to the defining characteristics of counseling psychology (i.e., emphasizing strengths over deficits, optimizing choice, valuing differences) should remain. I work very hard to instill these values in my students, and I appreciate the effort that the faculty at Ohio State put into instilling them in me.

On a more pragmatic level, I also developed, during graduate study, a distaste for keeping research within conventional topical bounds, an approach that has allowed me to pursue unconventional research topics throughout my professional life (although with qualms about not doing "counseling psychology research," particularly because I want to publish my research at least occasionally in the *Journal of Counseling Psychology*).

BEGINNING MY CAREER

I took a research interest in anxiety and cognitive-behavioral treatments to my first professional position at the University of Florida. There, I worked with several undergraduates on their honors theses in anxiety-related topics. Even within the conventional area of treatments for anxiety, however, I took a different road, stimulated in large part by the interests of my students. I worked with Jim Huber on anxiety from the perspective of Kelley's personal construct theory. (It would be hard to be a student or faculty member at Florida within the reach of Franz Epting's contagious enthusiasm for Kelley without at least *thinking* of personal construct applications, whatever one's interest area.)

Jim and I decided on a research topic for his thesis that investigated whether phobic individuals had constructs that incorporated threat at both poles of their construct dimensions or at only one pole, and the salience of the various dimensions to their overall reaction. To find a context for fear, we decided on snake phobia, and I acquired two boa constrictors, Chelsea and Tuppence (if you read Agatha Christie, the latter will make great sense). They lived in my office, in the letter bin during the day and a cage at night, and did double duty in keeping undergraduate advisees (of whom I had many) in the doorway asking very brief questions.

The research was very rewarding, partially because we had to invent new mechanisms for scoring the degree of threat in the construct dimensions and partially because I replicated the excitement I had found doing research in graduate school. I realized that part of the excitement for me in research was methodological, that is, in deciding *how* as opposed to *why* or *what*. Harking back to Ted Kaul and my primary course in research methodology, I remember that Ted posited two questions to the class that always had to be dealt with in each research project: What do you mean? and How do you know? I was realizing in Florida that the *how* was often as interesting as the *what*, and certainly was as influential from a scientific perspective.

This realization is related to a theme that has carried through my research to today. I would classify myself as a pragmatist in my orientation to research, particularly to such fundamental aspects of research as framing the questions. To me, the choice of method should be governed by the question. A field-based question demands a descriptive approach, a treatment comparison suggests an experimental study, and a methodological study seeks yet other strategies. Flexibility in method choice is as necessary for pursuing a series of questions within a research area as it is for advancing scholarship in general. Excellence in scholarship demands the best possible method and the best possible skepticism about one's findings. It seems to me that the debate over paradigm choice has shifted our focus away from asking and answering the best questions, with the best methods available for those questions, to predetermining the best methods and then choosing questions that match them.

Perhaps the most significant event in my research career, as random in nature as my choice of psychology as a major, occurred while I was at Florida, or more properly flying from Florida to another location. I sat in the airplane next to Warren Ross, an oncologist, who upon hearing of my research interests in anxiety and its treatment invited me to visit with him and his nurses at the hospital over a topic that was of great practical importance, anticipatory vomiting. Many of their patients developed this conditioning-based response to chemotherapy, and it interfered greatly with their treatment. Warren and I, along with an oncology social worker, investigated the phenomenon from a cognitive-coping perspective and treated the patients with a cognitive-behavioral approach. Both approaches were successful, and both resulted in publications. It is hard to overestimate the reward value of publications when one is untenured. Even if the research had not born such good fruit, however, I would still have been hooked on the importance of applying counseling psychology to health concerns, the excitement of working with patient issues in medical settings, and the value of collaborative and interdisciplinary research.

In the early 1980s, health applications were unusual in counseling psychology. The lack of role models forced me to develop an acquaintance with professional colleagues whom I might not have otherwise had the courage to approach, some of whom were quite senior to me and some of whom were outside counseling psychology. There also were few counseling psychology venues then for publishing this type of research. I decided to continue to pursue health psychology research topics, and also to maintain a balance of more publishable research in treatments for anxiety and in cognitive perspectives on anxiety.

ESTABLISHING MY CAREER AND RESEARCH PROGRAM

On my arrival at Iowa, I set out to replicate the research environment I had at Florida with patients undergoing chemotherapy and developing anticipatory vomiting. I was rather surprised that the oncology faculty at Iowa didn't find this to be a problem and, furthermore, weren't particularly interested in my research. This wasn't the first professional hurdle I had had to overcome, but it seemed more daunting than usual. I persisted and found myself invited to present my research at a journal club meeting. These meetings typically occur at 7 a.m. and, in spite of the name, are rather formal in nature. They are akin to giving a full-scale job colloquium, complete with slides, at 7 a.m. The talk on anticipatory vomiting, its development and treatment, was quite successful even though my discussion of stimulus transformation treatments went over the heads of all present. I acquired a new research focus that became available in the bone marrow transplantation (BMT) unit. I completed descriptive work on these patients' emotional and coping responses to BMT, a comparison of the comparative stresses of maintenance chemotherapy and BMT, and of BMT and renal transplantation. I have continued this work to my current involvement as principal investigator of a substudy on quality of life within a large multisite study of bone marrow transplant patients undergoing unrelated donor marrow transplantation, funded by the National Heart, Lung, and Blood Institute.

A second health-related interest came about when I was contacted by Wilbur Smith, residency director for radiology, who asked me to consult with them on selecting residents. At that time, I had a student who had done undergraduate work on behaviorally anchored interviewing who was interested in helping with this project, so Bill and I began a collaborative relationship that has lasted 15 years. Our research involves job analyses to identify critical components of physician performance. We have used accomplishment interviews to measure, at the time of selection, key variables that we followed up 3 years later in the residency. We now are close to having 10 years of data on radiologists and are following up these physicians in their careers. This area of research has been very rewarding in its expansion past radiology to pediatrics, obstetrics-gynecology, ophthalmology, and now to medical school selection. We have established in these many venues that traditional interviewing does not predict well, and objective predictors of performance, such as standardized tests, predict significantly but in the reverse direction (e.g., higher scoring applicants perform worse in a residency). Our accomplishment interview predicts well and suggests conscientiousness as a key variable in later effective performance.

I also developed an interest in psychological treatments for chronic low back pain after a request to develop a treatment program for pain patients proved too interesting to refuse. My research in this area, with several orthopedic surgeons, has been equally rewarding. For the first time, I brought counseling psychology to medicine in developing a treatment protocol for chronic low back pain aimed at fostering self-efficacy and coping acquisition, and in researching psychological variables as predictors of outcome in a clinical trial. The downside was that instead of one road less traveled, I was embarking on three, at least in my research program. At this time, I was an associate professor and was receiving lots of advice about choosing one, and *only* one, area of research for my focus. I resisted this advice and maintained my diverse interests. I have alternated low back pain and bone marrow transplantation in primary focus while keeping selection as an ongoing theme in the background.

Looking back, I have tried to fit reasons to my unwillingness to focus. At the time, I knew that my interest in each area was strong, and I found each area very stimulating both in content and in my research collaborators, who were typically physicians, my own counseling psychology graduate students, and other psychologists either here at Iowa or elsewhere. Each area also had its own unique challenges, all of which were quite intriguing. Furthermore, each area felt and still feels quite important in potential outcomes. Although research on selecting physicians doesn't offer the immediate potential for direct patient impact, as do the other areas, the influence on education and training outcomes has remained high, and there may yet be patient outcomes to be understood as a function of physicians' practice styles. More important, however, was my resistance to the idea that I couldn't do all of the areas well, that I had to focus if I was to achieve. This linear approach to research seemed quite uninteresting to me, and I resolved to let myself follow the directions that gave promise of more satisfaction.

The only way I was able to handle this challenge successfully was with the help of my students. At Florida and at Iowa, I have been gifted with students of great talent and promise who also possessed the ability to work well with me and to tolerate my eccentricities. I am sure that my students have many views on working with me, and they occasionally entertained me with stories of advice they got from more senior students such as "develop the ability to hide when you see her coming into the office." I regard my students as a primary professional reference group. They provide me with intellectual stimulation, they are emotionally supportive, they ask great questions, they need nurturing that takes me out of my own problems, and they choose me as an adviser, which I regard as the highest compliment. They have allowed me to pursue my multiple interests with some degree of success, and they have forced me to maintain a focus at other times. I am in their debt; the commitment and energy I have given to them have been dwarfed by the commitment and energy they have given to me. I want to thank them all.[2]

I suppose that one reason I feel so strongly about students' development is that I believe faculty in counseling psychology training programs too often try to replicate ourselves. We work to select students with promise in research rather than practice, and we bemoan our students' perceived lack of commitment to academic careers and their seduction by the lure of practice positions. It is more important for me to instill values in my students: the value of research in one's career, the excitement of new discoveries, the importance of following one's nose, and the critical nature of service in giving back to one's profession. These values should infuse whatever they do for a living, whether practice, research, or some blend, and indeed whatever they do in life. I very much appreciate the commitment my faculty colleagues at Iowa have made to these values as well. When a program faculty can agree on their values, working with students both individually and collectively is a great joy.

THE LARGER PSYCHOLOGY COMMUNITY

Another reference group that has played a critical role for me are my colleagues in counseling psychology, particularly in Division 17 of the American Psychological Association. My first experience with Division 17 was when I responded to a small notice in *The Counseling Psychologist* and volunteered for work on a Division committee. I was asked to serve on the Professional Affairs Committee, where I have Faith Tanney to thank for this early introduction to the Division and to its inner mechanisms. I have now been around the Division long enough to remember early Executive Committee meetings when the "MOMM cartel" (Minnesota, Ohio State, Missouri, and Maryland) was alive and well, and when committee chairs as well as committee members spent the entire time in one large and rather democratic group.

My service on the Professional Affairs Committee led to the Program Committee and several other related committees. My work on behalf of the Division culminated in my being elected treasurer, a great honor and an opportunity to work closely with George Gazda, Larry Brammer, Jim Hurst, and Naomi Meara while each was president. I discovered that being treasurer gave me a broad sense of responsibility for the well-being of the Division and a natural set of allies in all former Division treasurers, because treasurers are by nature conservative in regard to spending the Division's money, presumably because they think first of the existing account balance in response to any conversation about starting new projects. It also allowed me to form an abiding sense of respect and affection for the many people who commit themselves to the ongoing improvement of our profession.

The professional experience that had the greatest effect on me, however, was not in Division 17 but rather in the larger community of psychology as member and then Chair of the Committee on Accreditation. In the fall of 1992, the American Psychological Association embarked on a new venture vis-à-vis the committee. The committee structure was changed from a 10-person committee to a 21-person committee. Not only was the number larger, but the means by which people arrived on the committee also changed. When the committee was 10 people, they were nominated by various groups and selected by the Board of Education Affairs, and they tended to be pleasant folks with a heartfelt commitment to graduate education and a knowledge of how hard it is to reconcile multiple "agendas" on the committee. The 21 people, however, were nominated by defined constituent groups and therefore, presumably, would arrive with clear intentions for the committee based on their constituent representation. Furthermore, the new committee was charged with completely overhauling the scope, criteria, and procedures of accreditation while maintaining its usual workload. This charge appeared rather difficult to achieve.

Much to my surprise, the committee rose to the occasion and achieved all that had been expected. Keeping up with the regular workload of reviewing close to 70 programs each meeting, the committee also developed a new statement of scope, wrote new criteria for accreditation, and developed new sets of procedures for many aspects of accreditation, including program evaluation and site visitor training. In particular, the new criteria shifted from a process perspective to an outcome perspective, where the presence or absence of a particular training element was less important than its contribution to the program's meeting its own unique goals and its demonstrated effect on education and training outcomes among the students.

It is difficult to encapsulate my experience on the committee, both the 10-member group and the 21-member group. The topics were critical, and the ultimate outcome of this experiment in a larger, constituency-based committee was unknown. The interpersonal contact was intense, as committee members spend essentially every waking moment over 3 to 4 days together, eating every meal together and often finishing up the evening in the bar processing the day's events. The content was intense, as accreditation evokes passion, whether for or against, and strong opinions, both founded and unfounded.

Accreditation has undergone many changes over the years, as I discovered when I researched its history for a talk I gave at the 1995 convention on this topic. When the first committee began developing criteria, the criteria they articulated were open-ended and had more to do with principles and guidelines for effective training than with clear standards. Over time, the accreditation criteria have become more specified and, in the minds of some, less related to excellence than to minimal compliance.

I believe that certain principles have supported accreditation from the beginning: the notion of breadth as opposed to depth, the need for psychologists conducting training to have a high degree of competence, the integration of theory with practice and research, and an emphasis on the social implications of psychology and of training. The translation of these broad principles into mechanisms and processes of education and training, however, leads to conflict. For example, should internship, an intense training experience, precede or follow the granting of the doctoral degree? How much competence at conducting independent scholarly research should be required of faculty in programs that purport to train practitioners? How do models of training become developed and validated? Most important, what relationship does accreditation have with other processes in the psychological community (e.g., licensure)?

I learned many things in chairing the Committee on Accreditation. I learned that conflict is desirable, that people must speak their minds and be heard for compromise to be reached. I learned, too, that compromise is always in sight, and that the farther apart the sides are, the more room there is for finding a compromise. I learned that getting a group to work together and sacrifice individual agendas is hard work, both for me as chair and for them. I learned that I was more creative than I thought I was, in that problem solving became a creative endeavor for me. And I learned to appreciate Paul Nelson for his gracious leadership and patient approach to contentious issues. Paul is a great historian, and in my early days on the committee I would hear stories of the "old days" with little patience and inward sighs. It was amazing how rapidly that changed when I became Chair, and I was eager to hear how and why things were as they were to give me a sense of the history of the endeavor and the efforts of those persons who had worked at the task before.

At this point, what are my views of the profession of psychology? I believe we have lost sight of a unified value base as psychology has become more divided, with the various divisions adopting the values of various cultures, such as business, academe, and so on. I think the debate on the relevance of the scientist-practitioner model to training practitioners is emblematic of this divide. In moving toward a health care model of providing psychological services, some have argued that practitioners failed to appreciate the transitions that psychology, as a business, would undergo. I believe scientists, in turn, failed to understand practitioners' needs for applicable and clinically relevant data. If we are to establish a shared sense of psychology, it may be in the scientist-practitioner collaboration, where an application of psychology should rest on solid evidence of its effectiveness. (We may be seeing the beginnings of this solution in the definition of empirically validated treatments and practice guidelines.)

ACADEMIC ADMINISTRATION

My experience on the Committee on Accreditation served me well when I moved into my current position as Associate Provost of the University of Iowa. My responsibilities are those of a dean of faculty: I monitor searches, develop new faculty and new department chair orientation programs, manage mentoring programs, read annual reviews of probationary faculty, participate in tenure and promotion decisions, manage ethics complaints, and serve as the point person for grievances by faculty against the university or by the university against faculty. Everyday topics therefore are sexual harassment, consensual relationships, plagiarism, scientific misconduct, and other academic problem areas. Most tellingly, my work requires steady contact with the university attorneys.

I have developed a broad appreciation for the university as a community of people with ongoing expectations for one another and from external constituencies. I appreciate the role of faculty governance, peer review, due process, and procedures fairly applied. Paperwork seems important, too, as I sign off on all appointments and personnel forms, a pile that averages about 3 inches a day in my "in bin."

A recent book on the problems of being a woman in academe[3] describes with great clarity what it means for women in the academy to be caught in the bind of either trying to follow the unwritten rules, developed typically by and for men, or trying to forge a new path. Women do struggle in academe to find their place, and the politics of this struggle are both corporate and personal. I think it is impossible to live out one's career in academe as a woman and not experience at first hand the dilemma of choosing to follow the unwritten rules versus trying to establish the impossible proofs.

My initial experience of this struggle occurred when I gave birth to my first child and the University of Iowa had no policies governing such a "problem." Through a combination of misunderstandings and my own lack of assertiveness, I ended up with only 3 weeks off, one of which I spent in the hospital following a cesarean section. I subsequently received advice that female faculty who were mothers should be silent about this part of life so that their commitment to their professional life would not be questioned. I resolved not to allow this unwritten rule to dominate my attempts to reconcile work and family. Indeed, I once left a meeting with university administrators (on parenting issues, no less) because I had to pick up my children from day care and the meeting was scheduled at the end of the work day.

I do not see myself as an administrator, but clearly I have become one. My ongoing conflict between faculty roles and administrative roles is most evident in trying to meet—with limited time and patience—my students' needs for mentoring, support, and advice. I also have made a commitment to keeping my research going, even though on a reduced scale, and again appreciate my students' involvement in that task. What is most difficult about my current position, however, is the conflict it poses between work and family. This conflict happens because of the sheer number of hours I spend at work and my consequent inability to be at every event my children have; because they are 11 and 14 at the writing of this chapter, and are involved in sports and music, there are many such events. The conflict also happens because my energy and thoughts are consumed by work and less available for family. It is my unwillingness to give up my research coupled with my unwillingness to ask my family to continue to have my job dominate our life that led me away from other university administrative positions at this point in my career when they are a "natural" next step.

REFLECTIONS ON CAREER AND LIFE CHOICES

The writer of Ecclesiastes said that to every thing there is a season. To decide whether a particular road should be followed or not typically is complicated by the many agendas that get folded into any life decision. For me, many roads diverge in a yellow wood (literally, as it's fall in Iowa) and, while I regret that I cannot follow them all, I realize that the roads I have taken have led to other choices that I could not at that time have contemplated and that have resulted in most satisfying outcomes.

In reflecting on the roads taken to date, and considering roads ahead, my memories do indeed make for theories that are set into action by my conversation. Lisa Hoshmand posed a series of questions preparatory to the writing of these chapters, and one caught my attention: What is the relationship among the personal, social, and professional for you, and how should it be for all of us? I believe that the relationship among these facets rests on what one brings to them all, that is, how one integrates the domains. If one brings competition to these domains, for example, then there will be competition within each and among them. If one brings positive commitment, the ability to compromise, and a sense of excitement over the unknown ahead, as I hope I have, they seem to work well together. Certainly, it is helpful to articulate for oneself the values that underlie one's choices, and I have tried to discern and describe these in this chapter. For me, uncommon choices, looking back, had in common a sense of excitement and the opportunity to work with others in a collaborative way. I look forward to more of these roads ahead.

APPENDIX

Abbreviated Professional History

1973	BA (Psychology), Wheaton College
1975	MA (Counseling Psychology), Ohio State University
1977	PhD (Counseling Psychology), Ohio State University
1977-1980	Assistant Professor, University of Florida
1979	Professional Affairs Committee, Division of Counseling Psychology, APA
1980-1982	Assistant Professor, The University of Iowa
1982-1989	Associate Professor, The University of Iowa
1982-1993	Editorial Board, *Journal of Counseling Psychology*
1983-1991	Director, Counseling Psychology Program, The University of Iowa
1984-1993	Editorial Board, *Journal of Social and Clinical Psychology*
1986	Treasurer, Division of Counseling Psychology, APA
1986-1989	Executive Board, Council of Counseling Psychology Training Programs
1989	Professor, The University of Iowa
1990	Fellow, CIC Academic Leadership Program
1991	Associate Dean, College of Education, The University of Iowa
1991-1997	Associate Editor, *Contemporary Psychology*
1993	Associate Provost, The University of Iowa

NOTES

1. J. Martin, *The Construction and Understanding of Psychotherapeutic Change: Conversations, Memories, and Theories* (New York: Teachers College Press, 1994).

2. The author would like to name her students whose contributions she has so appreciated: Dave Bernstein, Jim Huber, Michael Weiss, Betty Yarris, Dave Priddy, Reggie Feldman, Peggy Bancroft, Cyndy McRae, Valerie Tarico, Anne Green-Emrich, Dawn VanVelzen, Jane Paulsen, Renee Redd, Randy Ross, Kate Morris, Candida Maurer, Andy Simcox, Miriam Meyer, Peggy Wood, Juan Aquino, Jane Cerhan, Kirk Mueller, Brian Johnson, Colleen O'Halloran, Amy

Stockman, Lolita Rhone, Sara Farnham, Michael Anderson, Tricia Henwood, Loreto Prieto, Jackie McMichael, Kiki Gorbatenko-Roth, Katie Ugolini, Luke Patrick, Lizzy Dew, Andrea Weiland and Lisa Streyffeler.

3. P. J. Caplan, *Lifting a Ton of Feathers: A Woman's Guide to Surviving in the Academic World* (Toronto: University of Toronto Press, 1994).

SELECT BIBLIOGRAPHY

With K. Moore and W. E. Ross. A pilot investigation of the psychologic functioning of patients with anticipatory vomiting. *Cancer, 49* (1982): 201-204.

With M. E. Meyer. *Applied specialties in psychology.* New York: Random House, 1985.

Processes in rehabilitation: A social psychological analysis. In *Social processes in clinical and counseling psychology,* ed. J. E. Maddux, C. D. Stoltenberg, and R. Rosenwein. New York: Springer, 1987.

With P. S. Wood, V. S. Tarico, and E. A. Franken. A prospective study of cognitive and noncognitive selection criteria as predictors of resident performance. *Investigative Radiology, 25* (1990): 855-859.

Research and practice roles for counseling psychologists in health care settings. *The Counseling Psychologist, 19* (1991): 342-364.

With R. D. Gingrich and M. A. Fyfe. Two-year adjustment of bone marrow transplant survivors. *Bone Marrow Transplantation, 7* (1991): 311-316.

With T. R. Lehmann, D. W. Russell, J. N. Weinstein, and C. F. Kao. The effectiveness of psychological interventions for the rehabilitation of low back pain: A randomized controlled trial evaluation. *Pain, 49* (1992): 329-335.

With D. W. Russell, C. F. Kao, T. R. Lehmann, & J. N. Weinstein. The role of self-efficacy in rehabilitation outcome among chronic low back pain patients. *Journal of Counseling Psychology, 40* (1993): 335-339.

With R. R. Ross. *Intervention in occupational stress: A handbook of counseling for stress at work.* London: Sage, 1994.

CHAPTER 6

A Personal Look at Psychology in My Life

DERALD WING SUE

I recall standing in front of my third-grade classroom speaking to my brother in Chinese. The school bell was about to ring when the teacher came out to close the door. Overhearing our conversation, my teacher gave us a disapproving look. She then turned to me and said, "Derald, you're in America! When you're in America you speak English. Get into the room now." I felt shamed and humiliated. What had I done wrong? Later that afternoon, when I returned home, my mother spoke to me in Chinese. I was curt with her, telling her that I never wanted to speak Chinese again, because that was the reason why people wouldn't accept us.

I am a Chinese American, a member of an ethnic minority group, who has suffered from prejudice, discrimination, and racism. I also have experienced poverty and stereotyping, and I have been made (or allowed myself) to feel self-conscious and inferior. Yet, in a strange sort of way, I believe that I also have benefited from minority group status as well. Although it may not make sense to some, my experiences as a minority group member have led to my own self-awakening and have profoundly influenced my work in life. Who I am as a psychologist cannot be separated from my personal identity. My work in multicultural psychology, minority mental health issues, multicultural organizational development, racial identity development, and concerns with social justice have their roots in many of my early experiences. Although many of these incidents were extremely painful, the lessons I have learned from them about life have proven invaluable.

THE EARLY YEARS

I was born in Portland, Oregon, to proud parents who believed in the primacy of the family and who extolled the virtues of hard work and achievement. I am the second oldest of five brothers and one sister. Interestingly enough, three of my brothers also have doctorates in psychology, yet my mother and father never finished the third grade. Despite my father's lack of formal education in the United States, he became a distinguished elder in the Chinese community. He immigrated to the United States by himself at the age of 13 or 14. He worked as a welder periodically but made his living as a professional gambler in Portland's Chinatown. As a result, our financial situation was always in flux; at times, surviving on a day-to-day basis was the norm, and at other times, my father would bring home large sums of money. My mother was a housewife who had her hands full in raising her family. Out of financial necessity, she worked at many different jobs: in laundries and canneries, and as a janitor. Whereas my father never learned to read or write English, my mother taught herself these skills. As I have gotten older, with children of my own, I have increasingly appreciated and realized how much my parents have accomplished in their lives. If I were to select some of the most influential experiences in my early life, they would be poverty, racial prejudice and identity, and being taught that work and achievement are important.

I can remember vividly how shamed my mother and father felt to have to ask for help to support their family. The male welfare worker would come to our house and would inspect our cupboards before he approved our application. He obviously was checking to see if we were really a family in need. After 6 months on welfare, my parents decided to quit the program even though that would create a hardship. They were too proud to endure the "humiliation." We all decided to work: My mother worked at the laundromat, and my brothers and I worked after school to supplement our father's income.

Economic hardship was a constant factor in our day-to-day existence. There was no doubt that we were poor and lacked many of the niceties of life that other families took for granted. There were periods of time in which our dinners consisted of the contents of giant cans of Campbell's soup mixed with white rice. Our presents to one another during birthdays often were food and candy;

gifts during Christmas and other holidays were always functional. We would wrap large cans of apple juice or giant Hershey bars of chocolate for one another and place them under the Christmas tree. We all contributed to the family budget by summer work, after-school employment, and other odd jobs. I can recall many times when the furnace would break down or our house would require repairs, which would upset my mother because it ultimately meant unforeseen expenses. Despite being poor, I do not remember a time when I went to bed hungry, nor can I say that I resented my parents for being who they were. I became very aware, however, of socioeconomic differences and how one's financial status could determine the amount of privilege enjoyed in our society.

Work was the norm among all members of the household. This was especially true for my mother. Not only did she raise a family of five sons and one daughter, but she cooked, did the laundry, cleaned the house, kept up the yard, and worked full-time outside the home. Of course, we were all expected to help. I believe that the work ethic was strongly instilled in all of us because of these early experiences. Indeed, my brothers, my sister, and I attended higher education without financial aid from our parents: I paid for my education through a combination of summer employment, scholarships, and loans. Although my parents never obtained even an elementary education, they instilled in us the need to achieve and to better ourselves through education.

Now, as a successful academician and consultant, I have achieved a high level of financial security, and my circle of acquaintances are generally well-to-do colleagues, neighbors, and friends. I have discovered how difficult it is for many of these folks to relate to conditions of poverty and how quickly they judge others by materialistic standards. More frightening is their tendency to blame the poor, homeless, and downtrodden for their plight. I must admit that there have been brief periods of my life when I, too, have been seduced by the comforts of monetary acquisition, but memories of my own early experiences of deprivation serve to counterbalance this tendency. I believe it is important not to lose the ability to understand poverty and the human toll it takes. It is important to be able to empathize with the financial plight of others and to understand that they may be victims of societal inequality and the forces that promote poverty.

As a child, I was made to feel inferior and ashamed of my racial identity and heritage. I remember being teased "ching-chong Chinaman" by classmates in Abernathy Grade School, being slighted by members of the opposite sex in dance classes, and so on. My parents were proud to be Chinese, but some of my peers, neighbors, and teachers operated from stereotypes and conveyed to me that to be White was better. Some of these stereotypes were that Asian Americans were good in the physical sciences, were good with numbers, and make good technical workers but are poor in interpersonal relations and inarticulate. For example, I can vividly recall my high school counselor encouraging me to go into the sciences because "you people are good at that." Worse yet, I became painfully aware that many women did not want to date me because Asians were considered "passive, nonsexual, and unattractive."

My experience with racial prejudice became acute when I entered my late teen years. I remember one specific incident involving Sharon, a blonde-haired girl I had met at work. I was on summer break and working at the cannery; we constantly flirted with one another until I finally worked up the courage to ask her out. On the morning of our planned beach outing, I arrived at her house only to be met by her father. He informed me that Sharon was not home. When I expressed disbelief, he exploded and told me never to come back, that he did not want his daughter to date "people like you."

I was always aware of being different, racially, culturally, and physically. As an "outsider" I felt excluded. I was always on the outside looking in, observing people and situations. In my youth, I wanted very much to be like all the other kids; to be accepted, liked, and respected. My brothers and I all went through this process and would frequently share our thoughts and feelings with one another. We seldom spoke about this to our parents. Our mother was aware of our feelings although she couldn't understand them. Our father baffled us because he was so proud of being Chinese.

I remember desperately trying to convince others and especially myself that I was not a "typical" Asian. As a young adult, I believed all the negative stereotypes about my race, and I was ashamed of being Chinese. The strong desire to be like my White classmates resulted in a denial of my racial heritage. I tried to be White and confined almost all my college dating to White women. Few opportunities ever arose for me to have social relationships with Asian women, and frankly I'm not sure I would have taken advantage of it. From early on I had witnessed the prejudices and discrimination meted out to me and my family. I believed then that we deserved it, having accepted the strong societal belief that to be different was to be deviant and that being White was better than being a member of any other culturally different group.

Throughout my life, I have experienced prejudice, stereotyping, and discrimination, some instances very dramatic and others more subtle. I have learned that one must endure and overcome if one is to lead a fruitful life and contribute something of worth to others. These experiences have played a large role in shaping my values, beliefs, and assumptions about human behavior.

RACIAL/CULTURAL REAWAKENING

During the latter part of my junior year in college, I abruptly changed majors from chemistry to psychology. I was fascinated with the field, having taken an introductory psychology course and being exposed to the topic of prejudice and racism. I began to discover that I not only loved the field but also could "think in a psychological manner." Whereas in my elementary and high school years I had believed that the physical sciences were my ultimate career (believing strongly the Asian stereotypes), many of the shackles regarding other vocational opportunities and possibilities began to fall away. I read and studied psychology continuously and took as many courses as possible in anthropology, sociology, and political science. I made a decision to go for my doctorate in the field even though my parents had no real idea of what psychology entailed.

Something changed for me, however, during my years in graduate school. It was, for some reason, a time of reflection and introspection. I began to realize that much of the knowledge base in psychology did not fit with my own experiences and views of the world. I was surprised that I began to use my family experiences, the silent teachings of my father, observations of my mother's hard life, and discussions with my brothers Stan and Dave to gauge the legitimacy of the psychology being taught. The theories of counseling and psychotherapy (my field of specialization), for example, appeared class-bound and culture-bound. Almost all of my fellow students seemed to want to go into private practice, and although they talked about social issues, it clearly was an intellectual exercise for most of them. At the risk of sounding self-righteous, they did not experientially or affectively understand issues of poverty and discrimination.

In actuality, the barriers to my awakening had begun to crumble even before graduate school. I was most intrigued with the Civil Rights Movement and particularly the teachings of Black leaders of the period. I could relate to the pain of oppression they experienced and the anger/rage they felt toward an intolerant society. Having no professional or political Asian American role models, I strongly identified with African Americans. My heroes were Black people: Martin Luther King, Malcolm X, Huey Newton, H. Rap Brown, and others. I read their writings extensively and was struck by the honesty and directness of their voices; many of the ideas resonated with my own experiential reality. One concept, however, had the greatest impact on me and constantly echoed in my mind: "Being Black is not the problem! The problem is society's perception of blackness." I began to ask myself "Could it possibly be that being Asian is not the problem and that it is society's perception of Asians?"

I was also greatly influenced by how Black Americans spoke of "Black is beautiful." This forced me to question myself: Why should people feel ashamed of who and what they are? It took years for me to sort this out and to come up with an acceptable answer. No group should be made to feel ashamed of their racial/cultural heritage. No group should have to justify their differences. No group should allow themselves to feel inferior. It was a long journey, but I finally concluded that minorities are not the problem—the problem resides in an oppressive and intolerant society. Any psychology that is directed primarily toward attempting to adjust clients to society should reconsider the fact that their reactions might be healthy, especially if the situation is "sick."

These realizations changed me completely. I began to take a very extremist position. Being Asian American was good! The problem was White society. It was reinforced when I accepted my first position at the University of California, Berkeley, Counseling Center. I had never been in the company of so many Asian Americans. I became involved with Asian American studies and became known on the campus as a "good counselor for Asian American students." I listened to the many stories of Asian American clients, some similar to mine but many quite dissimilar. I was struck by the fact that many of the Asian Americans were proud of their racial heritage, and this reminded me of my father. Little did my Asian American clients realize that their therapeutic journey was shared by their therapist.

I was at Berkeley, free and footloose, leading the life of a bachelor and dating many Asian women for the first time. My brother Stan called me one day and said he had just met a most attractive Asian American woman at a social function. At that time, I was still battling with White standards of physical attractiveness. He encouraged me to call this person for a date. I called Paulina and was struck by both her beauty and intelligence. In addition, I discovered she had never experienced racial self-hatred; she was proud of being Asian American. It was then that I truly realized how brainwashed I had been. She became my wife and bore me two children whom I hope will be proud of being Asian Americans.

▬▬▬▬▬ BEGINNING PROFESSIONAL YEARS

At the University of California, Berkeley, I embarked on a major study of Asian Americans that led to my first publications. Again, I noticed the almost complete lack of psychological studies on Asian Americans in the mental health field. Publications in those years dealt primarily with African Americans.

Several of these had a major impact upon my thinking: Grier and Cobbs's *Black Rage*,[1] Vontress's "Racial Differences: Impediments to Rapport,"[2] Thomas and Sillen's *Racism and Psychiatry*,[3] and Freire's *Pedagogy of the Oppressed*.[4] Reading the ideas of these writers was like water quenching a longtime thirst. They gave voice to my own thoughts, feelings, and experiential reality. As I have examined the major academic influences that have most shaped my ideas and work, I am struck by the lack of cross-cultural understanding in the theories and writings of traditional Euro-American psychologists. This is not to say that I was unimpressed with the writings of Skinner, Rogers, and other acknowledged giants in the field, but they spoke only to one narrow aspect of my reality.

My early publications dealt with Asian American identity, mental health, and personality. I drew parallels between the experiences of Black Americans and those of Asian Americans. There is little doubt in my mind that my research interests were related to my personal search: What was being Asian American, and what was the Asian American experience? My work was strongly tinged with a sociopolitical edge that many of my colleagues felt uncomfortable with. Indeed, I was often discouraged from pursuing research on ethnic/racial matters because it was too much "opinion" and not enough science. I was told that if I ever wanted to move up in academia, I would need to abandon my work on racial/ethnic minorities. Although these warnings bothered me immensely, I felt compelled to do research and publish on issues of oppression, prejudice, discrimination, and how racism influences identity development. My very first publication was coauthored with my brother Stan and concerned Asian American personality and mental health. It was published in an Asian American social issues journal and evoked strong reactions from many of the readers because it was very sociopolitical in nature. This publication was a crucial turning point in my life. I realized two things: I very much enjoyed writing and could put my ideas/feelings on paper well, and I was astounded at how words could influence and affect so many people.

Two other major events occurred during my early years that have affected my professional work. First, my brother Stan and I formed the Asian American Psychological Association (AAPA); I became its first president. We patterned ourselves after the other minority group organizations in psychology. Our goals were to promote the psychological study of Asian Americans, identify conditions that lead to mental disorders, and develop culture-specific approaches to ameliorating them. Although there were few of us in the organization during those early years, we were perceived by the American Psychological Association, the American Personnel and Guidance Association (now the American Counseling Association), and other mental health organizations as representing a significant constituency. I realized quickly that groups wielded more power and influence than individuals.

Second, my work in Asian American studies led me to propose a special feature on counseling Asian Americans for the *Personnel and Guidance Journal.* As a counseling psychologist, I had found this particular journal of special interest. Its editor, Leo Goldman, seemed receptive to racial/ethnic minority concerns and, indeed, seemed more committed to social justice issues than many of my Asian American colleagues. It was my communications with him and my past work with other White colleagues that increasingly led me to see them as potential allies. Working with Goldman was a rewarding experience. He seemed to understand the minority experience and encouraged me throughout the editing process. We published the special feature on Asian Americans, one of the early and few publications in the field at a time when everyone thought that race relations or cross-cultural matters were primarily Black-White. My enthusiasm for research on Asian Americans resulted in three subsequent publications in APA journals and numerous other articles.

In 1975, I was appointed editor of the *Personal and Guidance Journal,* the official publication of the American Personnel and Guidance Association. To this very day, I still do not have the complete picture of how I was chosen. Note that this occurred approximately 6 years after obtaining my doctorate and that an editorship generally is reserved for an elder of the profession with a distinguished publication record. My best reading was that my predecessor, Leo Goldman, had a major part in the selection process, and there was considerable pressure that it was time for a person of non-White descent to occupy the position. Whatever the reasons, I was both flattered and energized. I appointed an editorial board that truly represented racial/ethnic diversification, and I encouraged special features/issues of the journal on various racial/ethnic minority groups. In addition, my strong belief in making the journal understandable to readers (practical implications) and dealing frankly with topics such as human sexuality were well received by the readership. Letters poured in to the Association praising the new direction of the journal. Being new and naive, however, I came under criticism by the more senior and conservative members of the profession. Because the journal's direction placed higher priority on new topical areas, we declined to publish many traditional counseling-type manuscripts submitted by senior members of the profession.

Under my editorship, the journal challenged traditional values of counseling, guidance, and psychotherapy. My own worldview and those of my editorial board favored a nontraditional stance and approach. We believed strongly that prevention was more important than remediation, that the focus of counseling's future was in systems intervention, that the locus of problems often resided not in the person but the system, and that there was a strong need to change the sociopolitical makeup of society. This is still quite at odds with today's clinical orientation and was more so in 1975-1978. Perhaps I am unfair, but the "old boys network" within the profession apparently was threatened. After all, the gatekeeper of any journal wields tremendous power and influence (publications in academia are important for promotion and tenure). I really do not believe that they expected me to be so committed to changing the focus of the journal. It seemed better to have an Asian editor than a Black one (if one believes the stereotype that Asians "don't rock the boat" while African Americans will). After only 2 years of being editor, I encountered tremendous resistance from some key but influential elders in the profession. There was a strong move to censure me as the editor and to remove me from the position. Fortunately, many of my colleagues and friends worked on my behalf during some trying times. Nevertheless, after my first term (3 years), I elected not to continue for another.

Upon reflection, I must admit that my term as editor was a true learning and growth experience. I was both pained by the criticisms I received and encouraged by the results. Perhaps it was rationalization, but I began to understand that standing up for what one believes, when it flies in the face of the prevailing belief system, will evoke strong resistance and potential retaliation. Such forces are, oftentimes, very difficult to withstand. That was one of the reasons why I chose not to continue as the editor for another 3-year term. Although I have guilt over this decision (retreating in the face of opposition), I realize that the personal toll it took on me and my family would render me useless. So, I went into a period of hibernation. I needed time to collect my thoughts, and to reflect on what had happened. At that time, family issues were also pressing upon me. Suffice it to say that the consequences of such an intense and all-consuming involvement in multicultural psychology are not confined to one's professional life but may take a toll on a personal level as well.

THE ACADEMIC LIFE

After 3 years as a practicing psychologist, I came to realize that I enjoyed teaching, research, writing, and consulting. Some 4 years after obtaining my doctorate, I decided to go into academia and to accept a tenure-track position. It was during this period of my life that I also discovered I had a gift for oral communication. I had always known that I could write well, but being able to speak in front of groups was a true revelation. All my life and even today I consider myself to be shy, introverted, and basically a loner, an "outsider." I was always anxious when lecturing, but student evaluations were consistently positive. Even more flattering was being chosen "outstanding professor" during my first year at California State University, Hayward.

I found academia exciting and enjoyable. Students seemed to appreciate my disclosures about race, culture, and ethnicity. I developed courses on cross-cultural counseling and introduced multicultural concepts in all my classes. My colleagues, however, were less receptive and comfortable with my approach. They did not share, understand, or appreciate my worldview. Strangely enough, I found myself increasingly being able to tolerate their negative opinions of my work, teaching, and beliefs. During the years of my teaching from 1973 to 1980, I began to realize that many of my colleagues and especially White people were "hung up" about racial matters. In the past, I would have considered them adversaries, but I began to see that they, too, were victims of their cultural conditioning. Although my close colleagues were generally persons of color, I soon began to realize that some of my closest and respected friends were White individuals as equally committed as I to building bridges between the racial/ ethnic groups.

These multiple experiences resulted in seeing the field of counseling and psychotherapy quite differently from how many of my colleagues view it. My work became less ethnocentric and more liberated. As I have mentioned before, most of my early work was on Asian American psychology, but I soon felt it was too limited. Oppression, discrimination, prejudice, and stereotyping operated similarly across most minority groups. I refused to buy into the "us versus them" dichotomy or play the "we are more oppressed than you" game. I further fought against ethnic conditioning that emphasized group pride by derogating another's group.

My second awakening began to occur and resulted in seeing the implications of multiculturalism that transcend any one racial group, contributions on identity development and worldviews, identifying the generic characteristics of counseling/therapy, developing multicultural counseling/therapy competencies, developing a theory of multicultural counseling and therapy, and working in multicultural organizational development.

I received a long-distance call one day from a White male professor at a prestigious institution located on the East Coast. He told me that he taught classes on minority mental health issues and saw himself as "free of racism and bias." He then launched into a diatribe attacking my book *Counseling the Culturally Different: Theory and Practice*. He characterized it as "anti-White," biased, and likely to create greater misunderstanding and conflict between the races. How could I possibly write such a lopsided book? He would never use it and hoped it would find its way into "the gutter."

Although I had written several previous books, none represented such a labor of love as this one. It was written with great personal passion and to this day represents most clearly my thoughts and philosophy about the relationship of minority mental health and the sociopolitical nature of counseling and psychotherapy. I pride myself in being open and honest and in saying precisely what I believe. To tell others that they have biases, or to attack a "sacred cow" (their vision of psychotherapy), is extremely threatening and evokes a strong defensive reaction. Yet, I came to realize that many Euro-Americans have great difficulty with understanding the difference between my attacking white supremacist notions that underlie mental health practice and personal attacks. Later, I was to be exposed to the work of Janet Helms and Rita Hardiman on White identity development that so much resonated with these experiences. Several themes that reflect my personal and professional identity and work can be gleaned from the book.

First, persons of color, gays/lesbians, women, and other oppressed groups have a legitimate right to criticize the mental health field as having done great harm to minority constituents. Rather than educate or heal, rather than offer enlightenment and freedom, and rather than allow for equal access and opportunities, historical and current practices have often restricted, stereotyped, damaged, and oppressed the culturally different in our society.

Second, most mental health professionals have not been trained to work with other than mainstream individuals or groups. The theories they have been taught are both class-bound and culture-bound. Traditional theories of counseling and psychotherapy may become instruments of oppression, and helping professionals are not immune from inheriting the racial biases of their forebears. In other words, even the most well-intentioned helping professionals possess prejudices and biases that can harm their minority clients.

Third, mental health professionals need to question their traditional roles of the "one-to-one, in-the-office, remediation, and talking approach" to helping. Problems often reside not in the person but in the social system (racism, prejudice, poverty, sexism, discrimination). If psychology is to be truly helpful, intervention must occur at a systemic level, and the professional psychologist must take on the role of social change agent, consultant, teacher, advocate, and facilitator of indigenous resources in the community.

Reactions to the book and its adoption in many multicultural counseling courses propelled much of my other work on counseling/therapy before the professional eye. Although some White professionals like the one mentioned above reacted negatively, the book was well received by psychologists of color and by White colleagues who seemed to understand the minority experience. Indeed, several surveys[5] have identified *Counseling the Culturally Different: Theory and Practice* as a citation classic and as ranked by multicultural experts as the most influential publication in the field of multicultural counseling.

CHANGING THE SYSTEM

As my work in multicultural counseling and therapy became better known and better received, I began to get many invitations to speak on panels, give keynote addresses at conferences, and do training and consultation with various organizations. I quickly learned that antiracism training, diversity training, and sociopolitical analysis of the mental health field were equally applicable in the world of business and industry (or any organization for that matter). The language used by education, mental health, government, and business and industry might differ, but the processes and principles of prejudice and discrimination were the same from an institutional perspective. Like individuals, organizations also differed in their sensitivity and receptivity to culturally different workers or employees. In providing consultation and training, however, I began to notice that my classes and workshops on developing cultural competence were creating problems for many of my students and trainees, especially those most skilled in working with racial/ethnic minority clients. To understand the dilemma faced by many of these students requires a brief digression.

My multicultural mental health classes and the many workshops I conducted challenged the appropriateness of traditional mental health practices with respect to racial/ethnic minorities. My training consisted of teaching culturally appropriate or culture-specific intervention strategies that often violated traditional therapeutic "taboos" (such as a therapist does not give advice or suggestions, does not self-disclose, does not barter, does not accept gifts from clients, etc.) and involved playing different helping roles other than the conventional counselor/therapist role of in-the-office, one-to-one remediation primarily using "talk" as the medium for help. My philosophy and work opened students to the multiplicity of roles they could play: social change agent, advocate, consultant, teacher, or facilitator of community resources (neighborhoods, churches, clubs, etc.).

Over the years, many of my former students would return to share their experiences with me. They still believed strongly in multicultural counseling and therapy but found themselves at odds with the mental health organizations that employed them. They were often told by their supervisors or colleagues that they were "unprofessional in behavior," "had difficulty maintaining boundaries," "were involved in dual relationships," and "lacked good therapeutic skills." As a result, they often were given negative evaluations, not given deserved raises, and not promoted. It was then that I realized an important facet of change—it does no good to train people in multicultural competence when the very organizations that employ them do not appreciate it and may even be overtly antagonistic and punitive toward these helpers.

Although I had always been aware of systemic factors influencing human behavior, it was not until I began to do diversity training for organizations and listened to the stories of former students and trainees that I turned my attention and focus toward multicultural organizational development. I began to realize how impactful and controlling organizations are in our daily lives. They shape our perceptions, control our actions, define our roles, and set standards for appropriate behavior. This is accomplished via an organizational culture (most often monocultural in nature) that is manifested in their structures, programs, policies, and practices. For example, if we look at the American Psychological Association and the American Counseling Association, we will note that professional behavior is governed by a "Code of Ethics" and by "Standards of Practice." Both are predominantly Euro-American in origin and evolve from a particular cultural and political context. As such, they are culture-bound and may not be applicable to the many culturally different groups in our society. To rigidly impose and enforce these standards without the recognition of their limitations and biases will be to engage in cultural oppression.

Over the past 10 years, my focus has turned increasingly to systemic interventions beyond individual change. I have taken a much broader perspective in realizing that mental health and equal access and opportunities for all involve changes that go beyond just the individual. Indeed, I have begun to view change in a broader societal and cultural context. I see "ethnocentric monoculturalism" as dysfunctional in a pluralistic society like the United States. Ethnocentric monoculturalism combines Wrenn's "cultural encapsulation"[6] and Jones's "cultural racism."[7] Inherent in such a perspective is a strong belief in the superiority of one group's cultural heritage (history, values, language, traditions, arts/crafts, etc.) and a belief in the inferiority of all other groups' cultural heritage that extends to their customs, values, traditions, and language. The dominant group possesses the power to impose its standards and beliefs on the less powerful group. It is power or the unequal status relationship between groups that defines ethnocentric monoculturalism.

Ethnocentric values and beliefs are manifested in the programs, policies, practices, structures, and institutions of society. For example, chain-of-command systems, communication systems, management systems, and performance appraisal systems often dictate and control our lives. These systemic forces attain untouchable and godfather-like status in an organization. Because most systems are monocultural in nature and demand compliance, racial/ethnic minorities and women may be oppressed.

Because people are all products of cultural conditioning, their values and beliefs (worldviews) represent an "invisible veil" that operates outside the level of conscious awareness. As a result, people assume universality of worldviews: that their conceptions of reality and truth are shared by everyone regardless of race, culture, ethnicity, or gender. This assumption is erroneous but is seldom questioned because it is firmly ingrained in our ways of knowing.

I have come to the conclusion that individuals, organizations, and institutions are not immune from cultural conditioning and socialization processes. As individuals, we inherit the racial biases of our forebears. Organizations in our society are monocultural because they express the assumptions, values, and practices embedded in Euro-American culture only.

A PSYCHOLOGY OF SOCIAL ACTION AND JUSTICE

I believe strongly that the monocultural perspective of psychology has done great harm to culturally different groups in our society because it so clearly reflects the wider values of a monocultural Euro-American culture. This is not to say that Euro-American perspectives are "bad," but to indicate that a psychology that equates differences with deviance/pathology (implicitly or explicitly); fails to value racial, cultural, and ethnic differences; and minimizes systemic forces as contributors to human problems is seriously flawed. As psychologists, we have both a moral and a professional responsibility toward bettering the human condition, toward liberating those who are oppressed, and toward seeing that all groups—regardless of race, ethnicity, sexual orientation, gender, religion, and so on—have equal access and opportunity.

To accomplish such a goal means that our psychology and society must direct efforts toward the following four objectives, which are similar to the objectives of multicultural competence that were formulated in 1980 and were approved by Division 17 and later refined and adopted by two divisions of the American Counseling Association (AMCD and ACES).

1. Having mental health professionals become culturally aware of their own values, biases, and assumptions about human behavior.

2. Having mental health professionals acquire knowledge and understanding of the worldview of minority or culturally different groups and clients.

3. Having mental health professionals begin the process of developing appropriate and effective intervention strategies in working with culturally different clients.

4. Understanding how organizational and institutional forces may either enhance or negate the development of multicultural competence, and developing new rules, regulations, policies, practices, and structures within organizations to enhance multiculturalism.

Nearly all my professional work (education and training, community work, organizational consultation, and research and writing) at this time is directed toward these four objectives. Figuring out how to achieve these goals can be overwhelming, and achieving them can be met with much resistance from the status quo.

THE CONTINUING STRUGGLE

The police came to our house on a December morning in 1995. They had a search warrant for what they claimed to be stolen property in the possession of my 19-year-old son. Because my wife was running a carpool, no one was at home. The police broke down our front door and claimed to have recovered the missing equipment. My son was subsequently arrested and imprisoned on felony charges. These charges finally were dismissed after an outcry from friends, neighbors, and minority group organizations who saw the actions as an example of racism. What our family was forced to endure was extreme, unwarranted, and to me clearly in retaliation for our antiracism work in the community and/or a reflection of anti-Asian sentiment among certain elements in the city. I was positive that a White family in this affluent community would never have suffered a similar fate.

I cannot possibly convey to you the anguish and pain this incident has inflicted on my family and me. The pain associated with personal discrimination is different when a member of your own family is used to strike back at you. My wife and I had been very active in our community: I was a founding member of the city's Asian American Club, my wife put on diversity forums for the city, I had conducted pro bono multicultural education workshops for the school district, and we vocally expressed opposition to the formation of the Caucasian Students' Union, which evoked images of white supremacist organizations. The Asian American population in the schools had risen to 20%, and we constituted the largest racial minority group in the city. Space does not permit a more detailed explanation, but sufficeit to say that I interpreted the actions of certain city departments to have been motivated by racism.

I am certain that the city expected that we would retreat in the face of such force. The district attorney's office delayed filing charges, hoping that my son would accept a conditional diversion of the case. We refused every conditional offer even when it was minimal (they finally were willing to dismiss the charges if my son would do 10 days of community service). I believe that our refusal and our decision to risk a trial surprised them. With our decision to fight the charges and to go public, their case began to unravel. Some key city officials began to ask many embarrassing questions about the case, especially when the sworn statement of the chief accuser was contradicted by other credible witnesses, our family refused to bargain, a write-in campaign began from minority organizations threatening to make this incident public, and a well-known civil rights attorney entered the case.

Although the criminal portion of the case has been dismissed, our civil claim against the city for false arrest, false imprisonment, and violation of civil rights is still being processed. Although the city will never admit fault or apologize, we are heartened that responsible officials have begun to take certain actions on behalf of the city. For example, the city has started diversity training for its police force, one of the department heads has retired (encouraged to do so?), and the city appears to desire a quick resolution.

What I have learned from this unfortunate incident reinforces several lessons about the sociopolitical nature of working toward social change and justice that apply to almost every facet of societal functioning. First, whether one is challenging prevailing beliefs of the times, confronting people about bias and discrimination, or seeking change in unfair and entrenched policies and practices, one must always be ready for negative consequences. Commitment to social justice can result in a large backlash, resulting in personal and professional sacrifices. Second, no matter how committed and strong a person may be, it is not enough. Persevering to combat racism, sexism, and homophobia in the face of opposition requires the help and support of others—family, close friends, understanding colleagues, mentors, and those who have made sacrifices before us. This incident brought home strongly how important it was for our family to receive such unconditional local and national support. Such events occur every day, and many people do not have the resources or support from influential friends and colleagues. Third, I realize how difficult it is to effect change in the firmly entrenched racial biases of people and institutions. Thus, any diversity training program, or any course on multicultural counseling/therapy, that does not have an antiracism training component may be doomed to failure.

CONCLUDING THOUGHTS

As I have reread this manuscript many times, I am concerned that the telling of my story may make me appear embittered, that my life may appear to be a constant struggle, that I am an unhappy person, and that I see nothing good about our society and about the field of psychology. Nothing could be further from the truth. I am not an embittered person, but I am passionate and intense about my work and feel happiest when I am able to express my thoughts, beliefs, and feelings honestly and openly. It is precisely my commitment to our society and profession that makes me want to make it better. I have experienced many high points in my life and continue to experience gratification as I watch both my children grow and mature. Although my wife and I have tried to instill within them an ethnic pride and an understanding of racism, we realize that they will need to go forth into the world to make discoveries of their own.

My life is not always in turmoil, as my story may seem to indicate. I do believe, however, that it is struggle and conflict that have most shaped my identity. They revealed to me truths about my strengths and limitations and allowed me to find meaning in life and in my work. Another conclusion I have come to is that we will never eradicate racism, prejudice, and discrimination. I believe that, at some level, most people of color realize the reality of this statement. Strangely enough, this realization does not discourage me from my work in life because being true to oneself (doing the right thing) is as important as the goal (outcome). Martin Luther King had a vision that someday we would eliminate discrimination, and everyone would share equally in the fruits of society. Although I might desperately want to share that vision, I realize that it does not matter whether I believe it to be possible. For me, the striving is as important as the outcome.

Abbreviated Professional History

1965	BS, Oregon State University (Psychology)
1967	MS, University of Oregon (Counseling Psychology)
1969	PhD, University of Oregon (Counseling Psychology)
1969-1972	Counseling Psychologist, University of California, Berkeley
1972-1973	Assistant Professor, University of Santa Clara
1972-1975	President and Cofounder, Asian American Psychological Association
1973-1975	Editorial Board, *Journal of Counseling and Development*
1973-present	Professor, California State University, Hayward
1975-1976	Advisory Board, Minority Fellowship Program, APA
1975-1978	Editor, *Personnel and Guidance Journal*
1975-1978	Committee on Equality of Opportunity in Psychology, APA (Chair, 1977-1978)
1975-1978	Editorial Board, *American Association for Counseling and Development*
1977-1983	Consulting Editor, *The Counseling Psychologist*
1978	Board of Social and Ethical Responsibility, APA
1978-1980	Chair, Education and Training Committee, Division of Counseling Psychology, APA
1978-1983	Member-at-large, Executive Committee, Division 17, APA
1980-present	D. W. Sue, Ph.D., A Psychological Corporation (Assessment, consultation, and training for social service agencies, government, and business and industry)
1984	Chair, Committee on Racial/Ethnic Minorities, Division 17, APA
1988-1992	Consulting Editor, *Professional Psychology*

APPENDIX

Abbreviated Professional History *(continued)*

1988-1992	Chair, Professional Standards Committee, Association of Multicultural Counseling and Development, APA
1989-1991	Executive Committee, Society for Psychological Study of Ethnic Minority Issues (Division 45)
1989-1991	Chair, Committee on Multicultural Counseling Competencies, Division 17, APA
1990-1993	Training faculty, Columbia University Executive Training Programs in Managing Cultural Diversity
1994-present	Professor, California School of Professional Psychology, Alameda
1994-present	Editorial Board, Sage series on multicultural counseling and the counseling of women

NOTES

1. W. Grier and P. Cobbs, *Black Rage* (New York: Basic Books, 1968).

2. C. Vontress, "Racial Differences: Impediments to Rapport," *Journal of Counseling Psychology, 18* (1971): 7-13.

3. A. Thomas and S. Sillen, *Racism and Psychiatry* (New York: Brunner/Mazel, 1972).

4. P. Freire, *Pedagogy of the Oppressed* (New York: Continuum, 1972).

5. A. E. Heath, G. J. Niemeyer, and P. B. Pedersen, "The Future of Cross-Cultural Counseling: A Delphi Poll," *Journal of Counseling and Development, 67* (1988): 27-30; J. G. Ponterotto and H. B. Sabnani, " 'Classics' in Multicultural Counseling: A Systematic Five-Year Content Analysis," *Journal of Multicultural Counseling and Development, 17* (1989): 23-37; and D. Chih, J. Davis, T. Chilton, R. Olivera, T.L.D. Dones, J. Chow, M. Berardi, and T. Froehle, *Scholarship in Counseling Psychology: A Study in Significance* (paper presented at the 1995 Annual Convention of the American Psychological Association, New York).

6. C. G. Wrenn, "The Culturally-Encapsulated Counselor," *Harvard Educational Review, 32* (1962): 444-449.

7. J. M. Jones, (1972). *Prejudice and Racism* (Reading, MA: Addison-Wesley, 1972).

SELECT BIBLIOGRAPHY

With S. Sue. Ethnic minorities: Resistance to being researched. *Professional Psychology, 2* (1972): 11-17.

Guest editor for a special feature on Asian Americans, *Personnel and Guidance Journal, 51* (1973): 385-416.

Editorial: New directions in the *Personnel and Guidance Journal. Personnel and Guidance Journal, 54* (1975): 16-19.

With D. Sue. Barriers to effective cross-cultural counseling. *Journal of Counseling Psychology, 24* (1977): 420-425.

Eliminating cultural oppression in counseling: Toward a general theory. *Journal of Counseling Psychology, 25* (1978): 419-428.

Counseling the culturally different: Theory and practice. New York: John Wiley & Sons, 1980.

Barriers to cross-cultural counseling [media production]. North Amherst, MA: Microtraining Associates, 1990.

Cultural identity development [media production]. North Amherst, MA: Microtraining Associates, 1990.

Culture specific techniques in counseling: A conceptual framework. *Professional Psychology, 21* (1990): 424-433.

With D. W. Sue. *Counseling the culturally different: Theory and practice* (2nd ed.). New York: John Wiley, 1990.

With P. Arredondo and R. McDavis. Multicultural counseling competencies/standards: A call to the profession. *Journal of Multicultural Counseling and Development, 20* (1992): 64-88.

Confronting ourselves: The White and ethnic minority researcher. *The Counseling Psychologist, 21* (1993): 244-249.

With D. A. Atkinson and G. Morten (Eds.). *Counseling American minorities: A cross-cultural perspective.* Dubuque, IA: W. C. Brown, 1993.

Culture-specific strategies in counseling [media production]. North Amherst, MA: Microtraining Associates, 1994.

U.S. businesses and the challenge of cultural diversity. *The Diversity Factor, 2* (1994): 24-28.

Cross cultural communications in higher education [media production]. Cupertino, CA: DeAnza College Television Center, 1995.

Multicultural organizational development: Implications for the counseling profession. In *Handbook of multicultural counseling* (pp. 474-492), ed. J. G. Ponterotto, J. M. Casas, L. A. Suzuki, and C. M. Alexander. Thousand Oaks, CA: Sage, 1995.

Toward a theory of multicultural counseling and therapy. In *Handbook of research on multicultural education* (pp. 647-659), ed. J. Banks and C. Banks. New York: Macmillan, 1995.

Ethical issues in multicultural counseling. In *Ethical standards casebook* (5th ed., pp. 193-197), ed. B. Herlihy and G. Corey. Alexandria, VA: ACA Press, 1996.

With A. E. Ivey and P. D. Pedersen. *A theory of multicultural counseling and therapy.* Thousand Oaks, CA: Sage, 1996.

CHAPTER 7

A Professional Life in Family Context

BARBARA K. KEOGH

In her book *Composing a Life*, Mary Catherine Bateson[1] noted that we develop "by improvisation, discovering the shape of our creation along the way, rather than pursuing a vision already defined." Her observation is true for both men and women, but likely especially so for women, as the context of women's lives differs from that of men's. My own development as a psychologist was not based on conscious decision making regarding clear, predefined goals and strategies. Rather, until my middle years, my professional life was a series of improvisations and responses to changing family needs, to geographic moves, and to sometimes unexpected opportunities. As a consequence, my career path is a circuitous one, filled with gaps and wiggles, but fortunately with only a few major detours. Looking back, these demands were determining, and sometimes limiting, influences on my development as a psychologist. They also provided unique and valuable opportunities and experiences that I would not have known had my path been more direct.

AUTHOR'S NOTE: The author thanks Margaret Brown, Cindy Benheimer, and Ronald Gallimore for their thoughtful reviews, and Lisa Hoshmand for her helpful and sensitive suggestions and editing throughout the writing of this chapter.

My story in many ways may epitomize the role of intellectually and personally able women whose lives were embedded in, and in many ways determined by, the strong middle-class culture of America in the middle decades of the 1900s. In those years, social roles, especially gender roles, were well defined, and moral values were traditional and clear. Powerful social/cultural scripts provided guidelines for behavior, aspirations, and opportunities, serving to limit as well as to direct personal choices. Understanding the developmental pathway of a woman my age necessarily means taking into account the time period in which I lived.

PERSONAL BACKGROUND

I was fortunate to have an exceptionally stable and loving family. My father was a physician who headed a public health clinic in an impoverished area of Los Angeles, my mother a former teacher of high school mathematics. My maternal grandparents were both college graduates, my grandfather a Congregational minister who had earned a PhD in sociology at the University of Nebraska. During his graduate study years, he and his family lived in a settlement house in Lincoln, Nebraska, where he ran a program for disadvantaged youth. My father's mother was a social worker whose responsibilities were mostly in a depressed area of Los Angeles. My paternal grandfather was the editor and publisher of a political newspaper.

Despite the fact that my grandfather was a minister, as a family we were not strongly religious in an orthodox sense. There was, however, a powerful, although not formally articulated, sense of right and wrong and of social responsibility that was expressed in many specific ways and by adult example. The moral message was that the goal was "not only to be praised but to be praiseworthy," a distinction articulated by J. Q. Wilson[2] in his recent book *The Moral Sense*. As children, my sister and I were taught the homilies that in current times apparently make up the politically correct view of "family values." That is, we were expected to be honest, to tell the truth, to be kind and considerate of others, to do the best we can in whatever we attempt, to be respectful of our elders, and to be responsible for our actions. These behavioral codes had a strong moral basis that was transmitted primarily through the models of my family.

I have described my family in some detail because it helped me identify several major themes that have affected my personal and professional development as a psychologist. These themes are the importance of family and children, of education, and of a sense of responsibility for self and for others.

EDUCATION AND EARLY
PROFESSIONAL EXPERIENCE

Because of the social/cultural context in which I grew up, much of what I did and valued as a child and young woman just "happened" and was not the result of conscious decision making. As example, in many ways my decision about going to college was a nondecision, for as long as I can remember the question was not whether I would go to college but what college I would attend. A selective, small institution such as Pomona College was attractive because members of my family had graduated there, and there was strong belief that a liberal education was important. My first real decisions about education had to do with choice of career and graduate school. For several years, I seriously considered medicine, but I was unwilling to make the commitment required, as in those days it meant a choice between career and family, with few if any female role models who successfully combined both. Not to be underestimated, I had met my future husband in college and was in a serious relationship with him. I also recognized I wanted a family.

While a college student, I had become serious about the study of psychology, partly because it was intrinsically interesting and partly because of my experiences as a counselor in a summer camp for disadvantaged and disturbed children. This camp provided short vacations and respite for inner-city girls from San Francisco, many of whom were abused and/or neglected, and most of whom had serious adjustment problems. My experience as a "counselor" was upsetting, even traumatic, as I realized that I had neither the training nor the maturity to work effectively with these girls. Their worlds were different from the one I had known, and their problems were real and continuing. I was ill-prepared to understand them, and I certainly was of limited help to them. This experience, while at the time personally discouraging, increased my motivation to study psychology.

My master's degree from Stanford and subsequent years as an intern in a child psychiatry unit and as a clinical psychologist in a juvenile court provided me with good "hands-on" experience and contributed to my professional growth. After my marriage, my training also served as an economic resource through part-time employment as a school or clinical psychologist. The latter was important as we had begun a family and had made a number of geographic moves related to my husband's career. Thus, like many other women, my professional life did not follow a linear path, but was a series of improvisations, determined largely by geographic location, financial status, and family needs.

My doctoral study was another example of improvisation, as my husband's appointment to the faculty at Pomona College meant that we were in close proximity to the Claremont Graduate School, which offered a doctorate in developmental psychology. This program was ideal for me because of my age and my earlier applied experiences. I was able to tailor the focus of my academic work while meeting the traditional content required for all psychology doctoral students. I completed my PhD with a sense of having a solid background in the theory and content of psychology as a field, and with good analytic skills.

As a graduate student and young psychologist, my studies included the work of Freud, Hull, Skinner, Rogers, and Gesell, major "gurus" of the time. Behaviorism was becoming a dominant influence in psychology, and developmentalists focused primarily on documenting modal patterns of growth. I found myself more and more interested in the individuals who didn't fit the mode or who were "outliers" in experimental research. My summer camp experience with inner-city girls not only had pinpointed my own inadequate preparation but also had made me aware of the powerful effects of context and of the range of individual coping strategies. It is useful to describe expected (e.g., "normal") development and behavior and to know that we can change people's behavior using behavioral techniques. What is more impressive to me are the individual differences found within any group and the impact of these differences on development and behavior. Why are some individuals particularly responsive to particular treatments? How do individual characteristics contribute to children's social adjustment and affective development? What characterizes resilience? Such questions are of basic concern for both clinicians and researchers.

In his presidential address to the American Psychological Association (APA) in 1955, Stanford's Lee Cronbach definitively articulated two major streams in the science of psychology. His article "The Two Disciplines of Scientific Psychology"[3] is an important statement that in my view should be read by all psychologists. The nature of one's psychological orientation affects the nature of the questions asked; who and what are studied; the ways in which data and information are collected, analyzed, and interpreted; and the kinds of research methods chosen. I am clearly in the individual difference camp, as evidenced in my research and professional efforts.

PROFESSIONAL LIFE IN PSYCHOLOGY

My early work as a psychologist was basically clinical and with young children in schools and in hospital settings. Following graduate school, I spent a year as a psychology intern in the child psychiatry unit at Stanford University hospital in San Francisco. Our patients/clients were primarily middle-

and upper-middle-class children with emotional, behavior, and school problems, and psychotherapy, including play therapy, was the major approach to treatment. The next year provided dramatically different experiences, as I was on the clinical psychology staff of the juvenile court and probation office in Oakland, California. The juvenile court was a reality of a very different kind. The clients there were incarcerated children and adolescents; some were abandoned and/or abused, and others had committed violent felonies. The problems ranged in type and in intensity, and were in general different for males and females. Not surprisingly, the boys had arrest histories for aggressive misbehaviors, the girls for sexual promiscuity, for sexual victimization, and for running away. In general, the girls evidenced more signs of psychological pathology than did the boys, as the latter were often firmly entrenched in peer groups that provided support of a sort, and the girls were frequently isolates. Common to both, however, was a history of early and continuing school problems and a deep antipathy toward school and teachers.

Recognition of the contrast in problem behaviors in these two groups had a strong influence on my thinking, as the differences highlighted the relationship of psychological problems to gender, social class, and environmental and family conditions. The common negative attitude toward school and schooling was troubling, because in my own background school was a positive and valued experience. Equally troubling was my sense that our well-intentioned therapeutic efforts often were ineffective. These views were generally reinforced in subsequent years when, after marriage, I held a number of part-time positions as a school psychologist and as a clinician in a hospital setting.

I think my experience as a clinician was invaluable because it provided a solid "real world" base for interpreting psychological theory and for understanding problem behaviors. It also underscored the complexities and individual variations in the development and expression of problems and the seeming weakness of many therapeutic approaches. Over time, I found that information collected in clinical protocols often was irrelevant to the problem being considered and sometimes unnecessarily invaded areas of personal privacy. I also came to realize that many clinical practices were often inefficient and redundant, based on beliefs rather than on evidence of efficacy. These were discouraging observations that were reinforced when I became involved in special education, as there are many controversial and poorly tested interventions with exceptional children. I also found much of the practice of school psychology to be basically psychometric, limited by legalistic school district requirements and by school psychologists' strong testing orientation. I recognized the importance of treatment and interventions, but I became increasingly skeptical that we were getting the results we sought, be it in clinical or school settings. As valuable as practice was, these concerns were a strong force in moving me from practice to academia.

<hr>

LIFE IN ACADEME

While in England for my husband's sabbatical year, I was offered an assistant professorship in the Graduate School of Education at the University of California, Los Angeles (UCLA). The decision to accept was a major one, as for the first time since having children it meant full-time employment and a new and different set of responsibilities. I was uncertain that I would be comfortable in a school of education, as my experience in that field was limited. This appointment turned out to be a most positive personal and professional decision. For the first time, I held a stable professional position. I was fortunate to have excellent colleagues, and my own views were broadened as I worked with them over the years. My ongoing interactions with Frank Hewett were particularly important in my own professional growth, as he was extremely insightful about children with emotional problems. He also had his feet firmly planted in practical issues of treatment and intervention, and he was ingenious in developing programs for exceptional children in schools. I am also grateful for the opportunity to work closely with Ronald Gallimore, now both a valued friend and a colleague, whose concern for theory and for rigorous research addressing real world problems is admirable.

My appointment at UCLA began in the fall of 1966, a time of turmoil nationally and within the University of California system. The kinds of questions and issues raised by students forced many faculty, including me, to rethink both the content and the methods of teaching (more of Bateson's improvisation?). Changes in students' attitudes mandated a more participatory teaching-learning relationship. In my case, this led to an emphasis on conceptualization and analysis of issues and problems relating to exceptional children rather than on the presentation of descriptive information about particular problem conditions. My thinking about this approach was straightforward: Factual information is available in texts and journal articles, but doctoral education should be a constructive process, directed toward getting students to be better thinkers, that is, to be able to deal with future problems carefully, analytically, and responsibly. One consequence of this approach to teaching was that I learned a great deal from students, that I became a better thinker, and that I had a much clearer view of myself as a psychologist, special educator, and teacher.

It is often argued that teaching is a relatively unimportant part of university life, and some faculty members choose to teach as little as possible. I have a different view of the importance of teaching, as I think the process is critical in determining the content and structure of the knowledge to be studied and taught. It also leads to the construction of new ideas and insights. I found the opportunity to work with graduate students particularly rewarding. Many of these students are now well-respected professionals who are making their own contributions through college and university teaching and research, through administrative positions in governmental agencies, and as professionals who provide direct services to children and their families. I benefit from reflected glory. I am also fortunate that many former students have become personal friends and colleagues, and I attribute many of our long-lasting relationships to the mutual experiences we had in research and professional activities at UCLA, especially those inherent in doctoral-level study.

Doctoral study is not just a matter of going to classes and passing exams. The real heart of doctoral study is the dissertation, where for the first time students must take responsibility for their own intellectual work. This is a slow and sometimes painful process. The role of the teacher in this process is critical, as it is easy to be too directive or too laissez-faire. Referring to teaching creative writing, Wallace Stegner[4] noted that "the best teaching . . . is done by members of the class, upon one another. But it is not automatic, and the teacher is not unimportant. [The teacher's] job is to manage the environment, which may be as hard a job as for God to manage the climate" (p. 11). I agree.

Consistent with Stegner's comments, over the years at UCLA I found that the most productive intellectual activity for students, and my most effective teaching, occurred while using an interactive model in which the key was the joint constructive effort of students and teacher. This is not a didactic model of teaching in which the faculty member structures the content and dispenses information. Rather, it is one based in continuing interactions between teacher and student and student and student. In my case, the framework for this process was an ongoing seminar that continued throughout the full calendar year. In this seminar, each student presented at each meeting, and both students and teacher served as enquirers, critics, and sources of information. More advanced students served as models and mentors for those beginning their research. This is a slow process that is sometimes embarrassing for students, as their fuzzy thinking becomes publicly apparent. The process also built trust over time, so that students were able to acknowledge confusion, uncertainty, and discouragement, while at the same time coming to understand the topic they studied.

Although not dealt with on a conscious level, it was my impression that the ongoing interactions within the group contributed to students' awareness of the ethics of science, and these are both specific and broad. To name but a few, you don't fudge data, you report your findings honestly and fully even when they don't confirm your hypotheses, you don't take credit for other investigators' ideas, and you take seriously the rights of the individuals you study. Good science is a moral and public enterprise, and I believe scientific morality is not taught in theory, but rather is developed through the day-by-day interactions involved in the process of conducting research.

PERSPECTIVES ON WOMEN IN ACADEMIA

Like other institutions, universities are made up of many components and constituencies, and they serve many functions. Also like other institutions, universities reflect the social/political context in which they are embedded, and thus must deal with a number of concerns, including questions of equity and opportunity. Historically, universities have been dominated by men, although there are increasing numbers of women in faculty positions, especially in selected fields. I have found that overt prejudice or discrimination is seldom apparent but remains a subtle and powerful influence, albeit for the most part not on a conscious level.

As I noted earlier, the career paths of many women are not linear but consist of improvisations that are related to marriage and family. One consequence is that women with strong academic backgrounds are frequently found in part-time and/or in research associate or adjunct positions. Another consequence is that women often enter full academic life late; thus, they lack experience in the ways of the university and have not had opportunity or time to build up a working network of colleagues to be counted on, nor to build a systematic program of research. Not surprisingly, they are less likely than male peers to be appointed to "power" committees or to be considered for major administrative positions.

There are also subtle but powerful influences affecting women that have to do with the interactions of men and women in general. I refer to the findings of sociolinguists who have documented differences in the ways men and women interact and in the kinds of assumptions and perceptions they have about themselves and each other. According to the linguists, men are more comfortable than women with confrontation and argument; they are more apt to persist in espousing their views. Thus, faculty women may be less influential than men not only because of lack of sophistication in the ways of the university but also because of deeply ingrained patterns of male-female interactions. These differences in style are readily apparent in the workings of faculty committees and at conferences where women are outnumbered and where they may not forcefully nor persistently argue their views. I learned early on that to be effective it was essential to be prepared, to have done my homework so that I knew well the content of the topic under consideration. I also learned that persistent question asking was a more effective strategy than declamation and confrontation. In a sense, dealing with colleagues was similar to working with students in a doctoral seminar.

Women in the university are also affected by attitudes embedded in the culture in general: Men's positions are more important than women's, as men are the "real" breadwinners; women should be the primary caretakers of children and their jobs are secondary; women are less competent than men in organizational and administrative skills. These beliefs and attitudes become translated into behaviors and decisions that may limit women in academia. My own advancement to a tenured position was accelerated. In tenure review situations, however, I have heard questions raised about a woman's "commitment," questions that are rarely asked about male colleagues. I have also seen women ruled out of university responsibilities because it was assumed "she will not be interested," thus taking away the woman's right of choice. The irony, of course, is that faculty women, especially those at high professorial ranks, do more university service than do their male counterparts, as increasing sensitivity to possible discrimination mandates that women be included in decision making. Thus, women frequently do "double duty" in the university as well as at home.

Women faculty often feel a responsibility to take on additional duties as a response to historical exclusions, and I am a good example of that. I served on many major departmental and Academic Senate committees, including universitywide groups. Since moving into semi-retirement, I have continued to serve in ad hoc ways as consultant to senior administrators in problem situations involving women faculty. These experiences have contributed significantly to my understanding of the politics of academia, especially as they affect women, and have also provided an avenue for influencing, at least in a small way, decisions about university policies and practices.

I have been asked a number of times if achieving a successful career in the university was easier for women then than now. I honestly do not know, but based on my own experience I can attest that it was not easy. In my beginning days, the university, like the culture in general, placed a number of explicit and implicit limits on opportunities for women. I already have referred to the dominance of men, both in numbers and in influence. There were few women at senior ranks or in administrative positions, thus few models or mentors and little if any organized support for junior women. Indeed, in some instances high-ranked women appeared to adopt the attitude that "I got here on my own, you do the same."

Like other women with families, I had to accommodate my university life to the needs of children and the demands of home. This meant a very tight work schedule, a schedule that left little time for informal interactions or socialization with other faculty members. It also meant that interactions with students were highly focused so that we could use our time productively. Because of family needs, my academic writing was limited to late at night or during the hours my children were in school. I recognized early on that time management was critical, and I learned to direct my attention and to use my time efficiently.

Academic life for young women today may be somewhat different, but there are still stresses that are unique to professional women, especially women with families. Although many men now share in domestic activities, women continue to carry the major responsibilities of home and children, and like their older colleagues, this means demands on their time and energy. On the positive side, there is more recognition of possible discrimination and there are more resources for support. There is also the possibility of better mentoring and modeling, as women are increasingly found at higher professorial and administrative levels. On the downside, the university is still a male-dominated institution, and there continue to be implicit attitudes that limit women's opportunities. I wonder, also, if changes in opportunities and aspirations place additional stresses on women to succeed. In a sense, for academic women of my generation the goal was to survive. For many academic women today, the goals may be for success as defined within larger university and professional hierarchies.

RESEARCH, POLICY, AND PRACTICE

My research activity began before I joined the faculty at UCLA and, like a number of other experiences, was an example of improvisation. For economic reasons, I had accepted a part-time school psychologist position while my husband was in graduate school completing his doctoral degree. A good part of my job was to assess children with reading problems using the then standard assessment techniques of an intelligence test and a perceptual-motor measure (the latter often operationalized as the Bender-Gestalt and Draw-A-Person tests). Through these activities, I observed that the children's reading problems often were not strongly related to IQ, but that there was an association between reading level and perceptual abilities. This relationship prompted me to begin a study of reading and perceptual processes in kindergarten/first-grade children carried out with the then Director of Guidance in the school district. Our initial research became a longitudinal effort as we followed the children over a 6-year period, identifying differences in performance related to children's developmental ages and experience, and some suggestion of gender effects. We were particularly interested in the power of the early measures for predicting subsequent reading problems, as we hoped to develop techniques for early identification of problem learners. This research was the basis for my own PhD dissertation several years later.

My dissertation research had also advanced my understanding of early identification and prediction and became part of a program of research that included collaborative work with my husband while my family and I were in England for his sabbatical leave. During this period, I was fortunate to have a U.S. Public Health Service Fellowship for research and study that allowed me to develop my own research agenda. Our research involved presenting children with a novel task in which they were asked to translate two-dimensional designs into three-dimensional space. In specific, we asked children to "draw a design" by walking on the floor as if they had paint on the bottom of their shoes.

Our English studies were limited to samples of normally developing boys and to boys classified in the English system as educationally subnormal. I continued this research in a series of studies with UCLA graduate students in which we manipulated the number and types of cues provided the children and broadened our sampling frame to include both boys and girls and both typically developing and retarded children. Our findings dramatically documented real differences in how children perceived and interpreted the task as well as the strategies they used for solution. These differences were associated with age, cognitive level, and gender, and reinforced my sense of the importance of studying individual variations within groups.

This interest evolved further into research with UCLA graduate students that took into account a broader range of individual differences (e.g., cognitive styles, temperament) and that led to consideration of methodological issues related to sample variations. One 3-year project involved the development of a set of marker variables to be used in sample description in research on learning disabilities, thus allowing inferences about generalization across studies. A 5-year project addressed cognitive, behavioral, and temperament contributions to the development and adjustment of young children with delays, and tested the efficacy of early predictors. For the past 10 years I have participated with colleagues in the UCLA Department of Psychiatry in a longitudinal study of children with delays and their families, a project that has integrated child and family contributions to development and to developmental problems.

The change in my emphasis from traditional developmental research to more applied problems reflects in part the influence of students and colleagues on my thinking. My pattern walking research, for example, vividly documented individual differences in strategies and problem-solving approaches but did not address real problems facing atypical children and their families. In my early years at UCLA I became increasing aware of the need for systematic research on exceptional children and the programs that serve them. Thus, over the past 30 years my work has focused on children with special educational needs, particularly children with cognitive, learning, and behavior problems. Such children pose a range of research questions that necessitate consideration of individual and developmental characteristics as well as family and school conditions and influences.

My research activities also have led me to consider major ethical issues relating to children, especially children with problems. Many of these issues affect research efforts and have policy implications. I have long been interested in early identification of problem conditions, a seemingly obvious goal with many practical benefits for children and families. From the medical perspective, there is clear evidence to support many early identification efforts, as identification is linked to treatment. Screening for PKU is an obvious example. The early identification of psychological and behavioral problems, however, raises interesting and potentially troublesome methodological and ethical questions.

In practice, the early identification of mild problem conditions is limited by weak and often unreliable assessment and measurement. Furthermore, our work has shown that prediction generally is accurate for groups of children, but prediction for individual children is less certain. The within-group variations in the early (predictive) years and in long-term outcomes present intriguing but plaguing problems for the researcher. Finally, from a clinical perspective, identification of psychological or behavioral problems is not necessarily linked to specific treatments. The fact that a child is identified as "at risk" may affect his or her interactions with parents, teachers, and peers, as well as his or her own self-views. Thus, the moral and ethical dilemmas facing the researcher of at-risk conditions in young children include the potential negative effects of recognition, obligations to provide or help people get to services, determining what are proper services, and issues of privacy and subject protection as research findings are disseminated. There are also ethical considerations relating to the use or possible misuse of research findings as a way to influence public policy. Despite these potential problems, early identification is an area that must be developed, as the potential payoffs are powerful.

Psychologists can, and I believe must, contribute to our knowledge about early identification and intervention practices, and thus influence public policy relating to children. This is not an easy task, however, as most psychologists have not been trained in policy making. Like others, I found the foray into the public policy arena both rewarding and frustrating. My experience as a member of the National Advisory Committee on the Handicapped was eye opening, as for the first time I recognized how powerfully the sociopolitical context affected policy and services for children. An example with implications for current policy is Early Periodic Screening, Diagnosis, and Treatment (EPSDT), which was passed by the U.S. Congress in 1967. The history of EPSDT, a program directed at low-income, high-risk mothers and children, has a familiar ring as we hear the current debates about welfare mothers and children. The program has solid evidence to support it but was never fully implemented. Another current example of the impact of politics has to do with possible changes in IDEA, the Individuals With Disabilities Education Act of 1990, which mandates educational services for children with handicaps. Pressures to change IDEA are cloaked in ideology but have powerful economic underpinnings.

Based on my own experiences, I am not sure how psychologists can facilitate the development and adoption of policies and practices that positively affect children. I nevertheless view this as a major professional commitment, and I support the efforts of the APA in this regard. My own efforts have focused primarily on learning disabilities and on problems evidenced in the preschool and elementary school years, and I have achieved a certain visibility through my work. I have written for publication and have consulted about these topics with a range of federal and state agencies, and I have argued for the implementation of comprehensive and effective programs for children. I am an active letter writer to elected officials in the hope that substantive information will inform policy decisions. As an academic psychologist, however, I am not convinced that scholarly research has played a major part in decision making on a policy level, a discouraging inference. Politics and economics, rather than evidence, too often appear to determine policy decisions, but psychologists and others concerned about children must learn to be vigorous and effective advocates.

REFLECTIONS ON PSYCHOLOGY
AS A PROFESSION

I have spent my professional life as a psychologist, yet I am hard put to define or describe psychology as a profession. What it means to be a psychologist is not entirely clear, as psychology in the present day is a wondrous mix of diverse beliefs, activities, and strongly held positions. Considering the size and membership of the APA and the ever growing number of divisions, it is not surprising that as a profession we do not have a clearly articulated common purpose, that our goals are varied, and that the language and terminology of our discourse differ. The concerns of clinicians are different from those of academics, and there is an unfortunate lack of understanding, sometimes a seeming lack of respect, for different perspectives. Perhaps psychologists would profit from rereading Professor Cronbach's "Two Disciplines" article. Note that many academic psychologists chose to leave the APA to form the American Psychological Society (APS), as their interests and professional activities were not consistent with the strong clinical emphasis in that organization. This move was understandable and has had benefits for academic psychologists, yet it removed from the APA a constituency with a very important perspective.

The increasing diversity has led to a number of related but unresolved issues. At the least, these include questions of professional roles and responsibilities, education and training, and the efficacy of practices. In terms of training, it is ironic that much of the training for clinical psychologists is carried out in research-oriented academic institutions, with the exceptions the increasing numbers of schools of professional psychology. Training is, of course, closely tied to questions of professional rights and responsibilities. A current issue has to do with psychologists' rights to prescribe drugs. This proposed change is not just a legal matter but also has enormous implications for what psychologists should be taught, where, and by whom. It also raises questions about professional responsibilities and the monitoring of practices, a recurring theme in my own work.

As a psychologist focused on children with special education needs, I am particularly concerned with questions of efficacy, as I have seen a broad array of interventions and treatment programs, ranging from the mundane to the exotic. The limited research on efficacy unfortunately has led to the adoption of many programs and practices based on advocacy, enthusiasm, and economic considerations, rather than on demonstrated effectiveness. One consequence is that children and their families may not be helped, and indeed may even be harmed, by well-intentioned treatments; the profession of psychology is also diminished. Efficacy research is difficult, frustrating, and slow, but in my view it must be a priority for individual psychologists and for the profession as a whole.

AFTERTHOUGHTS

Writing this chapter has been more demanding and difficult than I had anticipated, as I have found that "making sense" of one's life requires both objectivity and sensitivity, as well as considerable honesty. For me, the effort forced an analysis of life events that were mostly positive but that sometimes recalled disturbing and painful experiences and memories, some of which may not be fully resolved or even resolvable. The content was partly shaped by questions posed by Lisa Hoshmand. Rather than respond to each of the questions separately, I have tried to touch on them as part of my narrative. I have also tried to respond to the questions from my perspective as a woman and as a professional. Thus, this is a personal story.

I have selected particular experiences and accomplishments, and post hoc have imposed an organization that might suggest that mine has been a reasonably orderly and planned life, and that whatever has been accomplished was done with ease. That would be an oversimplification. My professional life has been tightly woven with my family life, and for the most part these have not been in serious conflict. I am fortunate that my husband is a successful academic who encouraged me in my own career. More important, he is a man committed to family. This is not to say that there have not been stresses related to both family and professional demands, and that at times the combination seemed overwhelming. There has not been enough time to devote to each, and demands in each put limitations on the other, reducing my degrees of freedom. Certainly there have been times when questions emerged of "what might have been if things had been different."

In beginning this chapter, I referred to the notion of improvisation, and over time there have been many improvisations in my life, including those related to moving into semi-retirement. I find the "semi" aspect of retirement satisfactory, as it has freed up time for other interests, including continuing professional ones. I have become a member of the Advisory Committee for Exceptional Children and Youth of the U.S. Department of State, Office of Overseas Schools. This has provided me an opportunity to consider needs of exceptional children in other countries, and perhaps to influence educational practices in schools there. I am involved in a number of professional organizations. I serve as a consultant to governmental and private agencies and to schools, and I participate in policy discussions related to individuals with learning disabilities. I continue to be an active letter writer to governmental officials.

Currently, my major professional involvement consists of research in the Department of Psychiatry at UCLA. There are times I miss the ongoing and intense interactions with students, but I find the opportunity to focus on research both interesting and rewarding. I am one of a small group of researchers from several disciplines involved in a 10-year longitudinal study of children with developmental delays and their families. I have good colleagues who have broadened my perspectives and have added to my insights about children and families. The findings from our study are substantive and solid. They have implications for both researchers and practitioners, and eventually, we hope, for policies affecting children. I could not ask for a better finish to a career as a psychologist.

The final question Lisa Hoshmand posed was "What is the relationship between the personal, social, and professional for you, and how should it be for all of us?" I can answer only for myself, but I hope my experiences have some generalizability and will encourage other women to consider academic careers. As evidenced in my narrative, my early professional life was a series of improvisations, and my academic career started late. Improvisation is not necessarily a bad thing, however, and my different experiences as a psychologist contributed to my development in many ways. I suspect I would have a somewhat different view of psychology and my role as a psychologist had my career followed a more linear track. My move to academia was extremely positive, providing many opportunities and many benefits. On a practical level, the flexibility of university life allowed me to coordinate home and professional responsibilities (although often not easily), options that are even more difficult for women in other occupations. On a professional level, I was able to follow my own interests, to study what I deemed important, to be autonomous, and to work with able and interesting colleagues and students.

Looking back, I realize that there have been consistencies in my commitments and concerns over time, commitments that in part have their basis in my family background. These commitments have been expressed in the kind of research I have undertaken, in the substance of my teaching, and in my efforts to influence policy. My professional life has been driven by underlying values and beliefs about what is important, especially the well-being of children. I continue to be involved in research because there are important problems to be studied and because I find the research enterprise interesting and absorbing. I also continue to hope that solid evidence will lead to improved policies and practices for children. Said simply, I like what I do. I have been fortunate, and I wish the same for others.

APPENDIX

Abbreviated Professional History

1946	BA, Pomona College (Psychology)
1947	MA, Stanford University (Psychology)
1947-1948	Psychology Intern, Department of Child Psychiatry, Stanford University Medical School and Hospital
1948-1949	Clinical Psychologist, Alameda County Juvenile Court and Probation Department
1949-1950	Instructor in Psychology, Pomona College
1956-1958	School Psychologist, South San Francisco and El Segundo School Districts
1963	PhD, Claremont Graduate School (Psychology)
1964-1965	Clinical-Research Psychologist, Children's Hospital of Los Angeles
1965-1966	U.S. Public Health Research Fellow, England
1966-present	Assistant Professor (1966-1969), Associate Professor (1970-1974), Professor (1975-1991), and Professor Emerita (1991-present), Graduate School of Education, Los Angeles (UCLA)
1968-1978	Co-Director, UCLA-U.S. Office of Education Training Program in Special Education
1970-1974 and 1984-present	Advisory Board of the Division for Learning Disabilities, Council for Exceptional Children
1970-1976	Reviewer and Consultant, U.S. Office of Education, Bureau of Education for the Handicapped
1971-1976	Director, UCLA Special Education Research Program
1972-1974	Reviewer and Consultant, Maternal and Child Health Division, U.S. Department of Health, Education and Welfare
1974-1977	National Advisory Committee on the Handicapped
1976-1977, 1983-1984, and 1986-1988	Chair, UCLA Program in Special Education (retired, 1991)
1987-present	Senior researcher, Project CHILD
1991-present	Professor, Department of Psychiatry, UCLA
1995-present	Consultant, U.S. Department of State Overseas Educational Programs

━━━━━━━━ **NOTES**

1. M. C. Bateson, *Composing a Life* (New York: A Plume Book, Penguin, 1989).

2. J. Q. Wilson, *The Moral Sense* (New York: Free Press, 1993).

3. L. Cronbach, "The two disciplines of scientific psychology," *American Psychologist, 30* (1957): 116-127.

4. W. Stegner, *On the Teaching of Creative Writing* (Hanover, NH: The University Press of New England, 1988).

━━━━━━━━ **SELECT BIBLIOGRAPHY**

Guest Editorial: Working together: A new direction. *Journal of Learning Disabilities, 10* (1977): 13-16.

Children's rights in assessment and school placement. *Journal of Social Issues, 34* (1978): 87-100.

Advances in special education (Ed.). Volumes 1 and 2 (1980), 3 (1981), 4 (1986), and 5 (1986). Greenwich, CT: JAI.

With A. G. Wilcoxen and L. Bernheimer. Prevention services for at-risk children: Evidence for policy and practice. In *Risk in intellectual and psychosocial development* (pp. 287-316), ed. D. C. Farran and J. D. McKinley. New York: Academic Press, 1986.

Improving services for problem learners: Rethinking and restructuring. *Journal of Learning Disabilities, 21* (1988): 19-22.

With J. L. Swanson (Eds.). *Learning disabilities: Theoretical and research issues*. Hillsdale, NJ: Lawrence Erlbaum, 1990.

With L. P. Bernheimer and J. J. Coots. From research to practice: Support for developmental delay as a preschool category of exceptionality. *Journal of Early Intervention, 17* (1993): 97-106.

Linking purpose and practice: Social-political and developmental perspectives on classification. In *Better understanding learning disabilities: New views from research and their implications for education and public policies* (pp. 311-324), ed. G. R. Lyon, D. B. Gray, J. F. Kavanagh, and N. A. Krasnegor. Baltimore, MD: Paul Brookes, 1993.

With T. Weisner. An ecocultural perspective on risk and protective factors in children's development: Implications for learning disabilities. *Learning Disabilities Research and Practice, 8* (1993): 3-10.

What the special education research agenda should look like in the year 2000. *Learning Disabilities Research and Practice, 9* (1994): 62-69.

Transitions and transactions: The need to study the influence of schooling on students with learning disabilities. *Thalamus, 15* (1995): 3-9.

With D. Speece (Eds.). *Research on classroom ecologies: Inclusion of children with learning disabilities*. Hillsdale, NJ: Lawrence Erlbaum, 1996.

Strategies for implementing policies. In *Learning disabilities: Lifelong issues*, ed. S. C. Cramer and W. Ellis. Baltimore, MD: Paul Brookes, 1996.

With R. Gallimore and T. Weisner. A sociocultural perspective on learning and learning disabilities. *Learning Disabilities Research and Practice, 12* (1997): 107-113.

CHAPTER 8

Send in the Angel

ROLAND G. THARP

Knowledge, creativity, and moral vision as intertwining branches is an intriguing theme for an editor, a commentator, and perhaps for a reader. For the autobiographer, it is less comfortable. I think moral self-examination is universal but, like other basic functions, more pleasing when conducted in private. "Creativity" is equally problematic. Robert Frost said *poet* is a praise word, to be applied to others, not the self. Likewise, I think, "knowledge."

Otherwise, constructing this short story of my life has had some fascinations and surprises. Between genetics and early experience, most principal strands of a person's life declare themselves well before maturity. I doubt that a family or even psychologists can predict, then, which fibers will last and which will wear away, but at the end of the rope, we can make out the longest strands, down to the root. In my own case, four interests began early and have not abated: education, cultural complexities, human behavior, and the arts—especially but not exclusively poetry. Considering those four, hatched across and textured by issues of knowledge, creativity, and moral vision, produced a more coherent pattern than I would have imagined.

Of course it is a partial story, with the love life omitted, and almost all the private life, and all confessions. Those can be found, well summarized, in Frances Cornford's "Epitaph for Everyman":[1]

My heart was more disgraceful, more alone
And more courageous than the world has known.
O passer-by, my heart was like your own.

CHILDHOOD

La Marque, Texas, in 1930, was a sleepy railroad watering station of heat, humidity, mosquitoes, tall grass, and marshland in a monotonous 10-mile gradual descent of gray and green to the Gulf of Mexico and the county seat on Galveston Island. My grandfather had come down from North Zulch for the railroad, to be foreman of the "section," all the G, H, & H track from the water to 7 miles north of his home. My grandmother, grandfather, mother-to-be, and her brother and sister lived across the road from the passenger-and-freight station, in the railroad's section house, which stood as hen to her flock of shacks where the Mexican legals and illegals came and lived and mostly left. Across the street was a gas station, next to it a barber shop, then a grocery and feed store, which in one of its corners held the post office. Later, a doctor, a pharmacy with a lunch counter, and a beautician moved in. The section house remained central, though, both by its location and because of my grandmother Ila Keefer, who raised peacocks, guinea fowl, coon dogs, exotic bantam roosters, sick owls, and captured kits of foxes, and whose patience and love, generous bosom, and irrepressible imagination made field, yards, house, and her lap a kingdom where the pretended could transform the real, and the real was tangible and numinous.

Side by side with it, there was another kingdom, another La Marque, touching as close as a hand on a hard glass mirror. We didn't step through, not often, to what was called Colored-town by the more polite. I knew there were a store and cafe and roadhouse there, and their own school, but blacks and whites alike shopped at the one grocery and feed store, and came to the one post office window and train station. We played together, the Mexican children, my sister, and my cousin, when we were all young, around the dirt yards of the section houses. Ila was the daughter of Jolly Jim Matthews, a Cherokee, killed on the railroad in Waco; then she and her four sisters were raised by his brother. They were all proud of being Indian, thus so was I. Even though my grandfather ran a small herd of cattle and let me ride and brand alongside him, when we kids stalked each other through the high weeds I liked to be the "brave."

As young as 4, I remember being shushed and removed for saying "sir" to an elderly black man; I can still feel the embarrassment, both his and mine.

Relationships across the different groups were not simple, not the same in public as in private, and not easy to learn. Perhaps somewhere in that event, or in puzzling about others like it, in small-town close association, and regulated status, and shared space of living, are the roots of my continuing puzzlement about how to understand Otherness and how we all do and could relate.

In some settings and activities, relationships across the cultures were strong and lasting. In high school, I worked Saturdays and summers at my father's small and new lumber yard, most of that time at hard labor—unloading boxcars of 94-pound cement bags and tens of thousands of board feet of lumber, pushing a concrete barrow. Over many years, my father's Black foreman and longtime friend, Tom Neal, mentored me in the most basic of skill of them all: work. He taught how work took steadiness, skill, economy, grace, some singing, and a striding into it, because work is what men do. Tom Junior, in the boxcars at lunch rest, taught me steps to the new bebop music, and unaccountably to my friends, I became the dancingest white boy in town.

At about 20, in Frazer's *Golden Bough,* I learned that both past and present are a procession of Others and Others, in endless profusion, and it was only then that cultures became an object of thought. I haven't really stopped thinking about the "other" since, trying to understand of what "otherness" consists, and maybe improve the mysterious, necessary, and hurtful ways people live among one another.

SCHOOL

As a boy, 9 months of school wasn't enough, and during summer I dragooned a younger sister, even younger cousin, and the little girl next door into morning classes on whatever subject our collection of books would support. *The Book of Birds,* Volumes I and II, were frequent texts, and following my illustrated lecture, conducted on our living-room floor, the raggle-taggle class trooped out for a field trip in the hot sun. This, my first seminar, was maintained entirely by the incentive power of cookies.

I swam through school like a fish in the sea and, except for one short miserable time, have never left it. Last autumn, I returned to La Marque for our 50-year high school reunion. Sixteen of our 22 classmates are living, and most were there, aghast at each other's decline. Elaine Vauthier said there was no way to take pleasure in it, unless we view ourselves as ruined monuments, like the Parthenon.

Everyone told stories. I reminded them how my interest in psychology began. After puzzling and watching our dogs and cats and horses at play for many months, a "psychological" problem emerged: Do animals have a sense of humor? The question intrigued me, but our science teacher was not amused when I asked it aloud during class. He thought I was indulging my wise mouth (as usual, he might have said), and he landed on me with the full force of his out-of-sorts German-accented life. A right pedagogue might have assisted me in designing an experiment, but I can't blame him—my mind and mouth were too lively for the light harness I used on them.

Actually, we had extraordinary luck in our education. La Marque High was a nowhere school in a no-place town, but it was "undermanned," with more roles than people, and that meant that everyone got to do everything—from athletics to drama to the chess club to the newspaper, regardless of unusual gifts or talents. Participation was total, learning opportunities abounded, the faculty knew us, and a few of them cared about and taught us. The memory of that school is certainly a part of my vision of a reformed educational system, small enough for everyone to be known and for everyone to do much, working with friends and teachers, building community. The huge urban comprehensive high school seems to me a monstrous cruelty, an unjustifiable imprisoning and trivialization of youth who are already capable of productive involvement.

At the reunion, Violet Ober had saved a newspaper clipping for me. I was 5, crouched with my dog Tiny Mite, both of us smiling. The caption said that I had won the county Storytelling Contest. I can't remember it, but I can believe it. What a mentor of imagination I had. Ila hid under beds to shock us children with hand puppets. One Halloween she had herself "laid out" on the dining room table, with candles and flowers, a "corpse" too real to be enjoyed. She and my grandfather once greeted my aunt's new (and unwelcome) suitor with an extended improvised performance of family insanity, sending him fleeing in his open roadster back to Galveston Island and civilization. And she told stories. And she talked, with the others, late at night, telling old family tales, in even and soft voices that smoothed into a humming and my sleep.

And I wrote stories, and poems, and essays, and a school newspaper column. At 14, on summer lunch breaks at my grease-monkey job, a poem called " The Wall" resulted, some 30 morose stanzas of four lines each. It made a nice paper for English class that fall, and my teacher, Lois Moyer, read it, criticized it, and arranged for it to be entered in a national poetry contest for high school writers. She was a wonderful teacher, beautiful, elegant, cultured, sharp-tongued, and eternally challenging. At the reunion, I was shocked to find that the entire class had believed that they were her favorite. Her tour de force teaching must be one source vision of Ideal Teacher that has inspired my research and teaching in education.

Winning a national contest helped in getting the job I wanted, after graduation. Even I agreed that I was too young, at 16, to begin my studies in journalism at a university, but I could learn newspaper work by doing it, and got a job as copyboy and part-time reporter (high school sports) for the *Texas City Sun*. I wanted to write, and the job and the prospect of the university were to teach me how to write and write and write.

Then there was the matter of telling truth. Everyone went to church in humid La Marque, no matter how hot or how cold. Perhaps only my father could be called devout, but all the generations and most of the families congregated twice on Sunday, Wednesday nights, one week a year in "Revival," and a summer camp of Bible Study. I was taught to pray, both in praise and in supplication, and was taught and believed that God knows our hearts, so that we should speak and act with great care, so as not to compound our sins by trying to deceive the Almighty. One blistering summer day, about 1939, I stalled my bicycle entirely from excess concentration on the intractable problem of truth telling; I remember that some insincere prayer had sputtered into silence. So I resolved, with such frustration and desire that the feel of the gravel and the smell of the persimmon trees is still a part of it, to try and to always try to keep my mind on things, so as to speak about them truthfully.

Truth telling seemed a matter of effort and intention—as were all good actions, I then supposed. Among temptations, lying seemed the worst. That may have been a failure of imagination, because I did not yet comprehend the rich potentials in such opportunities for error as adultery, covetousness, and graving images. Of course, this struggle with the truth spilled into the human world as well. Deception brought punishment, but that was simple enough to avoid—by actually getting the chores done, or getting home just before the night swallowed up the twilight. As St. Thomas Aquinas taught, we best avoid sin by avoiding the occasion for sin. But God as audience was not so simple. . . .

That moral imperative of truth telling somehow organized all other standards of conduct—of personal honor, and of maintaining social and community relationships. Early on, I construed that truth telling was the what and the why of writing, especially poetry. I believed that only in such careful, nuanced expression could truth (always complex) ever be approximated. Later, science fit that model just as well: Pretense and deceit are poison worms not only to poetry but to science too, where the telling of things must be in such exact and honest terms that it will withstand challenge and provide proof, even to God.

I have come to understand it all quite differently now, but that is the very last part of the story.

━━━━━━━ **HIGHER EDUCATION**

One semester of delay was enough. Envy of college student friends, a general impatience for life to begin, and I was off to the University of Texas, in a blur of blind optimism, to learn how to write. What I found was a campus crowded with a far larger population than my hometown, thousands of war veteran men 10 to 20 years older, an acute shortage of classes and housing, and an indecipherable institutional structure; I never did understand that one had to officially drop courses—I thought neglect was an adequate disengagement. I learned much—evolution theory, Faulkner, the pleasures of beer and meeting new girls, but not much about how to work that world.

My parents were rightly worried. Two semesters of As and Fs (more of the latter), and they extricated me from my creaky rooming house and drove me back home, "until I was more ready." My father was glad to have me learn his lumber business. I married my high school sweetheart. I joined the Chamber of Commerce.

Within 3 years, I was miserable, reading classics, jealous of college student friends, and with such a hunger for knowledge my mind felt emaciated. My first night school class meant a commute of 40 miles each way to the University of Houston, watching the Music Appreciation lecturer fall gradually asleep, as I gulped down whole his recordings of Beethoven and Bartok. The second class was in Creative Writing, where I found my next crucial mentor, Ruth Penny-backer, who quickly swept me into her circle of students, the major "bohemian"-turning-"beat" crowd on the UH campus, and I was off and running; and I ran.

Those years of (mostly night) commuting were among the happiest ever. The writing crowd wrote and read and talked and drank and moved in and out with the painters and sculptors. I was deep into a Literature major, dreaming of being a small-college professor—it seemed a dream within reach, my poetry was making some splash, locally. And the *Atlantic Monthly* ran an annual national contest for college writing, where in the sophomore and junior years I won some honorable mentions.

I also was seriously engaged by Psychology 1A. This appeared to be a field where a young man could make his mark, there appearing to be so much about the mind and behavior just on the verge of being known. But I did not want to choose between psychology and literature, and so took a dual major—only the first effort to dodge that choice.

The psychology faculty was a fine one. Richard Evans and Loren Callicut liked and encouraged me, and I was having serious doubts about the study of literature—not about writing, but the life of literary critic and teacher began to seem fey and irrelevant, compared to the vigorous burgeoning of psychology's inquiries. In those mid-1950s, psychology graduate students had the highest GREs of all disciplines. For that brief time, those young men and women shone the brightest, and I wanted to be one of them.

For graduate school, I chose the University of Michigan, and in 1957 I prepared to enroll in its famous Social Psychology program. But literature again intervened; I had won the *Atlantic Monthly*'s Grand Prize this time, with an essay on Romanesque sculpture. The prize was indeed a grand one: an expense-free summer of study at Middlebury College's Bread Loaf School of English. The faculty were in the pantheon of American letters. The teaching and learning of that summer were a privilege of which I had not even imagined. That, and other Vermont summers to come, allowed me to be acquainted, and often friends, with most of the major poets of my generation. Of course, I did not want to leave, and I wondered if I had erred.

Then, in Ann Arbor, the experience was parallel. Our first year pro-seminar lecturers read like the author list of the Annual Review, presenting a high-heaped table of ideas and activities to meet any student's taste. I learned that Michigan offered Clinical as a "Professional Specialty," attachable to any "Field Specialty," such as Social, so I quickly added Clinical to my program, probably because the first-year lecturers were so urbane, self-confident, and forever immersed in high drama and bizarrerie.

My principal intellectual struggles developed within personality theory and clinical issues. Psychoanalytic writers, and our faculty's psychoanalytically oriented practitioners, seemed to spin further and further out and away from any evidence and indeed from common sense. I began to read the existentialists and the Dutch phenomenologists, who were no stronger on evidence, of course, but at least discussed the therapies in terms recognizably tied to human experiences. The faculty appeared to enjoy my dissident role and mild fencing with them, and appreciated, I think, the importing of some literatures not commonly read there.

It seems to me that this constituted the first halting independent step in my intellectual journey. Rejecting psychoanalysis and moving toward existentialism/phenomenology was an almost tropic reaction toward constructs based on the life-as-lived-in-the-world, and away from conceptually tortured screens of an analyst's language.

In Ann Arbor, there were wonderful debates on ideas, roaring disputations and verbal tugs-of-war, in the classes and in the beer halls—even more intense and informed than at Houston. Faculty and students of 1990s universities seem oblivious to the terrible loss they have inflicted, in their suppression of debate, by their sanctimonious, exquisite social control. Nor have they noticed that their goddess of political correctness is a corpse. Ann Arbor was, for me, a living cathedral of ideas.

I rode to school in beret, beard, and bicycle, more often than not frosted with snow, and learned statistics, testing, psychopathology, sociology and role theory, and anthropology. I can remember almost no details, until the dissertation preparation. That is almost certainly because I was not involved closely with any laboratory or professorial group. Although I had as many student friends as anyone, my daily routines were more like those of an ordinary man, with a family and social life, than those of the apprentice scientist. Not until decades later, when I knew something of sociocultural theory, did I understand what was wrong with those years—there was none of the joint productive activity that builds intersubjectivity and the sense of community. Some of my classmates did have that, in their research teams and labs. Now I try to create a much better atmosphere for my own graduate students than I had (than I chose) in those years.

On most days, a ration of time was saved for fiction or poetry, and in the second year I entered a competition again. The poetry won me the Frost Prize, which was a scholarship back to Bread Loaf for another summer, so I was in the odd rhythm of doing graduate studies in psychology in the academic year and literature graduate study in the summers. As the Frost scholar, I was taken to Robert Frost's cabin in the woods and left alone there with him for 2 hours of talk, mostly about poetry and poets.

I had a personal thing I wanted to know from him. Was it possible that these two ambitions, psychologist and poet, could be achieved together? He moved his lips in thought for a while, then said he saw nothing to prevent it; he even talked about a psychiatrist friend who sometimes dictated verse along with his case notes, dashing from office to ward. There was one problem, he said. I should be careful, because the Freudians had things badly wrong. Sex is not the main thing in life, he said, not even during youth. "No, the main thing for people is gossiping and guessing about each other."

I have found that to be profoundly true. Even sex is subordinated into the continuously negotiated social nexus of explanation and control. So there was no better place to study clinical, than in social psychology. A lifetime of work has convinced me of nothing different: There is no help to be given or taken, other than in a negotiated social context of some community. At Ann Arbor, I took a minor in cultural anthropology and had the privilege of working with Leslie White and David Aberle. Even so, I don't know a better short line for it than "gossiping and guessing about each other."

A DECISION

I had always done school better than anything else, and by now I presumed that my grades would be high. In the second Bread Loaf year, for the first time ever, I did not excel. By reading and reflecting on other students' work, it became clear that I was competing against students who were doing literature full-time, with full commitment, and that standards were being moved up. They knew things I did not know and had conceptual language that I lacked. I could identify in their papers the domains of discourse that would have to be learned if I were to continue seriously in my doubled life. Having made the discrimination, the valences were immediately clear: I did not want to know those positions and those genres, or at least I had no desire to devote myself to their acquisition, nor to their practice. The great heaps in the storerooms of the world's literatures were unsurpassed treasure, but the keys were kept by monks and castrati, their practices cabalistic, their domains small as a garden.

Perhaps the harshness of that judgment was needed by a young man in bad need of making up his mind. But how could a life of criticism compete with one in psychology, in which all was possible? We psychologists could work anywhere, at anything, in any domain or role, bringing relief to the suffering, knowledge to the benighted, science to the superstitious, and power to ourselves—like the ironic description of the missionaries to Hawaii, we could expect both to do good and to do well. All that was true, for a time, almost all of which I was able to enjoy. My judgment of that other life was absurd; now I mostly long for a small garden and some quiet regularities practiced with great care. But the choice then was inevitable, unproblematic, and confident.

Of course, I had no intention of giving up writing. Each summer at Bread Loaf, when the Summer School stage was struck, the Writer's Conference swirled quickly into the cabins, halls, and meadows. To that I returned many times, for interludes of deep and sometimes dramatic significance to my personal development. In 1959, however, I was ready for the drive back to Ann Arbor. It was late summer, but Bread Loaf is high country, and the leaves had already turned.

<hr/>

SERIOUS WORK

I had no ambition and little respect for psychological research. Research in psychotherapy was pitiful, and I had not been interested enough, or pursued enough, to engage with other research groups. But a dissertation had to be done, and I remembered that E. Lowell Kelly had described his long-term and longitudinal study of marriages in our first-year pro-seminar. Love, marriage, and all that did interest me, both as a confused participant and as a neophyte social psychologist. Lowell welcomed me into his team, and I began by writing our required "third-year paper," titled *Psychological Patterning in Marriage*. Role theory was dominant in the social program and characterized Lowell's inquiries. He had asked his couples before marriage (and again at intervals thereafter) how marriage should be enacted, both in its mundane aspects (who should take out the garbage?) and in its social and emotional responsibilities and domains. I learned the marriage/relationships literature (largely from sociology) and role theory (Talcott Parsons and Theodore Newcomb), and I wrote about the possibilities and questions that arose when the two were considered together. That was my first piece of serious psychological work, and the writing of it had a transformative effect on my view of human behavior and experience. It became clear that the notion of "personality," upon which psychotherapy depended, was by no means so fixed as then supposed, because so much behavior was contingent on role occupancy. Various and apparently contradictory "traits" were regularly exhibited by the same individual, depending on the social role being enacted. The analyses of the Kelly data, done in my dissertation, showed that there was, for his couples, over decades, a stability of the patterning of those role expectations, a stability that certainly equaled the presumed continuities of personality. This position had obvious and deep implications for the theory and practice of psychology, and I moved permanently toward analyses of individuals in social interaction settings (at this time, of marriage and family) as a more authentic and inclusive frame for understanding human behavior and experience.

Before completing the doctoral program, I went away for a year's clinical internship, to the Palo Alto Veterans Administration (PAVA) Hospital (then on the Menlo Park campus), taking these "radical" ideas with me. Oh my, I did not know what radical was, but I soon found out from PAVA's resident geniuses—from the new behaviorism of Ullman and Krasner, to the ecological psychiatry of Gregory Bateson, the community psychiatry of George Fairweather, the communication-based family therapy of Don Jackson, the psychotropic "model psychoses" drug experimentation—this was heady stuff, and it fit exactly with my new interests in psychology understood as relationship patterns, communication patterns, and behavior exchanges, and in therapy as interventions on those levels and in those modes.

The next return to Ann Arbor was with new confidence, a determination to get on with thought and practice in ways that no one had yet fully envisioned. I graduated in 1961 on my 31st birthday.

Lowell Kelly was accommodating and generous with me. I admired him greatly, but I did not want to be like him. In fact, I never wanted to do another piece of research, which I had experienced throughout graduate school only as an isolated grinding of data, and a trivial pursuit, compared with wild swimmings in floods of experience and ideas. I'm not sure what I had in mind to do exactly. It must have been to do psychology in different ways, to observe carefully, to think hard, to express precisely, and to tell the truth, regardless of current orthodoxy. Research, I supposed, was something much duller, perhaps something one did to prove to others that one had been right in the first place.

But I was going to write, too. Michigan was as lively in the language arts as in the social sciences, and it awarded the Hopwood Prizes annually, arguably the most prestigious university-level writing awards in the nation. A big festival surrounded the ceremonies; Robert Graves and Saul Bellow were among the Hopwood speakers during that time. My novel was ignored, but my collection of poems was given a "Major Hopwood," as it was called, on the next day after defending my dissertation. That was a week among weeks, its pleasures including the astonishment of the psychology department at this revelation of a secret and double life.

PSYCHOLOGIST AT LAST

Getting back to San Francisco Bay was my ambition, but there were no jobs open there. (In fact, I did not achieve that ambition until 30 years later.) Kelly thought I should go to Indiana, but I much preferred Arizona, because the offering there was half university teaching post and half staff psychologist, for the first, model Community Mental Health Center, the new initiative of the National Institutes of Mental Health under the Kennedy administration. Tucson also was richly multicultural—half Mexican American, and thick with southwestern Indian tribes and cultures, many of which I had studied with such fascination at Michigan.

The Southern Arizona Mental Health Center, as it came to be called, started its life in an abandoned motel on South 6th Avenue, more oriented to the barrio than to the University of Arizona. The group included Robert Shearer, the psychiatrist-director; Arnold Meadow, clinical director at the university, as lead psychologist; a new PhD in anthropology, Bill Holland; a cadre of clinical graduate students, and me. Holland and I were immediate allies: It was easier for me, with my role and communication theories, to seek an accommodation of practice with the cultural patterns of our clients than it was for our senior and more psychodynamically oriented colleagues.

We studied Mexican American folk medicine, interviewed *curanderos* and extended family groups of Mexicans and Indians, and made some gestures toward a culturally compatible approach to services. By translating the scale items from my dissertation into Spanish, we studied the transformations of marriage role expectations through the course of acculturation of Mexican immigrants to Tucson.

Yes, I was doing research. Neil Bartlett, Head of Psychology at Arizona, enjoyed my fiction and poetry but felt obliged to remind me, however gently, that young faculty members were expected to publish. In psychology journals. So I sent in my "third-year" paper to the *Psychological Bulletin*. That experience was so painless that I was hooked, sent off the dissertation, and have kept sending things off, more or less ever since.

For the first few years, there was great excitement in the cultural studies. Soon it became clear that any real culturally based transformations in practice were not to be realized in that particular Tucson institution, but putting together what could be found in the literature and practice of psychotherapy, together with social role theory and communication theory, and crafting it all into some kind of culturally attuned way of interacting with clients—that was a task worth engaging. Others, particularly at the University of New Mexico, later made more progress at it.

I was to take up those questions again, in another time and place, but in Arizona, I needed most to be immersed in that soup of ideas. Bill Holland shared all his dissertation data with me, wanting a psychologist-partner to help make sense of the healing practices of the Highland Maya of Central America, using the concepts of psychotherapy. We published that article in the *American Anthropologist*, but I wanted to know more, see for myself, and make sure we had told it right. So Bill and I went to Mexico; drove to Chiapas and environs, through the Mayan country of Guatemala; and flew into Tikal; all with his principal informant, a Mayan Xotcil *curandero.*

During those months, I was immersed in Otherness, more than at any other time. The experience is with me still almost entirely raw, not cooked by analysis. I've written about it only in poetry:

> *Flapping silent, then a moment's feather*
> *Rasp, a bird,*
> *Mayan, gazed down,*
> *Treading on its roost.*
> *There is on that stone*
> *That bird. "Death," the Indian*
> *Whispered in his tongue, "It brings*
> *Death," and gestured us beyond.*

This was in the Tikal jungle. Bill said, "Nah, pay no attention, they believe that bird comes just before a death. He'll be all right." But the guide wasn't all right; he was clearly and severely anxious until we all separated later that week, the Mayan on the bus back to Chiapas, me back to Tucson, Holland on to Honduras, where the next day, climbing the highest pyramid in Copan, he died.

For many reasons, my cultural work did not mature until 10 years later.

▬▬▬ HUMAN CHANGE PROCESS

Conventional psychotherapy continued to worry me, and I first responded by trying to gain more skill. Good senior supervisors were around, and one of them urged that we select together a long-term case to be my principal arena for learning. The client turned out to be an emblem of her era—a brilliant young photographic fashion model, who after a bad time in the Cambridge parties of Timothy Leary crashed in an acid-triggered psychotic episode of the most bizarre, coherent, and compelling content, and was slowly inching her way up the ladder back into a New Age. She had a history, a beauty, and a mentation of mythic dimensions; small wonder, I can now see, that I scheduled her appointments too often, for too many months. For a while, I was completely self-deceived, but after reducing her role as "patient" it seemed clear that she moved more quickly into a richer and more complex real life. I was shaken by the implications and more than ever determined to devise a professional role with greater clarity, more guidelines against drift, and more provisions for keeping one's mind on things and for keeping the patient's needs in the forefront. I saw all around me in psychotherapy a troubling vagueness of purpose, looseness of explanation and theory, and deliberate mystifications. Perhaps it was my own limitation, but as a profession, surely (I thought) we would do better to avoid the conditions most likely to produce self-deception.

The work on a role-based treatment, though, went forward rapidly and productively. By then, there was actually little left to work out. For normal subjects, marital satisfaction is highly and negatively correlated with the difference between marriage role expectations and perceptions of actual role enactments. Why not then work in therapy to reduce that disparity, helping couples to negotiate role disputes and to achieve compromises and resolutions to maximize role satisfactions? Personality and psychopathology need not be treated directly, but much symptomatology could be expected to mitigate as this most important of human relationships was eased of its tensions. We (my students in this work were Gerald Otis and Marge Crago) had no trouble devising procedures; we had a measurement instrument ready at hand, and our clinical experiences were highly positive, leading us to push the approach further and further into (apparently) more "pathological" cases and into full-family groups.

What would have developed from that work, had it continued? It had inherent limitations—not those with which it was then challenged, but deeper ones, deriving from role theory itself, which is static and descriptive, lacking a dynamic component, and inadequate to explain developmental processes. There were no conceptual tools available at that time to take the theory further. Now there are, and as role theory comes to be absorbed into more general sociocultural analyses, which will provide the developmental concepts, I expect to see the return of role-based treatments, manifested as a focus on the everyday realities of social life, and with negotiated exchanges and work on developing semiotic congruence—that is, helping groups to label, interpret, and understand their shared events in common terms, achieving what we now understand as intersubjectivity.

At the time, though, I was satisfied. My standards were met: It was work that had evidence of effectiveness; the descriptions and explanations were transparent, leaving little to be concealed behind speculative smoke; and the likelihood of countertransference and therapist's self-deception were lowered.

Others liked the work too. I turned down several fine positions. At Harvard, my recruitment host was the venerable father of community psychiatry, Gerald Kaplan. We talked a long time in his office, on a late cold night. He told me what life at Harvard would be like: the rigorous expectations and schedules, the necessity of achieving steady output and solid prominence, and the pleasures of arguably America's most elevated intellectual climate. I told him I wanted all that, and I coveted the cachet. But there was the real possibility that I might do better, back in Arizona. Because there was no one there of great importance or great power, I could work as I saw fit, and if I were allowed the way and the pace best suited to me, I expected to find something. He said that he knew well the advantages of "one's time in the desert." I knew of his years in Israel, where he had done his fundamental thinking and writing. "Well," he said, "you have a difficult choice," but his smile told me he knew it was easy.

Back in Arizona, two young psychologists, Ralph "Bud" Wetzel and Montrose Wolf, migrated down from the University of Washington, that hatchery of behaviorists, and changed my life course. I had no prior close encounters with applied behaviorism, but Bud and Mont made up for that, and soon the entire membership of the movement visited the Arizona cell, bringing news and messages of their plot for the next revolution. I liked their zeal and their puritanical expurgation of "everything that could not be seen, counted, and reported." What behaviorism I know was learned from them, first in argument, later in joint work. Behaviorism fit well into what I was doing and seemed to differ mainly in the centrality of the management of contingencies. In any event, we were friends, and over a period of time we gradually evolved a plan for a project together.

At the Community Mental Health Center, we initiated a program for early intervention with "pre-delinquent" boys and girls. Mont Wolf set up a behaviorist classroom on the premises, and Wetzel and I began the Behavioral Research Project, working in homes and schools to observe parent-child interactions, and designing intervention plans to purify the structure of behavior and contingencies. Much of the work involved complicated communication activities between home and school. The collection of data and the interaction with parents and teachers were all carried out by young BA-level generalists, trained and supervised by us. We operated in the "triadic model" of consultation, in which we psychologists supervised the BAs, who counseled and supported the "mediators" (parents and/or teachers), who actually delivered the instructions and reinforcers, who set the rules, rewarded and ignored, and collected the data. None of the professionals interacted directly with the problem kids. Thus, we were doing *Behavior Modification in the Natural Environment,* the title of our book that reported on the project. Published in 1969, it had a considerable influence. The procedures we devised for treating young children who were beginning to act out became such standard protocol that they are perceived only as a part of received wisdom, not something psychologists think of as having been invented. They are still sound, at least as an extreme example of how human service can be offered in ways that do not disrupt natural relationships, but enhance them.

This work represented to me an even further movement toward a more inclusive settings-analysis, of school and family. The theoretical language of behaviorism offered an honesty and simplicity that came near a full disclosure to clients and left the real agency of change to the families and schools themselves. During that time, the work on marital and family therapy continued. I had developed a small private practice, of the academic's usual one day a week, seeing clients of that kind entirely, trying to hone my skills and understanding, collecting case material and some deepened understanding of the way their and our relationships worked, and worked best. In 1967, I had about half of a book manuscript ready.

About that time, my personal world fell into shambles. After a disastrous divorce, nothing in my life was left standing where it stood before. I ended my cases as quickly as possible, threw out my manuscript, and broke off any intellectual activity concerning marriage and family treatment. It was less a loss of confidence than a certitude that I could not think objectively about these matters and would not be able to do so again for the foreseeable future. I indicted my own theories, at the very least for ineptitude, if not for being feloniously wrong. Some of this was depression rhetoric, but I know I was right to leave it alone, for at least a while.

CLINICAL PSYCHOLOGY IN HAWAII

As a part of the cataclysm, I moved to the University of Hawaii as Clinical Director. When the plane landed, and I saw from the tarmac those blue mountains and green hills, I never thought I would live and work in that strange and beautiful place for more than 20 years.

The Hawaii faculty were interested in my behavioral approach to clinical work and my commitment to cultural adaptations. There is no better place to do the latter than Hawaii, so often called a "natural laboratory" for multicultural studies. As it turned out, it was good ground too for growing an original and new-mold doctoral program. There was no problem in recruiting fine people to Hawaii, both faculty and students, and for a while at least, the values of objectivity, clarity, and working with natural relationships, with families and communities and diverse cultural groups, permeated our new program. If not unique, it was certainly among the first to base clinical practice not on psychotherapy but on practices affecting larger groups. We were accredited within 4 years, and I was ready to do something new.

Those 4 years were largely intellectual consolidation. I taught not only behaviorism but also comparative psychotherapies, and so continued to consider the wisdoms of existentialism, phenomenology, and even psychoanalysis, particularly Jung. It was also a time of personal healing, living on a sailboat, teaching, institution building, re-creating a personal life, playing handball—and writing poetry, almost every day. Through the Hawaii Literary Arts Council and the university English department, I was able to find a lively and competent society of poets and writers, and of course every writer from everywhere passed through Hawaii, the most pleasant station on the Readings Tour. Some Bread Loaf summers served for networking too. My poems were by now appearing with some regularity in the good journals. I wanted to be praised by the title "Poet," worked hard to earn it, and accumulated a record close to tenurable in the English department (or so it has pleased me to think—I certainly never indulged that braggadocio in their Kuykendall Hall). My two lives enriched and even refreshed each other—their energy seemed stored in different tanks.

In psychology, studies of the pathological, or indeed of the exceptional in any way, now seemed too limiting, too small a canvas for painting the entire scene. As Social was the best place to study Clinical, then the best place to study Social was in communities, institutions, and cultures. I resigned as clinical director, left clinical entirely, and have never returned.

THE KAMEHAMEHA EARLY EDUCATION PROJECT (KEEP)

The Kamehameha Schools is a private institution, for the education of Hawaiian boys and girls. It was then the 10th largest eleemosynary foundation in the world, its wealth arising from the legacy of the last of the Kamehamehas, Princess Bernice Pauhi Bishop, included in which are the residual royal lands of that dynasty. The Kamehameha Schools was then (and as of this writing, is again) a boarding-and-day academy for Hawaiian and part-Hawaiian children, who are admitted competitively for the purpose of educating a cadre of most-able Hawaiian leaders.

In 1970, the educational plight of most Hawaiian/part-Hawaiian students was worsening, particularly among the urban poor, and recent studies by social agencies had made the case that school performances of Hawaiian children were abysmal. Jack Darvill, President of the Schools, had called my psychologist colleague Ron Gallimore, who had done ethnographic and experimental work in a Hawaiian community, to ask his advice; Ron in turn called me. We took a small contract to survey the situations of Hawaiian students in schools across the state. Darvill put the problem to us simply and clearly: "Why do Hawaiian children have such trouble in learning to read?" and "Is there anything the Kamehameha Schools could do about it?"

After a year's work, site visits to many public schools on all the islands, and interviewing anyone who might be in position to clarify the issues, we answered his questions this way: "No one knows," and "Yes."

What the Schools could do, in our proposal, was study the question by building a special small school, kindergarten to third grade, populating it with at-risk, poor Hawaiian/part-Hawaiian students, then observe events carefully, vary the teaching methods according to carefully plotted time-series measurements of academic progress, and by this experimental method discover what works. Of course, we also would consult every possible national and international expert for the most promising forms of instruction. We were confident that part of the problem lay in the cultural patterns of the children, which were certainly not what the public schools expected nor enjoyed. We had no idea what the critical cultural aspects might be, nor how they might inform school practices.

I spent the next 16 years working on those problems, in that laboratory school. Gallimore moved to UCLA shortly after the school opened, but he remained active in the research and scholarship of the program for the entire time. The most complete report of that work is contained in our book *Rousing Minds to Life: Teaching and Learning in Social Context.*

The discoveries of the Kamehameha Early Education Program are too extensive even to list here, much less discuss. As principal investigator, I was the CEO of the unit, reporting directly to President Darvill. At the height of our activity, KEEP had more than 200 employees, about 40 active researchers and research assistants, 120 students in our school, and field site "colonies" in 10 public schools on three islands, serving a total of 5,000 students a year. There has not been anything like it before or since, and now years after the program ended, it is still regarded as perhaps the only true test of a culturally adapted, integrated total school reform program for minority at-risk students.

Such success came about for a few very good reasons. We had enough long-term funding, a multidisciplinary staff, a coherent set of operating values, and an absolute commitment to evaluation data made public. We had political protection (for a time) and license to freely design all aspects of schooling. We all knew it could never last, but those unique conditions held just long enough to solve the basic problem.

It was a near thing. It took us 3 years to crack the nut, a much longer time to "creatively fail" than is allowed to almost any other social scientist. But time was needed, and is often needed when many elements are a part of the solution. Ours included a balanced reading program, with a strong emphasis on comprehension, adapted for children who had little early home experience with literacy activities. It included a social organization much like Hawaiian society, with simultaneous multiple activity settings in classrooms, requiring strong student initiative and responsibility, just as in Hawaiian culture. Like Hawaiian culture too, a pattern of dialogue between teacher and students allowed co-narration, overlapping speech, and voluntarism. Our program also included a continuation of the strong evaluation component, with frequent assessment of student progress, and staff support to teachers to ensure the fidelity of their performance to program standards.

For the trajectory of my own work and thought, it represented a confirmation of my earliest earned intellectual position: that the adequate plane of analysis for human service delivery (whether educational or clinical) is not the individual considered as an isolated unit, but the individual in the context of social interaction. Of course, the KEEP work represented a significant forward movement from role theory or behaviorism, toward more inclusive settings-analysis, into home, community, school, and cultural contexts, as well as a movement toward a more comprehensive theoretical language, achieved by interdisciplinary analyses.

That this was the chance and work of a lifetime became clear to me in the early 1980s, and it required my full energies and commitment. In the meantime, it seemed to me that I had struck the ceiling of my ambitions for poetry. Rising to the next level would also require full energy and commitment, but I also believed that I lacked genius for it—not an improbable judgment, certainly, because so very few have. And not that I suspected genius in psychology/education, either, but the opportunity to do a great thing there was at hand, unique, and within my capacities, as I judged them. So at that point, at about 54, I finally chose.

So then came the last giant step in my personal intellectual pilgrimage. In integrating the enormous mass of data from the KEEP project, I believed that we needed a lingua franca, one that would articulate observations in many domains and disciplines. I had done research using concepts from Luria, and in 1980, I read his mentor Vygotsky, and that was the major transformative event of my work life.

That "sociocultural perspective" was a culmination of inclusiveness. The appropriation (and participation in) the theoretical development of the sociocultural perspective—which includes the psychological, the interpersonal, and the community, including the cultural-historical, as mediated by language and other semiotic systems—gives over entirely to the participants the action decisions for their own developmental goals. Well. That did it all.

The sociocultural perspective also enabled the formulation of a general theory of education, which remains (so far as I know) a unique achievement. This was published in *Rousing Minds to Life,* and I like to think that the integrated theory in it was a large reason for that book's success.

▬▬▬▬ MOVING ON

All good things end, and so did KEEP. The Kamehameha Schools came under new leadership, which decided to return the Schools to an exclusive concern with the most able of Hawaiian students. From the point of view of science, the best of the work had been completed anyway. It was time to move on.

I had a brief stint as Academic Vice President of United States International University, to which I was drawn for the opportunity to work with cultural issues in education on the international scale. The work in Kenya, Mexico, and London was enormously exciting and, on a day-to-day basis, the most enjoyable job I have had.

In 1990, I moved to the University of California at Santa Cruz, because a group there had just won the competition for the National Center for Research on Cultural Diversity and Second Language Learning, one of the national R&D centers of the U.S. Department of Education. Because they had based their proposal heavily on my work and theory, it seemed a natural alliance, so I took up residence in Santa Cruz and operated as a kind of guru—the kind that people point out but are not obliged to converse with, no one understanding his language.

Those years of return from Hawaii and from KEEP were enormously frustrating. Educational development work in California and in the mainland United States generally was far behind the work we had done at KEEP a decade earlier. Culture and education had become a battlefield in the national culture wars. The university (not only the University of California, but the American academy in general) was no longer a place of debate, but of the suppression of debate. It became clear nationally that actual change in educational practice was enormously difficult to achieve, and that every constituency of education was heavily invested in the current stream of benefits more than in doing any hard work for the improvement of student achievement.

Schools, especially in California, from which the virus is spreading eastward at an alarming rate, are pervaded by the "whatever" attitude that to educate children is to oppress them, and that the schools should work in students' "comfort zone," so as to unduly disturb neither student nor teacher. In the 7 years since leaving KEEP, I have seen no instance of the kind of "hard teaching" that was routine in that Hawaii program.

A general disgust with education at every level, and a parallel dismay at the general decline of standards in American (and global) culture in general—these complaints began to sound, even to me, like the predictable, disappointed bitterness of an aging man. There is some truth in that, but I do deny it as sole source. Even the baby boomers' own children, themselves now gaining full voice as social critics, are challenging the mindless disestablishmentarianism with which the now-dominant intellectual elite continues to operate.

Looking at my career of study of the nature and the rights of the Other, both friends and critics assume that a cultural relativism is my value position. It is not. As I understand the distinction between cultural relativism and cultural pluralism, as drawn for example by Isiah Berlin, pluralism involves a respectful consideration of sets of values, as developed by others, who are recognizably human, in response to their own unique challenges and circumstances, without in any way reducing one's own value commitments, and certainly not reducing the validity of values per se. As a cultural pluralist, in considering the values of self and others, I believe I am obliged to assert the primacy of the highest pan-human values that I can discern from diligent dialogue with human history. When the values of my sister cultures are seen to be lesser, my appropriate action, if any, is to assist in removing the conditions that have drawn forth that lesser response from my recognizably human brothers, understanding fully that I would in all likelihood, in their place, have chosen as they chose. That is, moral man does not erase the distinction between the right and the wrong; rather, with St. Thomas, he assists with the correction of the conditions that make wrong behavior adaptive.

Cultural relativism, on the other hand, considers values themselves to be the subject of valuation only within their own contexts, and not suitable for comparison across cultures. The latter, now the dominant cultural assumption, necessarily eliminates the possibility of standards for conduct across contexts. Because there is no metric for value, value has no value. It has been only a short logical and developmental step into the dark alley where children shoot one another at random, their elders dazed by violent hypodermic television, and the controlling elite systematically razing every wall where there are two bricks of standards left stacked.

It is much harder to be a cultural pluralist, there being few, and those cursed into silence. It is even harder to work for the values of education in a society that has no firm grasp on the absolute value of hard work, high learning, and the achievement of the highest potential for all. "I mean, really, who are you to say that anything's any better than hanging out?" For me, it is impossible to sustain energy and drive forever, in the absence of a supportive community of fellow workers. My own supportive community, increasingly scattered, had grown smaller rather than larger. I have begun a novel, a utopian novel (which are always about education), thinking that the world of ideas is the only one left in which a difference can be made. I have also begun to question my career insistence on action and ideas: It is plausible that a career in ideas alone would have had a greater good.

In 1996, I was eligible for retirement, and ready for a small garden and a return to literature, but in one last reflex of stubbornness, I agreed to take the lead among our small companion band, to try to assemble a much larger national team and compete for the next R&D center, this one for diversity and at-risk students. So like Diogenes with his lamp, we searched the nation for a team of like-minded scholars, of every age group, who were not only brilliant but also personally agreeable and desirous of forming a collaborating research community. My goal was to submit a plan of work that would be to the highest standards I could devise, theoretically, practically, and scientifically. If we won the competition, there would be once more that rare, almost unique opportunity of engaging in great things in the company of a like-minded community. If we lost, there awaited a retirement to the novel and garden. I shipped off the proposal not quite knowing which would be best. (If only I could again be doing both. . . .)

We have just begun the first of our 5 years of that Center for Research on Education, Diversity and Excellence (CREDE). The work itself grapples with the problems of the major cultural groups of the United States. The integrated program of research and educational development includes the psychological, social, and community planes. It is a formidable challenge in its inclusiveness. We 100 colleagues are by and large an able, affable, committed, and enjoyable community of workers; it is company in which ideas are debated, companionship follows, and (most of the time, when we are not too tired) truth is sought. There is no lack in the conditions: Any error will be my own most grievous fault.

There is one loose strand left in the story, the raveling "truth" thread. I am truly thankful for receiving the idea of truth as the high value; on a value more lofty I would surely have foundered even worse and sunk. At keeping my word, old-time Texas-style, many have done worse; at the general matter of truth telling, many have succeeded far above me. Nowadays, I give little thought to it, other than trying not to mock that boy-and-man's simpleminded notion that truth could be uncovered by careful attention, an earned inclusiveness, and a mastery of language.

After Wittgenstein, Vygotsky, Bakhtin, Ecco; after knowing language as the instrument of intersubjectivity, that all propositions are rejoinders, that symbols and their meanings are fluid constructions of working communities—after finding that among the criteria that any sign system must meet, in order to be true language, is falsifiability: well then. "What is truth?" I no longer know, except that "truthing" is an activity, not an achievement.

As can be seen from that tangled paragraph, "truthing" may be easier in another kind of writing:

CONTAINING THE LIE

a poem or play or film

by

Roland Tharp

Being an interview between a young chimpanzee and a graduate student, in which they explore common ground.

The setting is a small theaterlike room with semicircular seating raked upward. The audience is already seated as the cast descends down stage-right and takes their places in furniture arranged for a homey interview.

Cast of Characters

Chimpanzee	An experimental primate who has been taught a language system in a normal human home environment
Mommy	The adult female of the home
Cousin	The infantile female of the home
Audience	A surrounding, intent group of primates
Author	A bearded, surly primate
Graduate Student	A seeker of knowledge

All the characters and the audience are normally attired, except the Chimpanzee, who appears to be a human actor in a Chimpanzee suit, and the Graduate Student, who appears to be a chimpanzee in a Human suit.

The Graduate Student interviews the Chimpanzee, whose human family members are in close attendance. The Author is walking about, intensely, rather like a director of his own fantasy. The Graduate Student speaks first, the Chimpanzee answers:

Graduate Student: Q. When did they first admit that you used language?

Chimpanzee: A. On a Thursday. I had said a thing a second way, offered an alternate phrasing. They found that *generative*.

They continue:

Q. That did it?

A. No, I called my cousin "Shit-face." They found that *inventive*.

Q. That did it?

A. No, I said Shit-face broke the teacup. That did it.

Q. Why?

A. They found that a lie. Language falsifies. Ergo, I . . .

Q. Is that true? Must language to be language tell a lie?

A. When Mommy scolded Cousin, I felt powerful and sad, as if a branch had come off in my hand.

Q. Do you believe a chimpanzee will ever write a poem? Which takes intellect, and which poets say is for truth telling?

A. I would say, judging from life with Mommy and Cousin, that such a thing would want a lie in it.

Q. Why?

A. When the next cup fell, I called myself Shit-face. I believe I dropped it; I should have dropped it. Cousin sat in her high chair, looking solemn.

Q. Well, you must type it out, to have a poem.

A. That's no problem.

Audience: Just a moment please. Which one of you is the chimp?

Author: Really, must you interrupt? That is the reason they wear masks. Please attend to his point: that the poem must contain a lie.

Graduate Student: Q. If we may continue. Now this word "contain." Do you suppose Author means the lie is limited, as by an enclosure, a pen, a zoo?

Chimpanzee: A. I think "contain" means held, careful-not-to-drop.

(Laughter from Mommy and Cousin)

CONCLUSION

So, any complaints? No, this story (so far) is of good fortune in the extreme. The dream of another, different life, not chosen and perhaps regretted—that imagined me almost always to appear as a visual artist, usually a painter. In such reverie, I offer a bargain—take away the words and bring pigments, drive out that succubus "truth" and send in the angel—who swings open the door to this moment's carved actuality.

Perhaps after a morning's writing, there will be an afternoon for watercolors, in the corner of a garden with just a few gray-silver weeds. . . .

APPENDIX

Abbreviated Professional History

1957	BA, Cum Laude (Literature and Psychology), University of Houston
1958	MA (Psychology; Minor, Anthropology), University of Michigan
1961	PhD (Clinical/Social Psychology), University of Michigan
1961-1967	Staff Psychologist, Southern Arizona Community Mental Health Center; Director, Psychology Department, 1964-1967
1961-1968	Assistant Professor to Associate Professor, University of Arizona; Founding Director, The Psychological Clinic, 1964-1965
1968	Diplomate, American Board of Examiners in Professional Psychology
1968-1989	Associate Professor to Professor, University of Hawaii; Founding Director of Clinical Studies, 1968-1972
1968, 1969, and 1974	Visiting Psychologist, American Psychological Association
1969-1986	Founder, Chief Executive Officer, and Principal Investigator, Kamehameha Early Education Program (KEEP), Center for Development of Education, Honolulu
1971-1972	President, Hawaii Psychological Association
1978	President, Hawaii Literary Arts Council
1986	Cofounder, PETOM Program (Preservice Education for Teachers of Minorities), College of Education, University of Hawaii
1986-present	Board of Directors, Intermountain Center for Human Development, Santa Fe, New Mexico, and Arizona
1987-1989	Founding Director, Center for the Study of Multicultural Higher Education, University of Hawaii

APPENDIX

Abbreviated Professional History *(continued)*

1989-present	Professor Emeritus of Psychology, University of Hawaii
1989-1990	Dean, School of Human Behavior, United States International University; Provost and Vice-President for Academic Affairs, 1990
1991-present	National Evaluation Advisory Panel, Early Intervention Systems for Navajo Children and Families
1991-present	Professor of Education and Psychology, University of California, Santa Cruz; Chair of Board of Studies in Education, 1991-1995
1995-1996	Codirector, National Center for Research on Cultural Diversity and Second Language Learning (OERI-USDOE and University of California at Santa Cruz)
1996	Director, National Center for Research on Education, Diversity and Excellence (OERI-USDOE and University of California at Santa Cruz)

NOTE

1. Francis Cornford died in 1960, shortly after self-publishing a small book of poems, *On a Calm Shore*, including "Epitaph for Everyman." The author has been unable to locate the holder of the copyright, if any, but the poem is widely quoted.

SELECT BIBLIOGRAPHY IN PSYCHOLOGY AND EDUCATION

Psychological patterning in marriage. *Psychological Bulletin, 60* (1963): 97-117.
With D. Otis. Toward a theory for therapeutic intervention in families. *Journal of Consulting Psychology, 30* (1966): 426-434.
With R. J. Wetzel. *Behavior modification in the natural environment.* New York: Academic Press, 1969.

With D. R. Watson, D. R. *Self-directed behavior.* Pacific Grove, CA: Brooks/Cole, 1972. (revised editions in 1977, 1981, 1985, 1988, 1992, 1996)

With A. J. Marsella and T. Ciborowski. (Eds.). *Perspectives in cross-cultural psychology.* New York: Academic Press, 1979.

The effective instruction of comprehension: Results and description of the Kamehameha Early Education Program. *Reading Research Quarterly, 17* (1982): 503-527.

With R. Gallimore. Inquiry process in program development. *Journal of Community Psychology, 10* (1982): 103-118.

With M. Note. The triadic model of consultation: New developments. In *School consultation: Interdisciplinary perspectives on theory, research, training, and practice* (pp. 35-51), ed. F. West. Austin: Research and Training Project on School Consultation, The University of Texas at Austin and The Association of Educational and Psychological Consultants, Austin, Texas, 1988.

Psychocultural variables and constants: Effects on teaching and learning in schools. *American Psychologist, 44* (1989): 349-359.

With R. Gallimore. *Rousing minds to life: Teaching and learning in social context.* New York: Cambridge University Press, 1989.

Cultural diversity and treatment of children. *Journal of Consulting and Clinical Psychology, 59* (1991): 799-812.

The institutional and social context of educational practice and reform. In *Contexts for learning: Sociocultural dynamics in children's development* (pp. 269-282), ed. E. A. Forman, N. Minick, and C. A. Stone. Cambridge, UK: Cambridge University Press, 1993.

Research knowledge and policy issues in cultural diversity and education. In *Language and learning: Educating linguistically diverse students* (pp. 129-167), ed. B. McLeod. Albany: State University of New York Press, 1994.

Intergroup differences among Native Americans in socialization and child cognition: An ethnogenetic analysis. In *Cross-cultural roots of minority child development* (pp. 87-105), ed. P. Greenfield and R. Cocking. Hillsdale, NJ: Lawrence Erlbaum, 1994.

SELECT BIBLIOGRAPHY OF LITERARY PUBLICATIONS

Romanesque Sculpture: A Study in the Hideous, and The Cosmogony of Dylan Thomas, *The Atlantic Prize Papers,* 1956-1957.

Cat-House (short fiction), *Voices,* Summer 1963.

Bald She Walks Among the Peacocks (short fiction), *Arizona Quarterly,* Summer 1964.

Colding Nights; Because; and Essay on the Evolution of Social Influence, *Prairie Schooner,* Winter 1974-1975.

From the Woods, *Shenandoah, 26*(4), Summer 1975.

Kyrie Eleison; Ogive; and Tremor Harmonic, *Quixote, 9*(9), 1976.

Highland Station: Poems by Roland Tharp. Texas City: Poetry Texas Press, 1977. (2nd printing, 1978)

The Piero Poems, II: The Baptism; and The Piero Poems, III: The Nativity, *Christianity and Literature,* Spring 1978 and Winter 1979.

Carpenters, Waterfall, Stream, Sea; The Ageing Friends; Sack-of-Bones; and Two Incantations of Ill Will, *Prairie Schooner*, Spring 1980.

Before the Storm in Progresso, *Hawaii Review*, 1984, no. 16.

SELECT VISUAL AND PERFORMING ARTS PRODUCTIONS

In Celebration of Eros (poetry/drama). Manoa Valley Theater, Honolulu, May 1978.

Scenes From the Life. Athens International Video Festival, 1982.

My Aunt May. American Film Magazine Award, Hawaii International Film Festival, 1990.

PART III

SUMMARY AND DISCUSSION

CHAPTER 9

Summary
and Analysis

LISA TSOI HOSHMAND

The autobiographical accounts, interpreted in the light of the interview data and supplemental information, provide coherent pictures of each participant's career and life in psychology. The consistency between word and deed has been reassuring, given both narrative constructions in the participants' accounts and actual enactment in their published works, professional presentations, and past and continuing activities. To the extent that these accounts stand on their own coherence, I see my task of summary as largely one of organizing what is given in the text by topics of interest, and commenting on noticeable patterns. Before giving a summary of the interview data and the contributed chapters, however, some notes on methodology are in order. Rather than leave them for subsequent discussion, I wish to present considerations of method and process as a context for the summary observations that follow.

ISSUES OF METHOD
AND PROCESS

My ideas of method and concerns with the present methodology have changed somewhat over the course of conducting this study. Initially I was concerned about the subjectivity of a narrative interpretive approach. As I gathered more information, the convergence of data has lessened my anxiety about the risk of misinterpretation. Re-reading interview notes and the authors' written accounts, as well as listening again to interview tapes, had been helpful in keeping me grounded in the descriptive accuracy of my summary. At the risk of appearing to be short on method, I have found this project overall to require little consciousness of technique. The natural flow of inquiry and the proximity of the research questions to the questions posed to the participants are perhaps characteristic of most narrative studies.

Given the premise of the multideterminacy of lives, I did not try to formulate singular hypotheses about individual motives or search for particular antecedents according to a given theory. Rather, I simply followed the biographical principle of relating the professional commitments, career, and life of each person to his or her sociocultural and historical context. This inductive, broad framework may have set me apart from dynamic schools of psychohistory and some of the personality theorists who use psychobiography as a method of theory building. I am perhaps closer to other narrative researchers who rely mostly on examples and the internal coherence of the text to derive general statements. The summary and conclusions, however, were read by the participants, whose comments gave thought to an epilogue.

Although there is no attempt at narrow forms of hypothesis testing, this project has involved applying a broad conceptual framework for linking epistemic and moral commitments to professional identity and creativity. I am aware of the dangers of conflating theory and data, but I also realize that there is theory-ladenness in any set of data, narrative or otherwise. The fruitfulness and robustness of this framework is for others to judge. For myself, the interpretations have come readily because the various texts seem to require little interpretive effort when examined within this frame. This ease of contextualization may have resulted in part from the procedural effects of asking the participants to begin with a life line and presenting them with interview questions that include consideration of context. Although some of the authors might have followed mentally the blueprint implicit in the questions, I have tried to emphasize that there is no uniform structure or format for writing the autobiographical chapters. In a few instances, when I found the initial drafts of the chapter to be more analytical than narrative in style, I encouraged the person to engage in more "storytelling." To the extent that my editing suggestions have not been excessive, these facilitated autobiographical accounts may be considered to be consistent with the spirit of narrative self-interpretation. The authors have lent intelligibility to their stories with their own philosophy of life, before my recounting and summary on the common points of reference.

In reflecting on my interactions with the participants, I realize how generous each has been in sharing personal views and sentiments. I was very much aware of the fact that all of them have to select from the past those experiences they are willing to present in a public forum, some of which are difficult and even painful. By leaving the decisions to them and respecting their need for privacy, I hope that I have managed this dialogical process with sufficient sensitivity. The only times I made suggestions for content were those instances when an author had spoken about a pertinent issue in our interview and had not included similar comments or elaborations in the chapter. Even then, the final decision on content was the author's to make.

My relationships with the participants have varied, partly because of different histories. I am quite certain that the degree of rapport in each case has had some effect on the quality of information and depth of disclosure; however, in no case did I feel that the interaction was not authentic. Although it was easy for me to identify with the experiences of the women and their personal conflicts about work and family commitments, I did not feel a great deal of gender-related differences in my interactions with the informants. The fact that I had no prior relationship with four of the participants also meant that I had fewer preconceptions about them. The person with whom I have had the longest relationship is Roland Tharp. In this case, I found myself wondering whether certain views he expressed are consistent with my knowledge of him and our shared experiences. For example, when in our interview he spoke of the negative sequel to the 1960s, I recalled the optimism and air of liberalism that he conveyed as a professor to me when I was a graduate student in the late 1960s. I wondered privately how his present view contrasts with my earlier impression. Yet, in the late 1960s, I had only the perspective of a not very mature student, and the context was not comparable to the present. My reaction to the apparent shift suggests that interpretations are perspectival as well as a function of the temporal and relational context in which the interlocutors share a space of understanding. (Tharp has subsequently clarified that he was optimistic in the 1960s and has seen some of his own vision and goals eventuated. The current disappointment stems more from what he considers to be failed possibilities in our common social and intellectual life.)

Other narrative researchers have discussed ethical concerns in their work. I consider the very process of posing questions on ultimate concerns to the participants, and comprehending their lives in a mutual existential context, to be an ethical encounter. Besides the invasion of privacy and the possibility of misrepresentation, my main concern is whether I have done justice to the careers and lives of these remarkable individuals. The abbreviated professional histories and select bibliographies appended to each chapter were constructed by me from the participants' life lines and curriculum vita, and approved by them. Although I asked for, and have obtained, their reactions to the summative interpretations, I continue to worry about the fact that there is always minimization and oversimplification in reducing data to a manageable form. More important, this was a multiple-case study based on autobiographical sketches; it did not allow the depth of analysis possible with whole biographies.

On the other hand, I do not feel that there was a shortage of data, and rather regret not being able to present in the group summary the richness of ideas and actions found in the collected samples of these individuals' work. My fear is that the uniqueness of each person's contributions might be obscured by the multiple-case presentation. In recounting their stories, I also might have rounded out plots and overextrapolated. In the sense that the collective narrative is a reconstruction, its validity may be more in terms of pragmatics and the effects on the readers, including the participants themselves. On the whole, the participants have indicated that they find the project to be of value to them, and if so, it may be considered an ethical consequence of this endeavor.

The part of the methodology that I feel least confident about is the deconstruction of text, including the reconstructed arguments in the present summary of the individual accounts. Reflexivity can be mundane or informed, and it is always perspectival. My own commitments and interests are apparent in this process. The fact that I am in agreement with many of the expressed views limits my ability to question their assumptions, as would their likely critics. Even though the present findings reveal shared concerns and disappointments with the present state of psychology and American society, to construct a comprehensive critical theory from such cultural and political observations is beyond the scope of this project. Past the intellectual exercise and reflections, I am left with mixed emotions and a dialectical experience of optimism and pessimism. The individual dialogues and written narratives have merged into a complex group conversation in my mind. In unpeeling the layers and embedding them at the same time in the larger context of the profession and our society, I am not certain that I have captured the tonality of these multiple voices. Following the hermeneutic metaphor, however, one can expect the cycle of interpretation and critical deconstruction to continue beyond this writing.

PROFESSIONAL IDENTITY
AND PERSONAL PROJECTS

The autobiographical accounts and the manner in which developmental stories of professional identity were told convey, for the most part, a quality of purposefulness. I was struck by the intensity of commitment and sense of destiny in some cases, notably that of Derald Sue, who clearly described his professional goals as being intertwined with his own cultural awakening and personal identity development. Though downplaying his instrumentality in certain developments, Leo Goldman spoke of his two "crusades." One can readily identify the causes to which each psychologist has made contributions throughout a significant portion of his or her professional life: Derald Sue's and Leo Goldman's promotion of diversity and contribution to counselor training, Jill Reich's and Donald Peterson's work in psychology education, Barbara Keogh's public policy efforts and research in special education, Elizabeth Altmaier's application of psychology to health-related research, and Roland Tharp's research and program development in education as well as in culturally and ecologically inclusive theorizing. Personal projects and professional identities as educator, advocate, researcher, theorist, and reformer appear to be inseparable.

It appears that these identity projects were associated with a personal conflict or moral issue, and involved the working through of such conflicts or resolution of a value question. Sue's cultural identity conflict as an Asian American was paralleled by Goldman's identity experience as a "New York, ethnic Jew" on the fringe of what he considered to be mainstream America. Peterson identified conflicts he felt about academic psychology failing to prepare students to meet the demands of professional service, along with subsequent disagreements with both those skeptical of alternative professional education for practitioners and those who are overconfident about the effectiveness of professional schools. Jill Reich was concerned with the separation of service from teaching and research in the academy. Barbara Keogh felt conflicted about her initial preparation for practice and the less than adequate validity of practice. Tharp was disenchanted with recent trends in psychology and mental health and the relative inattention of the profession to social change. He reported experiencing continuing tensions in choosing alternative arenas for creative efforts that could make a difference. By prolonging his double life in literature and psychology, he pursued projects in both realms. Elizabeth Altmaier described the pull of conflicting roles as administrator, faculty mentor, researcher, and working wife and mother. All discerned value implications in their conflicts. All found ways of dealing with the sources of conflict, or ways of sustaining particular interests that represent what they value. In the process of carrying out their personal projects and enacting their commitments, these individuals apparently have evolved the kinds of professional identity that represent who they are.

In following the life paths of these individuals, we can detect changes in self-knowledge with experience. Sue spoke of shifts in attitude toward other ethnic groups in the course of his own cultural identity development. Goldman realized his own strengths and limitations in leadership roles. Altmaier reported changes in life perspective and an acknowledgment of complexity as characteristic of adulthood. Reich described both the differentiation and integration of professional roles. When asked to identify when they began to have a sense of identity and place in the profession, the participants typically traced their journey back to points of confluence of events and activities that signify personal growth and accomplishment. It would not be difficult to identify nuclear episodes that preceded the development of life scripts of commitment in these cases, especially if the informants were asked to provide more information on their early experiences. It was not my purpose, however, to investigate what some would regard as concealed stories. The authors themselves have traced their subsequent commitments to early influences.

Developmentally, these psychologists are all reflective of generativity, not only in terms of the stage of their careers and lives, but also in their desire to make a difference for the future. Tharp had communicated in our personal conversations a concern about not having sufficient time to accomplish what needs to be done. Sue was anxious about being able to fulfill his extensive professional commitments. Elizabeth Altmaier was reluctant to compromise a productive research program and her mentoring of students by taking on more administrative responsibilities. For Jill Reich, promotion of education reflects a broader agenda than meeting the immediate needs of the profession. It is intended to reorient the enterprise to the larger context of its future role and relationships with the community, as well as to keep pace with the accelerated changes in technology, our own knowledge base, and social needs and demographics. Barbara Keogh and Leo Goldman were not ready to retire; they continue to enjoy their professional involvement as well as volunteer work. More than half of the personal work cited in Peterson's chapter was published after his retirement, and he had plans for additional writing in the future.

These professional identities and lives of generativity are embedded in the state of the profession and the needs and social issues of the times. Several authors commented on the changes in the profession: the separation of academic researchers and practitioners, the proliferation and economic drivenness of practice, and the growing social expectations of the profession that are both exciting and daunting. All are interested in the education and training of future generations of psychologists in response to social needs. Jill Reich advocated service learning as an important component in education and professional socialization, as did Elizabeth Altmaier. Reich has continuously emphasized the importance of teaching and reminded psychology educators to address the increasing diversity among students and the society in which they have to work, a project that has consumed much of Sue's energy as a counselor educator. Altmaier and Keogh stressed value socialization in the education of psychology students. Peterson conceived of our role as reflective educators charged with preparing a future generation of reflective practitioners. The majority of the group expressed a deep concern about social inequities and the presence of racial prejudice and disharmony, committing themselves to addressing these problems in action. Their moral outlook and views of the profession will be further discussed later. Although there is little doubt that personal intentionality and the embedding life context interact in the shaping of professional identities, it is interesting to consider how these authors of their own lives perceive their careers.

CAREER PATHS, GENDER, AND SOCIAL FACTORS

Career paths present as choices that call for both prudence and risk taking, leaving some degree of regret over roads not taken. Not all authors expressed anxiety, however, about giving up career opportunities and life paths that could have been chosen. When such angst was present, as suggested by the interviews, it was concerned with the consequences of allowing certain possibilities to be potentiated and forfeiting others of equal promise. Like other professions, careers in psychology are subject to the impact of historical events. Peterson and Goldman chronicled some of the postwar developments in the field of psychology and subsequent shifts in funding for education and practice. Society and the times offer opportunities as well as resources that afford education, programs, and jobs for psychologists. Jill Reich provided a historically situated perspective on psychology education and its changing mandates, as did Peterson on the professional school movement.

Barbara Keogh gave us glimpses not only into the related field of special education but also into the role of women in academia and the climate for professional women of her generation. Not surprisingly, social conventions have imposed constraints in the form of "typical careers" for women, as reported by Keogh and Altmaier. Both testified to the importance of family commitments in moderating career ambitions of women in their cohorts, even as they expressed greater optimism for the next generation of professional women. I have mentioned the initial difficulties of finding women with accomplished careers to participate in this project. The lower participation of women in high academic and professional ranks was verified by those who have witnessed gender bias and the struggles of women in academia. Although Jill Reich did not personally experience barriers, she acknowledged having had female role models early on, as well as mentoring in her career as an academician and administrator.

Keogh's perceptions of the career choices of women were validated by Altmaier, who made a conscious decision to forgo an opportunity for advancement as an administrator because of family obligations. Perhaps characteristic of their cultural background, Sue and Goldman also commented on the impact of their professional commitments and career moves on their families. Both the men and the women referred to the role of chance factors in entering and pursuing psychology as a career. Although intentionality and goal-directedness are found in all cases, the gender difference seems to consist of the degree to which women, relatively less than men, attribute career outcomes to preplanning and careerist motives. Both groups acknowledged influential others in their professional and career development, as well as the formative nature of the values, knowledge, and wisdom of their mentors and colleagues. Perhaps as another gender characteristic, the women seemed to attribute career fulfillment more to teaching and the nurturing relationships they have had with students. Although the men probably had similar relationships with students, they did not speak of them in quite the same way. It also is interesting to note that these women gave special attention in their chapters to my question about the relationship between the personal, the social, and the professional.

Barbara Keogh made a strong point about how her career exemplifies the ways women tend to improvise in effecting a viable combination of work and family commitments. In viewing these flexible adaptations as offering diverse experiences that have enriched her professional knowledge and identity, she shows us that the professional activities and settings in which she has participated were engendering of her particular professional identity—one that combines the worldviews of teaching, research, and practice. By necessity, women tend to weave multiple strands into their lives, resulting in a rich tapestry of experience. One may conclude that plurality is an inherent quality in these lives of multiple responsibilities. Elizabeth Altmaier emphasized harmony between domains of responsibility as a superordinate value, an attainable ideal provided that one is able to articulate the value base of each commitment and to see the different domains as complementary rather than competing. This fostering of plurality and harmony may well be a source of metaphoric inspiration, not only for professional women but also for their male counterparts.

Keogh also stressed the importance of social support in managing multiple responsibilities. The social environment of professional lives plays a significant role in shaping careers and achievements. Organized groups and professional networks have been a powerful force. Although Goldman and Sue did not claim membership in the same network from which Altmaier received support as a junior faculty member and a subsequently successful academic, they found networks of their own. Social forces of a different sort can be seen in Peterson's account of the development of the professional schools. The organization of the National Council of Schools of Professional Psychology has been essential to legitimizing the voices of those involved in this alternative model of graduate education and training. Keogh's involvement in organizations has allowed her to assume an advocacy role in special education and to have input on public policy. When Goldman and Sue found themselves holding offices and editorships, they were able to promote the diversity lacking in the worldview and knowledge of the profession. Reich's applied developmental research led her to a position of working with the legislature in setting social policy on children and families. Tharp's grantsmanship has opened doors of opportunity for his research associates and students, as well as enabling him to build a strong platform for social action. The formal recognition of accomplishments provides access to important forums and those in control of policy decisions.

Important as they are, membership in formal organizations and formal recognition of achievements are only part of the key to professional effectiveness. These psychologists' participation in informal groups also has aided them in accomplishing what is deemed important. As a respected senior female colleague, Barbara Keogh is able to exert influence on behalf of women at her university. By building teams, Jill Reich and Elizabeth Altmaier were able to manage their leadership in areas of responsibility that involve multiple constituencies. Tharp, who now views himself as marginally affiliated with the psychology profession, is connected with a multidisciplinary network that keeps alive a constant stream of ideas and problem-solving scholarship. Altmaier and Keogh reported that students are an important part of the learning community that sustains research efforts in their careers. The importance of community in sustaining productive discourse and scholarly practice is evident.

As private citizens, these professionals belong to additional communities reflecting personal commitments, such as in Altmaier's work for her church,

Sue's civic activities in promoting diversity, and Keogh's and Goldman's volunteer work and activism for their respective causes. If professional activities and memberships have been engendering of identity in adult life, these additional projects and memberships probably have played a similar role. All the participants are grateful for the rewards of both professional and civic commitments. In reviewing their careers and lives, all have expressed a genuine appreciation of the opportunities and autonomy they have had, and consider themselves most fortunate.

History has shaped careers as well as perspectives on one's work and place in the social order. The decade of the 1960s was consciousness raising in more than one sense for Sue's minority consciousness and for Keogh's approach to teaching. It also was identified in our interview by Tharp as having ushered in an age of self-absorption and the relativistic debunking of traditions. Tharp's concern is that developments in the decades following the 1960s have eroded the forces of cultural integration and the capacity of society to engage in rational dialogue and problem solving. His projects may be viewed in part as attempts to re-create structures and a social consciousness for problem solving that is informed by knowledge and values. Peterson, who was involved in the study of racial tensions on the university campus in the same period, has made it a personal project to continue with researching the history of prejudice. The research and writing of Keogh, Tharp, and Sue are meant to address social and educational issues. Thus, professional activities and knowledge seeking are in fact responses to societal problems in particular historical contexts.

PERSPECTIVES ON KNOWLEDGE

One of the central themes of this book that is also evident in the autobiographical accounts concerns knowledge. Several in the group expressed dissatisfaction with the prevalent methods for developing knowledge in psychology and the relative inability of psychologists to produce or apply useful knowledge. Goldman took an antitraditionalist stance in questioning the experimental tradition and the positivistic assumptions of psychology. In his writings and professional presentations, he has argued for the broadening of epistemic approaches to include alternative forms of research and psychological assessment that are more relevant to practice. A similar loss of faith in what psychologists are able to accomplish with our theoretical and research-tested knowledge was experienced by Keogh with respect to some of the interventions used in special education and clinical practice, as well as in the policy area. Peterson became involved in the PsyD model of professional education also because of the limitations of traditional research-based knowledge in preparing psychologists for practice. He saw the need for a more versatile epistemology in the disciplined inquiries of professional service. Sue challenged psychological theories and the existing knowledge on counseling diverse populations, in terms of their applicability to minority groups. These critical attitudes toward knowledge are matched in every case by an intense desire to learn and to know.

As a thematic concern, issues of knowledge appear to have fueled the intellectual lives and productive activities of these psychologists. The theoretical and methodological writings, as well as the substantive research and application throughout Tharp's career, clearly reflect efforts to grapple with issues of knowledge. Tharp sees knowledge not so much in terms of definitive truth claims but as an organic development of an increasingly inclusive and coherent framework with which to make sense of human experience and to articulate interrelationships. In our interview, he conveyed a pluralistic view of knowledge whereby different forms of knowledge are expected to serve different purposes. Included in this view of knowledge is the granting of a human capacity to dimly perceive what we cannot fully cognize and express. Tharp is rather hopeful about the increasingly pluralistic approach to knowledge among social scientists. He cites as evidence the breakdown of disciplinary barriers and the contributions from anthropology, sociology, linguistics, and history to the sociocultural and historical approach to developmental and educational theorizing and research. It is from years of experience in such research and evaluation that Tharp has distilled ideas for a metamethodology for applied research and program development.

There is an openness to multidisciplinary knowledge among members of this group. Peterson and Sue have found readings of authors outside psychology to be both inspirational and informative. Peterson, Reich, and Tharp have strong roots in liberal arts education. A Jamesian view of psychology seems to be endorsed in the discussion of knowledge in more than one case. The researchers in the group have worked in multidisciplinary settings: in education and health, and, in the case of Reich, in collaboration with sociologists, medical professionals, and architects and city planners in decision-making research. Reich conceives of a translation paradigm that allows knowledge and skills in one domain to be applied to other domains. She expects psychologists to be more active in the public policy arena by becoming more able to do such translation. The valuing of multidisciplinary knowledge within this group stems from the experience of working with problems that benefit from the cross-fertilization of ideas and perspectives.

Rather than concern themselves with paradigm debates, most of the participants indicated in their interviews that they have taken a pragmatic approach to knowledge. In trying to find a viable science-practice relationship in professional education and practice, Peterson has arrived at pragmatism as a philosophical frame. It is also self-evident to Altmaier, Reich, and Keogh that psychologists should be open to a range of methods and follow epistemic approaches that "work," while being cognizant of the strengths and limitations of each. They, along with Tharp and Peterson, recognize that the nature of a given problem should drive the choice of method and approach, a point implicit in the objections Sue and Goldman raised regarding the profession's traditional theoretical and methodological orientations. A fair conclusion to make is that these psychologists have learned from their professional experiences that pragmatism is an appropriate approach to knowledge and an appropriate philosophical principle on which to base their work. Altmaier credited this perspective partly to the epistemic training provided by her mentor, who emphasized the "how" of research and inquiry in addition to substantive questions. She finds it ironic that for a profession that avoids religious issues, there seems to be a great deal of received truth in our knowledge system.

The goal of producing useful knowledge is shared by all in the group. For Jill Reich, this is crucial to the viability of psychology as a discipline and to our meaningful participation as members of a science-based profession. She has tried to convey to students the importance of knowing how to ask relevant research questions and determining who can use answers to the questions researched by our discipline. Just as Tharp has derived metamethodological principles from his experience with applied research, Reich has evolved a way of understanding applied research in terms of its impact on those who will have a stake in the profession by the fact that they need answers to problems we can help address. She feels that in today's world, academics can no longer afford to indulge in seeking knowledge only for the sake of knowledge. She attributes psychologists' reluctance to apply knowledge partly to uncertainty and partly to a separation of the researcher's role from that of a consultant.

Reich suggests that it is "a hard line to walk" between healthy skepticism and certainty in the knowledge that we produce. In inquiry and the application of knowledge, we need to move through periods of uncertainty and conviction. Staying always in one mode (such as to publish research results but withhold application) can become problematic, as it takes conviction for one to spring into action. She makes it very clear, however, that certainty is not the same as arrogance. Our conversation on this point was linked to issues of faith. In her view, there is a developmental necessity of having beliefs and paradigms from which to act on one's knowledge with some degree of confidence. Considering the discipline as a whole, each cohort of students learns the discipline differently at a given point, yet knowledge and beliefs are not to be static, as new paradigms can offer different ways of conceptualizing problems. To move on in the cycle of questioning and asserting, a qualified type of certainty is more functional. In her words, "you need to be certain about your uncertainty . . . but I don't think you can go through life and do anything constructive without some certainty." Through an examined intellectual life, we can advance a better life for all.

The position shared by this group, that knowledge should be useful and improve the human condition, reflects more than a heuristic value. Many of the statements and expressed sentiments reflect commitment to non-epistemic values. There is an interest in accomplishing something that contributes to social good (a transcendental goal?), such as the reduction of illiteracy and racism, the promotion of health and human functioning, and the correction of conditions that make wrong behavior adaptive. There is also the recognition that knowledge is social in its creation, application, and justification. Keogh described the intimate interactions involved in the teaching and learning of inquiry. She and everyone in the group acknowledged the social milieu in which their work has continued to evolve. The power of editorial boards and funding agencies in the legitimization of knowledge is recognized, as are the influences of economic and political forces in delimiting the effects of knowledge claims. Although knowledge depends on community, the creation of community also can be supported by knowledge, such as found in the work of Peterson, Reich, Sue, Keogh, and Tharp. They have argued for the importance of broadening our focus from individuals to the social system and the larger ecological context of problems.

In contrasting the picture presented by this group and what I had found in my previous project on applied epistemology, I feel that there is added evidence of shifts in psychologists' epistemic orientation toward a pragmatist, multimethod (often multidisciplinary), pluralistic approach. Informed by their experiential knowledge as researchers, practitioners, theorists, and educators, this group has come to endorse a view of knowledge that is dynamic and evolving. It is perhaps this type of increasing sophistication and openness about inquiry that one can consider to be indicative of progress in any knowledge enterprise. The related question is whether psychology has within its communities of inquirers the rational capacity for self-critique and open dialogue about the state of the profession and its inquiry practices.

========== **RATIONALITY, VALUES, AND
STATE OF THE PROFESSION**

This project has been based on a desire to explore the meaning of human rationality in the hope of broadening current conceptions that are strongly influenced by scientific rationality and its cognitive emphasis. By examining the epistemic and non-epistemic values held by the present group of psychologists, I suggest that we can derive certain hypotheses from emergent patterns. What has come through clearly are the academic values and professional values held by these individuals. Peterson and Keogh articulated a number of standards and codes of conduct that represent epistemic values and moral codes constituting what may be considered academic integrity. Intellectual honesty was valued by Goldman and Sue in those instances when psychologists have to face the limitations of their knowledge and methods of inquiry. Reich spoke against intellectual arrogance in our interview. Altmaier considered it her responsibility to instill intellectual curiosity and a healthy skepticism in students. For Tharp, truth telling is just as important in science as in the arts. The group views professional values of practice largely in terms of the integration of science and practice. In addition, Peterson stressed reflectiveness and social responsibility in professional education; Reich, service learning at all levels of education; and Sue, the emancipatory role of practitioners in alleviating conditions of social oppression and injustice.

What is significant is that these psychologists appreciate both the moral certitude of the epistemic and cognitive values that inform their academic and professional actions, and the fact that they do not offer a sufficient moral base. Peterson and Goldman spoke of their atheistic orientation. Each independently expressed some degree of regret at the inadequacy of moral resources in secular life. Tharp and Peterson are interested in theology and spiritual and ethical inquiry. Tharp, who had received Southern Baptist teachings in early life, eventually found the Church of England to be more consistent with his life as an intellectual. Theology to him, however, can never be more than metaphor. In the process of understanding the relationship between the moral and the spiritual, both Tharp and Peterson have immersed themselves in projects that point to moral questions.

Altmaier and Reich, who attended sectarian schools and came from families with strong religious convictions, seem to have traveled different distances from their origins. Altmaier commented in her interview that she is still "Old Testament" in matters of principle and continues to derive much meaning from her involvement in the church. Reich regarded the Catholicism in her background to have served as a powerful system against which to "rebel" and to consolidate her own ethical outlook which is still indebted to her roots. Keogh, who has religious vocation in her family occupation, attributed her moral sense more to the same types of homegrown values that Peterson identified in his early life. The social and cultural appropriation of values is seen in every case, including Sue's internalization of civil rights ethics and moral leadership from the Black leaders of the 1960s. Sue's bicultural background is reflected in the values he has adopted from his parental heritage and the cultural environment in the United States during his early adulthood.

What kind of value system exists in the current culture of psychology? The majority view from the interviews is that the profession lacks a shared value base and communal commitments beyond its guild interests. Altmaier and Reich, who have been involved with accreditation, and Goldman and Peterson, who also have been involved in the formal workings of professional organizations, perceive psychologists as divided and not unified in a moral direction. Sue and Tharp do not regard psychology as any more capable of cultural integration than the rest of society. It is a challenge to facilitate conversations among different constituencies in the profession who represent diverse and sometimes competing interests. In this regard, there is a continuum of opinions as to how hopeful we can be about the profession and the prospect of communal dialogue in search of common commitments.

Jill Reich considers herself an optimist. She sees psychologists as having knowledge and talents that can enable us to accomplish social goals and define ourselves as a worthy profession. She finds it unfortunate that even though most of us enjoy conceptualizing problems, we are not good at taking the next step in problem solving. In her judgment, this is due in part to the youth of the discipline. The current framing of professional identity issues as "scientists versus practitioners" is misleading in the sense that most psychologists will be involved in a variety of activities at different points in their careers. All of us need to be able to contribute in a socially significant way. She feels that neither the arrogance of science nor the complacency of practice will serve us well. Her hope is that the voices of those who can find linkages between science and practice will prevail, such that we can work together in moving the profession out of its current state. This view is echoed by Altmaier, who expects greater collaboration between researchers and practitioners in offering the public empirically validated intervention approaches.

Altmaier and Keogh have areas of skepticism toward the profession but do not seem to allow this to color their faith in effecting changes that are worthwhile.

Altmaier feels that the historic trust that the public has in the professions is being violated. Psychology has lost its historic good because it has not been nurtured, honored, and maintained. Like Goldman, she does not think that it is human nature to sacrifice individual interests for the collective good, especially if the collective is not important enough to people. Goldman believes that it is not enough to be critical, but that one also must offer a blueprint or structure for change. Sue sees the profession as having a long way to go in terms of understanding human diversity and exemplifying a commitment to diversity. Individualism and guild interests are seen as putting the survival of human society at risk. I have heard from more than one person the opinion that psychologists have failed to apply the knowledge of the discipline to ourselves, whether it is in our teaching, in our group decision making, or in resolving our internal conflicts. To earn credibility, psychology must get its own house in order.

Tharp views psychological science as too narrow in its theories and concerns, and psychological practice as not sufficiently grounded in its empirical science base. He reports finding most psychologists to be perfectly willing to acknowledge the limitations of their theoretical positions and to be open, for instance, to expanding the conceptual unit of psychology beyond an individual focus. He is less optimistic about the prospect of psychological practitioners evolving themselves into a profession of kindness and helpfulness. The self-policing and critical evaluation of practice seem secondary to individual financial motivation. Peterson is similarly concerned about the degree of psychologists' willingness to critically evaluate professional education and what we do as professionals. Although they favor a realistic optimism, he and Goldman and Sue are skeptical of our ability to change the social realities of interracial intolerance. This serious concern further points to the pressing role of psychologists as critics and change agents in the social order.

In spite of a critical tendency and expressed skepticism, which may be healthy facets of rationality, none has allowed the lack of unqualified optimism to stand in the way of taking affirmative action toward what is believed to be appropriate. Notwithstanding what he described as his explicit pessimism, Goldman wondered if the fact that he keeps fighting battles for change implies a kind of optimism. He considered his own belief in a moral obligation to the community at large to be a rationalization of emotions felt deep down, which, together with his convictions, may constitute a kind of faith. Sue spoke passionately of having faith in the ideas he works with and faith in the integrity of doing what he believes is right. Jill Reich considers herself a doer and a facilitator of group efforts. She expressed faith in society and the world, just as she has faith in psychology as a profession with enormous potential to give to human life. To her, the question of faith is a matter of consciousness of problems and perceived efficacy in overcoming the problems of one's era. Perhaps it is the sense of self-efficacy and collective agency that will help to strike a balance between optimism and otherwise pessimistic forecasts of the future.

One may ask, what evidence of noncognitive sources of rationality can be found in the moral commitments of this group of professionals? Indignation about social injustice, caring for human suffering, and empathy for the disadvantaged and the discriminated can be found in the stories told as well as the historical actions taken by the group. Without their thirst for knowledge and the intellectual power of their critical capacities, however, these psychologists might not have been able to develop and implement their own sense of rationality about the human condition. In my conversations with them, I have found each to be highly reflective about our existential concerns and the process of defining the place of the profession in the social order. It seems within the reach of their imagination and my own to conceive of a productive collective dialogue both among psychologists and with others who have a stake in the professions and our society.

If the reflective accounts of this group and my conversations with them are indicative of how this may be achieved, the search for common horizons does not seem impossible. Among the diverse perspectives and achievements of the present group are common commitments to the academic values of intellectual integrity and critical inquiry, as well as prosocial values in the service of human betterment. All have concerns about what is not right. All are supportive of diversity and inclusion. As Jill Reich sees it, the knowledge we seek and create enables democracy to thrive. We should incorporate diversity in all that we do. Tharp spoke at length in our interview about the inevitability of pluralism in the face of mass migration and changes in worldwide communication. People with different cultural expressions in living present modes of existence not intelligible to other groups, and this fact requires that we make an effort to understand such pluralism and to search for common ground. Unlike relativism, a critical pluralism entails the evaluation of different forms of diversity. Tharp believes that there is error as well as validity in every culture, and that the politically correct position that all individual and cultural forms of existence are equally good (i.e., an uncritical pluralism) is not viable in the long run. Without a respectful pluralism as a theme of social coherence and cultural integration, he fears that American society with its current popular culture will continue on a destructive path.

Considering the fact that certain institutions have permitted individual and corporate interests to prevail in recent decades, system changes and a radical overhaul of current institutions and practices are being suggested by some in the group. What is unclear is whether the requisite changes will come about through gradual evolution or revolutionary measures. For this group, psychologists and other professionals have an obligation to correct social inequities and environments that are not empowering of individuals and communities. Without necessarily being self-proclaimed liberationists, they envision a knowledge base and professional practices that serve emancipatory interests. Rationality is not only an instrumental form of scientific knowing but also an affective and embodied consciousness of our social nature and the freedoms and constraints of cultural living.

EXISTENTIAL CREATIVITY
AS VISIONS OF THE GOOD

What have we learned about creativity? Creativity as responses to problems of living and the social and cultural givens of human existence is found in every life story of achievement and every journey of identity development. Although each actor may assume a different role or choose a different project, all use as medium what is available from the cultural environment in navigating career/life courses and crafting professional/personal identities. It is the manner in which this process evolves that perhaps distinguishes different forms of creativity.

Consistent with research on creative persons, there is definitely in these cases an element of innovation and rejection of what has been the norm. Peterson, Goldman, and Sue were critical of existing traditions and the status quo. Each persisted in the face of opposition and applied creative energy to overcome resistance in implementing new ideas, journal policies, and models of education. Keogh and Tharp conceived of new theoretical possibilities, programs, and practices as alternatives to existing ones that have not adequately addressed problems. Reich and Altmaier pursued forms of applied research not typically well received in the traditional academy. They also attempted to create the conditions for collective problem discussion and problem solving in their lives as administrators and officers with organizational responsibilities. As Altmaier remarked, it is when she is able to bring about compromise and resolve conflicts between parties that she feels most creative. In such instances, the implication is that a collaborative approach has prevailed over competitive approaches to issues. Her own choices of research topics and venues were driven by inquisitiveness and the ability to follow her interests even when safer choices are available. The ability to turn down the temptation of power and prestige for what Tharp refers to as "one's time in the desert" also seems critical in maintaining a creative focus. Each of the psychologists has alluded to the necessity of overcoming professional hurdles and contending with personal costs in pursuing what is considered worthwhile.

There are learning experiences and personal qualities that contribute to the ability to achieve in exceptional ways. From the fertile soils of cultural diversity and apprenticeships in storytelling in his youth, we can surmise where Tharp the writer had taken root. In the underdeveloped environment of his hometown, Peterson learned that the world could be changed when improvement was needed. Jill Reich reported in our interview that she learned early to be self-reliant and to seek out opportunities to do what she wants. Her experience as a research assistant and her early exposure to the application of research to problems of high-risk infants seem to have given her a sense of efficacy in the role of an applied researcher. At the same time, her encounter with mothers who needed answers she could not give for the proper care of their at-risk children led to a realization that much more is needed to solve problems. In subsequent years, Reich became involved with creating early opportunities of research apprenticeship for students and worked with legislators on public policy concerning children and their families. Thus, creativity comes with the necessity of responding to real-life problems. Although I did not search for precursors of creativity in early life in every case, it appears that a mind-set that is accepting of ambiguity and encouraged in this respect, such as by a mentor in the case of Altmaier, may dispose one to more effective problem solving.

Ambiguity also is significant in the sense of the current flux of society and the uncertainty of what is called for by way of commitment. Tharp indicated that in being highly skeptical of the existing apparatus and action lines in the field of education at any given time, his response to ambiguity always has been to base his choice on the valuing of possibilities in making a difference. In other words, creativity is identified not so much with commitment to particular structures and solutions, but with the search for new possibilities itself as a value. Of all the informants, Tharp reported the strongest existential misgivings in contemplating choices he has made in renouncing other lives that he can fully imagine, including in this case the possibilities of pursuing his creative writing and filmmaking. He is acutely aware of the existential importance of moral choice, feeling that we are at a historical point of greater ambiguity than ever.

Developmentally, there is evidence of shifts and new self-knowledge as a benefit of experience. Sue's work illustrates attitudinal and affective changes over time from one of in-group promotion to an inclusive multiculturalism. In other words, creativity entails growth and self-transformation. In the process, the concomitant achievements have transformative effects on the environment. This could not have occurred without an openness to experience. Psychology as a discipline and profession is subject to changes in the world of which we are a part. Through inquiry and education that are responsive to these changes, Reich sees us as potentiating our own development. During the interviews, I was struck by the fact that many of the creative efforts of these individuals have gone unreported. As Reich explained, she and others like her are often too busy to write accounts of their experience with uncommon projects for publication and dissemination. With stories of personal learning and the creative process remaining untold, few lessons have been made available to others. Such accounts deserve greater attention in the professions and in the study of creativity, particularly because they involve transcending the creative constraints of existing arrangements in the professional environment.

I have noted previously the embedding context of extraordinary forms of generativity. Support, mentoring, and communities of collaboration constitute conditions of creativity that also should be considered. Tharp, Sue, and nearly everyone else in the group acknowledged the importance of community in maintaining a space of creativity and in sustaining individual efforts that go against the norm. Herein lies the dialectical significance of autonomy and community in creative ways of living. Creativity involves channeling our energies into forms of individual expression that are valued by a certain rational community in whom we have moral and epistemic confidence. Considering the development of psychology as a relatively autonomous profession, our cultural creativity still depends on how well we are integrated into the larger community, and to what extent our contributions are valued.

In terms of the participants' verbal definitions of creativity, the interviews produced responses such as approaching issues in a new way, having a vision of what could be, creating the context for conflict resolution and group problem solving, finding new ways of connecting ideas or serving as a bridge between separate domains, and "we have been creative in the way we have created our lives." As expected, excellence and high standards are associated with these examples of uncommon achievements. Apart from the obvious fact that this is a highly accomplished group honored for works of distinction, each person has striven for quality and high standards. The strength of commitment derives partly from what appears to be the intrinsic reward of a fine product, whether it is one's students in teaching or a program of one's creation. It is no accident that all have contributed as educators. What characterizes such commitments are goods internal to the activity rather than external goods. In this sense, one may consider creativity to be a special form of generativity. There is a willingness to take the long view and to build on projects that have cumulative impact. The individual chooses certain ends for intrinsic goods and not just for short-term outcomes that are rewarded by society. This points again to the link between creative living and the moral.

From the creative work and professional lives of these individuals, we can glean visions of the good toward which they are aimed. There is a boldness in envisioning, a realistic sense of efficacy, an investment in the process itself, and a quality of care and deep concern. Research questions are framed in terms of envisioned possibilities. Models and programs are developed to broaden options. New working structures are experimented with that enable learning and problem solving not possible before. Much satisfaction comes from being able to engage in the search for possibilities. The self-creation of identity projects entails in nearly every case a tension or working through of conflict that involves making value-based choices. Each choice, with its related practices and lived experiences, appears to have an engendering effect on the person's moral development. Although individual talents play an important role, creativity as observed here is not an intrapsychic phenomenon coming from a mysterious personal power It is a way of living that responds to what is given in the fabric of life, which in turn creates valued possibilities for living.

Moral ontology consists of the social living of cultural beings. This is captured by Tharp's depiction of his life work as an interest in understanding "otherness." Both in his creative writing and in developing an inclusive theoretical language for human experience, Tharp has shown us the prime motive of intersubjectivity. He left us with our paradoxical and delicate relationship with language in the human search for meaning in exercising existential creativity. As moral philosophers have come to realize, intersubjectivity and the language with which we interpret human experience and social action form the basis of morality. Our vulnerability and social nature by necessity call for an immanent normativity in living.

Returning to the issue of separation of ethical theory and practice, one may conclude that existential creativity, as the motivated enactment of visions of the good, bridges theory and practice in the ethical realm. The psychology of moral living illustrated in this multiple-case study can lend intelligibility and substance to concepts that otherwise would remain abstractions in moral philosophy. The clarity of action and self-consistency in the individual lives examined here reflect a synthetic unity that is perhaps characteristic of ethical understanding and practice.

CRITICAL VOICES AND
THE DECONSTRUCTION OF TEXT

In reaching the present set of interpretations, I am faced with the task of deconstructing the individual narratives and my own rendering of collective meanings. It would seem that the deconstruction of text should include not only the autobiographical accounts and the interviews but also the texts of living enacted by this group. The process of deconstruction can begin with the critical voices and subtexts of discontent present in these narratives.

One of the critical concerns is with the profession's lack of a unified value base from which to exercise moral leadership. Political and guild interests are apparent, for example, in the experiences of Altmaier, Reich, and Peterson with accreditation. Attempts to obtain collective agreement on standards of self-regulation and their implementation have been fraught with difficulties. Altmaier is critical of academic psychologists' tendency to replicate themselves in the education and training of students, as opposed to socializing students in more universal values of an epistemic and social nature. These tendencies and hierarchical relations represent questionable motifs in the academic career culture. A related critical concern is our self-justification as a profession. What kinds of social roles will we have if psychology continues to avoid value issues in our scientific teachings? How could we claim special knowledge when the foundations of our historical authority are in question, and when our methods have not always yielded useful knowledge? Reich is particularly concerned about the profession losing sight of the interrelationships among teaching, research, and service. The separation of these activities has made it more difficult for psychologists to ask for and expect political or public support. Peterson considers it irresponsible of the profession to produce large numbers of practitioners without sufficient attention to program standards and the quality of graduates. Tharp and Keogh are weary of the proliferation of practice and the seeming lack of concern on the part of practitioners with the critical evaluation of their knowledge base and claims of effectiveness.

The subtext seems to be that the viability of the profession depends on whether the lack of reflexive evaluation and self-monitoring can be balanced by the development of a critical capacity that is inherent in the cognitive values of the academic tradition. There is a concern that rationality is losing ground, with a concomitant mistrust of practices that are not informed by knowledge and appropriate values. There is also the opinion that within both psychology and society at large, the cultural capabilities for collective agency have been undermined. At the same time, a critical pluralism, not relativism, is valued as a strength. Peterson, Goldman, Sue, and Tharp have spoken against the forces of hegemony that disempower minorities. They remind us that we first have to be able to understand and live with our own diversity. They also cast doubt on the present organizational ethos and existing system mechanisms in terms of supporting change. Keogh challenges the assumption of sameness and calls attention to the social-ecological conditions that contribute to individual differences. She has realized the power of asking questions about the status quo. She and Altmaier have been critical of social attitudes and practices that limit the participation of women.

Part of the unease with the profession comes from the sense that it should be making a greater difference in a troubled and divided world. Sue feels that ethnic wars and racial tensions are signs that the world is on a dangerous collision course. Psychology and society need to come to terms with multiculturalism. Goldman refers to the human drive for power, material gains, and technological progress and our inability to psychologically and sociologically keep pace with such ways of living. He attributes the rise of fundamentalism and other forms of guru worship to fear and a desire for the security offered by authoritative rules. Although he prefers a communal process of rational problem solving, he is doubtful that most people will trust in the process because they mistrust others with different worldviews.

If there is no identity of value stances in contemporary society, there is also no single answer as to the proper means of enhancing ethical rationality. For the most part, this group continues to believe in the intellectual powers of education and inquiry, though with qualified faith in the models of knowledge traditionally found in psychology as a discipline. Tharp and others propose a broadening of horizons to include the discourse and methods of other disciplines. The hope may be that the plurality of creative means emergent from multidisciplinary endeavors can offer some possibilities of cultural integration and reflexive understanding that are presently lacking. In their mediating roles, Reich and Altmaier view conflicts as opportunities for productive compromise. This type of sensibility seems aimed at facilitating visions of the good that encourage people to set aside individual agendas for the collective. Interdependency as an existential given is clearly understood.

This is not to overstate the sense of community experienced by the group, particularly among fellow psychologists. Goldman and Sue have been confronted with problems of inclusiveness and view themselves as minorities. They find community with others who share similar values, such as in working for environmental issues, civil liberties, and human rights. Tharp expressed disappointment over the minimal sense of affiliation he feels toward psychology as a profession, something he never expected at this point in his life. He has, however, created his own community of coworkers among a circle of researchers and professionals who are committed to educational reform. Community is bound not just by interests but also by common values. A psychological sense of community is sustained by commitment to the present and future purposes of a larger collective. In creating one's own society at a time of fragmentation and alienation, the metaphor followed is that of reconstruction.

To what extent this group has appropriately rested our future on communitarian interests is for the reader to decide. It is fair to ask of any communitarian proposal, which community and what kind of values and common interests are being represented. A morally domineering monolithic community may be no more desirable than an uncritical pluralistic community. In the absence of consensual contexts of evaluation, all manners of self-justification can be at risk of self-absorption and self-promotion. For the present group of psychologists, the lack of a universal framework of moral understanding does not seem to be as disconcerting as the difficulties of communal dialogue in search of common horizons.

Freedom of debate and serious dialogue have diminished in the politically correct climate of the American academy. It is feared that the formal texts of the professions may not be adequate forums for communal discourse. Professional journals and editorial practices modulate the extent of critical dialogue and the legitimization of voice as well as knowledge claims. Methodolatry and hegemony not only constrain creativity but also set limits on the communal process by favoring only certain discourse practices and subcultures. We need to examine other forms of text—those living texts of everyday practices that are not solely accountable to the institutions from which they derive legitimacy, but are accountable to the larger human community.

The life texts available here point to affective sources of commitment to the social, in those who have experienced the wholesomeness of communal living and service to others in early life, as well as those who have experienced marginalization and discrimination by society. Each of these social actors has found community to sustain creative projects that are in the service of the community at large while also engendering of identity. Their ways of living are contrary to liberal assumptions of an individual autonomy that centers on the individualistic self away from community. A communitarian ontology, however, does not guarantee the attainment of communitarian ideals, unless there is the appropriate type of intentionality and collective agency. Each person in this group is a generative professional, capable not only of reflective existential dialogue but also of exercising agency in collaborative problem finding and problem solving in the interest of the community at large. The texts of living they present hold up as tenaciously as the moral arguments in their autobiographical narratives. No further recounting is necessary.

CHAPTER 10

Epistemic and Moral Viability in the Postmodern Age

LISA TSOI HOSHMAND

This project has been an attempt to link issues of professional knowledge and individual commitment with the cultural and the social, in the hope of bringing realism to theories on moral development and moral existence. Having summarized what was learned, I would like to place the project in the context of the philosophical and social discourse that has influenced my thinking. The unease that led me to embark on this project and to search for understanding from others in the profession stems from the ambiguities of contemporary life. The restraint I have found necessary in interpreting the postmodern condition comes from a simultaneous awareness of its promise and perils.

THE POSTMODERN CONTEXT

The Postmodern age (Lyotard, 1984) has been viewed as providing a liberalizing condition of openness and opportunity for change, as well as causing social disruption and perpetuating those aspects of modern life that are questionable. It is also a time when human society is showing a high degree of differentiation. As universal foundations give way to pluralistic conceptions of human possibilities, ideas about what is appropriate in all aspects of life have been radically transformed. The cultural forces of a divergent pluralism, coupled with a relativistic climate, have resulted in an attenuation of communal sources of unity (Selznick, 1992). Some charge that postmodernism has been ahistorical and nihilistic in attitude, and has inadvertently supported unproductive skepticism and inaction where commitment is needed. Others feel that the intellectual and social freedom as well as valuing of change that it promises are necessary for progress. These different perspectives on postmodernism are associated with different forms of relativism, ranging from the extreme to more moderate positions (Harré & Krausz, 1996). Whereas extreme relativism implies that it is impossible and inappropriate to evaluate or reconcile incompatible worldviews, a weaker form of relativism allows for the possibility of evaluative judgments in the negotiation of horizons.

In the area of knowledge, because judgments about claims of knowledge and professional practices based on such knowledge involve the evaluation of theories and other normative considerations, we are faced with issues of justification. (Thus, this project is partly aimed at clarifying the positions that can be taken on matters of knowledge.) The postmodern rejection of monistic theories and universal foundations has undermined preexisting systems of justification in a way that makes it difficult to make epistemic judgments. Philosophers of science have framed this as a problem of incommensurability, in that it is impossible to evaluate and compare theoretical claims that are based on incompatible conceptual systems and frames of reference.

The epistemological concerns arising from relativism as an alternative to foundationalism have been approached, respectively, from a social constructionist and a pragmatist position (Hoshmand, 1994). Rather than assume universal methods and standards of knowledge, multiple practices and interpretive possibilities are granted on the basis of social construction. Yet, knowledge has to be fallible. A strong form of relativism or a totally divergent pluralism whereby different groups hold different epistemic criteria and standards is problematic in rendering judgments (Harris, 1992; Hoshmand & Martin, 1994). The pragmatist view is that a contingent set of meta criteria derived from the experience of practice may be helpful in adjudicating knowledge claims and evaluating progress (Bernstein, 1983; Margolis, 1991). This view is consistent with a naturalistic approach to the evolution of research praxis and how issues of knowledge are dealt with in inquiry with the benefit of experience (Hoshmand & Martin, 1995).

In a similar vein, the discussion of morality has shifted from a universal principle-based ethics to a contextualized relativism. Traditional institutions have not been replaced adequately by technocratic values of logical efficiency or the ethics of individualism in modern Western societies. With the postmodern debunking of universal foundations and standards, social theorists and moral philosophers, like philosophers of knowledge, are faced with the same problem of finding a viable basis of commitment. This parallel problem is made acute by the fact that philosophers of science have provided only partial answers to the problem of epistemic justification. Scientific principles and procedural norms do not address directly how the application of knowledge affects human society. As stated in the first chapter, if knowledge making is motivated by non-epistemic values and transcendental goals, there comes a point when we have to move from considering only epistemic standards to considering broadly philosophical and axiological concerns.

This reaching beyond what is ordinarily the discourse of science-based disciplines and the philosophy of science has been viewed with suspicion by those who fear the return of metaphysics. The modern age of science has left a certain degree of skepticism toward metaphysical theses in Western industrialized societies. This mistrust of metaphysics has extended to metanarratives in general, with consequences for the discussion of normative issues. As critics in the humanities and the social sciences try to deconstruct the grand narratives of their disciplines to question their implicit assumptions and value orientations, their voices tend to be marginalized in the dominant discourse. Commenting on this state of affairs involves discourse about discourse (or meta-discourse), which is also necessary for enabling coordinated social action. As reported by the professionals in this project, however, it has been difficult to find a common language, acceptable to all points of view, with which to negotiate differences in perspective such as encountered in professional life.

Thus, the problems of judgment are compounded by difficulties in discourse across diverse epistemic and moral communities. Viability of judgment is not simply a matter of settling differences in our definition of rationality. When intelligibility is desired in epistemic and moral decisions, neither a normative form of rationalism nor a contextual relativism has been found adequate (Bohman & Kelly, 1996; Hollis & Lukes, 1982). This is because all understanding is perspectival and evaluative. Conditions of truth as well as conditions of right and wrong are linked to human communication and the negotiation of horizons. A tolerant climate that encourages open dialogue and fair-minded criticism is necessary to sustain epistemic and moral discourse (Myerson, 1994). Also necessary is a special effort to understand the goals and actions of others who may not necessarily share our own values and standards. This type of intersubjectivity, though not easy to achieve, is an essential human basis for rationality. I have argued in a previous article, proposing cultural psychology as a metatheory and a form of meta-discourse (Hoshmand, 1996), that in the absence of universal frames of reference we still have to endorse certain criteria as if they matter. How particular values and symbolic processes enter into normative interpretations and judgments in a communal context, and whether epistemic and moral viability can be reinstated, have been the subjects of ongoing debate.

COMMUNITARIAN, HERMENEUTIC, AND PRAGMATIST PROPOSALS

To reiterate, a common problem in the current discourses on epistemology and moral ontology is that the postmodern rejection of universal standards has made it difficult to uphold particular forms of judgment or to justify one's commitment to particular positions. Alternatives to universalist standards are likely to be tangled with the logical and social problems of relativism. Even as we undertake a contingent evaluation of institutionalized practices and their foundational assumptions, we are not free of the problems of judgment. The question becomes whether it is possible to assert what is good, without appealing to transcendental norms or invoking certain ideals that are ideological and political as well. Social theorists from the Frankfurt school and the French poststructuralists are divided on how this question can be answered.

Habermas (1979, 1984) located normative possibilities in ideal forms of interpretive and discursive communities. Presuming the ideological norm of democratic participation, he conceived of an ideal free speech situation as enabling members of a community to work together in negotiating common goods. Habermas's communitarian proposal based on communicative rationality was criticized by Lyotard (1984), who considered all metanarratives and grand narratives as rhetorical language games that legitimate particular forms of truth. In the view of the poststructuralists, not only are ideals of free speech and democratic participation constrained by the realities of power differentials in everyday life, but those who offer critical insights and alternative interpretations of social realities may assume an elitist position. Habermas (1990), on the other hand, proffered the hopes of a gradually evolved communicative ideal that would transcend political community. The issue remains as to whether a given community is capable of collaborating for the sake of common goods without neglecting the welfare of less vocal members or society at large. (This is the question I am posing to my own profession and other professions with this project.)

Blaug (1996) cautioned that discursive democracy as a utopian ideal may not be a panacea for hermeneutic failures. Issues of judgment cannot be settled purely at the level of language games or rhetorical analysis in the face of irreducible plurality. Regarding the adjudication of knowledge claims, Bhaskar (1979) proposed a distinction between epistemic relativism and judgmental relativism, suggesting that we can be pluralistic in method and relativistic in standards without giving up all basis of judgment. The pragmatist view on pluralism is that epistemic and moral judgments, even if contingent and evolving, can be linked to concrete circumstances of living and cultural constructions of the human condition. Besides engaging in communal dialogue as a way of developing intersubjectivity, we have to consider the realistic effects of human action in social context. It is for these reasons that in both the epistemic and the moral domains, naturalistic study of human intentions and practices, with grounding in our sociality and cultural existence, seems appropriate as attempted here.

In grounding all judgments in cultural existence, the hermeneutic tradition (Gadamer, 1975) claims that human beings are governed less by universal principles than by particular histories as understood within particular cultural assumptions that can be evaluated critically. The cultural, hermeneutic approach adopted here moves from a language-analytic philosophy to empirical inquiry into the actual cultural pragmatics of our epistemic and moral discourse. As Ricoeur (1980) argued, it is the concrete utility and existential function of a given text that matters in life. The study of cultural pragmatics means using a "vocabulary of practice rather than of theory, of action rather than contemplation" (Rorty, 1982, p. 162). Also very important is that "the pragmatist knows no better way to explain his convictions than to remind his interlocutor of the position they both are in, the contingent starting points they both share" (Rorty, 1982, pp. 173-174). This pragmatist view of cultural living, which has informed the present project, retains a contingent form of transcendental argument without presuming an immutability of cultural norms and practices.

The fact that we live in a culturally diverse postmodern world places us in what the philosopher Taylor (1989) referred to as an inescapable space of moral questioning. Our contributing authors acknowledge the current lack of cultural integration and moral coherence. From the standpoint of multiculturalism, communal consciousness and dialogue are necessary to find appropriate ways of being in a pluralistic society and world order. The philosophical and value base of multiculturalism itself (Fowers & Richardson, 1996) has been contentious because trust in an interpretive framework proposed by others does not come readily. Again, reflexive understanding of our cultural ways of knowing and being may furnish a contingent form of meta understanding (Hoshmand, 1996). This understanding has to be embodied, in the phenomenological sense, and grounded in the realities of everyday living. A phenomenological ethics, which I mentioned in Chapter 1, complements the cultural hermeneutic proposal by stressing that moral consciousness evolves from the natural process of living with our human predicament.

LOCATING THE PRESENT PROJECT

In summary of the various proposals, the cultural hermeneutic approach to moral ontology parallels naturalized epistemology and pragmatism as an answer to how we can avoid the extremes of dogmatism and relativism in rendering judgments in the realm of knowledge (Hoshmand & Martin, 1995). It enables us to reframe the philosopher's mistrust of both authoritarian moralism and relativistic subjectivism as questions about social practices and human consciousness. In the absence of cultural unity and universal standards of rationality, the ontological assumptions of our sociality and capacity for self-interpretation would still hold as conceptual necessities. The ways by which a group structures and implements particular visions of moral coexistence, and how individuals create their identities within the constraints and resources of their changing cultural environment, can be subject to cultural psychological study (Hoshmand, 1996; Hoshmand & Ho, 1995).

The present project is an attempt at understanding professional identity in relation to moral and epistemic commitments within the embedding context of the professional, sociocultural, and political realities of a person's life. To the extent that there are varied intentions, values, and ongoing debates within the professional community and the larger community, issues of judgment and consensus must be considered in a critical, hermeneutic fashion. To direct social and philosophical critique at any study of moral ontology is consistent with the conception of lived experience as a social and reflexive process. Gadamer (1976) considered philosophical hermeneutics an ontological discipline that examines the fundamental conditions of living underlying our efforts to make sense of human existence. In comprehending another person's story or action, no one has final authority. Understanding is "an event over which the interpreting subject does not ultimately preside" (p. xi). Jameson (1981) further cautioned that we do not reduce a person's narrative to a single interpretation according to a dominant metanarrative or the paradigm of another narrative as a master code (p. 22). We may impoverish it and our interpretive understanding by doing so. This point of view is consistent with the recognition that social interpretation and moral coexistence imply an irreducible plurality. It is also consistent with the view of culture as always multivocal and overdetermined (Rabinow & Sullivan, 1987). These views have set the context for presenting the narratives and interpretive summary in this volume.

If there is no privileged perspective or final recounting, how does one evaluate a given set of interpretations such as those emergent from the present project? It would seem that a certain dialectic is involved in juxtapositioning the narrator's point of view and other perspectives that aim to take the process of interpretation beyond the horizon of the person's own existential situation. The evaluator's role is to explicate the context and totality of cultural meanings, being cognizant of the fact that one's inquiry is caught in the same web of signification while possibly changing and expanding it. In assuming that narrated texts of identity are individual attempts to cope with existential problems and moral conflicts, we also grant that there is a referential dimension to such texts as cultural constructions. I called attention in the previous chapter to the texts of living behind the autobiographical narratives. Each of the professionals included here has demonstrated the effective enactment of epistemic and moral commitments in living with the postmodern condition.

A dialectic of pessimism and optimism, experienced by critical theorists who have attempted to deconstruct and critique cultural texts (see Jay, 1973), also is found in the present project. We can hope that a reconstructive process will be possible with new forms of intersubjectivity, as Gadamer (1987) emphasized, that unify ethics, social practices, and contingent professional knowledge.

IMPLICATIONS FOR EDUCATION AND PROFESSIONAL SOCIALIZATION

The foregoing and what has been learned in this project have implications for education and professional socialization, not only in psychology but also in related fields and other professions. Given the embeddedness of any knowledge enterprise, as educators we have to examine continuously the assumptions and models of knowledge that inform our efforts, as well as the moral implications of our practices in particular political and sociocultural contexts. If we are to follow a pragmatist approach to knowledge, our curriculum and teaching should be evaluated constantly in terms of developing problem-solving abilities and socially relevant knowledge. Most educators would also agree that changing demographics and technological advances call for the reform of schooling and educational practices at all levels. As some of our participants noted, in responding to diversity and the need to integrate technology with multidisciplinary knowledge, we have to work toward reducing the likely discrepancies between our rhetoric and actual practice in support of substantive and system-level changes.

In the case of training for professional psychologists, the unresolved polemics about PhD versus PsyD models suggest not only continuing difficulties with understanding the evolving historical contexts and values associated with each approach but also an inability to acknowledge the strengths and weaknesses of both models as implemented. These kinds of difficulties, seen in graduate education and other levels of schooling, are indicative of the general problems of communal discourse. They reflect, as well, problems in the relationship between society and the professions in which social accountability and ethics are increasingly compromised by political power structures and economic arrangements. The points made by the group of educators here, in terms of integrating service values into all aspects of professional work and emphasizing a communal ethic of collaboration, are well taken.

In spite of well-intentioned educational efforts and examples of professional integrity in every field, the current difficulties in education and professional socialization stem from the lack of a shared context of values. Although disciplinary norms of scholarship and professional codes of conduct can provide some guidance, they are no substitute for genuine epistemic and moral dialogue, nor can they have as much impact as the socialization provided daily in academic institutions and professional subcultures. Until members of every academic and professional education program can engage in critical communal dialogue, we will not have sufficient standards of judgment or clarity of mutual actions. The purpose of such dialogue would be to develop genuinely shared principles and values as a context not only for teaching and learning but for all interactions that are otherwise governed by political and economic considerations. In addition, until there are mutually acceptable values informing the relationship between the professions and the public, there will be no firm basis of accountability. These values would have to extend beyond the utilitarian and technocratic to the broadly humanitarian and prosocial.

The kinds of serious communal dialogue and informed discussion needed will entail attention to process and personal courage to engage in interactions that may involve political and social risks. They will require reflexivity and a form of rationality that is sensitive to cultural differences and political constraints on social discourse. Knowledge as a social enterprise requires ways of knowing and relating that are ethical, and positions of knowing that are worthy of virtuous citizens. To the extent that educators and professionals can model these qualities and an ethic of care in their interactions with colleagues and students, and to the degree that those with less of a voice can be empowered, we may be able to promote such ideals in serving the public.

FUTURE DIRECTIONS

Would it still be possible for us to have any pancultural, universal human standards? Some may appeal to transcendental ideals from their particular cultural heritage, while others look toward the ongoing discourse of their symbolic communities and the changing cultural landscape in setting the boundary conditions of rationality. A critical pluralism, however, implies that relative perspectives are subject to evaluation and comparison. Furthermore, whether institutions and practices are developed to implement a priori standards or contingent ideals, they have to operate within our existential givens. From an empirical, historicist standpoint, these boundary conditions may be regarded as human constants to the extent that they are found in diverse modes of consciousness and ways of life.

It remains for social scientists and cultural historians to bridge the gap of philosophical theorizing about our moral potentials—with empirical understanding of how communities provide symbolic socialization and institutional practices for negotiating and implementing shared standards of accountability; how individuals appropriate meanings and action alternatives from an increasingly pluralistic consciousness that is continuously self-interpreted and self-created; and whether particular cultures and societies are capable of maintaining critical dialogue, a condition that some of us consider necessary for epistemic and moral viability. An important part of the process will consist of the critical evaluation of our ideas, institutions, and practices for their adverse effects as well as contributions to the social good. With proper socialization and effective moral dialogue, the culture of particular professions (though derived from the society to which they belong) conceivably can help to shape the values and practices of society at large—through the actions of its members and its contribution to normative societal discourse. This may represent a form of creativity in the professions that transcends technological and economic interests.

As demonstrated by the participants in this project, professional identity has to be fashioned creatively within the dialectics of freedom and constraint in the postmodern context. Transcendence and reasoned commitment are possible with the help of critical, caring communities. Epistemic and moral viability can be attained by developing and improving on our sources of intersubjectivity.

Epilogue

This project has involved probing ultimate questions in an attempt to understand the transcendental goals of professional lives and how a number of psychologists, in this case, have fashioned their identities in the context of 20th-century society. The individual narratives and dialogues are a reflection of the culture and issues of American psychology, as well as the broader concerns of the times. My hope is that personal reflections and communal dialogues will be stimulated, not only in psychology but also in other professions that aspire to improve the human condition through knowledge, ideas, and purposive action.

The text presented for consideration has been subject to a certain degree of deconstruction. Further critical analyses may prove useful, as suggested by one of the contributing authors after reading the summary chapter. My own experience of the dialectic of hope and doubt in seeing both possibilities and failings in social living is resonated by the authors, yet we can take comfort in sharing common concerns and developing intersubjectivity as a basis on which to build the future.

By grounding ourselves in the narrative meanings and lived realities of identity projects, I hope that we have begun to bridge the divide between moral philosophy and practice. To understand the moral is to become fully attuned to the other. In using primarily the language of the social sciences to describe this experience and the understanding that ensues, I have felt some limitations. Perhaps another time and another medium might find me suitably in awe and wonder of the subject.

References

Albee, G. W. (1986). Toward a just society: Lessons from observations on the primary prevention of psychopathology. *American Psychologist, 41,* 891-898.

Allport, G. W. (1968). *The person in psychology: Selected essays.* Boston: Beacon.

Arasteh, A. R., & Arasteh, J. D. (1976). *Creativity in human development.* New York: John Wiley.

Aristotle. (1980). *The Nichomachean ethics* (D. Ross, Trans.). Oxford, UK: Oxford University Press.

Bakhtin, M. M. (1973). *Problems of Dostoevsky's poetics* (2nd ed.; R. W. Rostel, Trans.). Ann Arbor, MI: Ardis.

Bakhtin, M. M. (1981). *The dialogic imagination: Four essays by M. M. Bakhtin* (M. Holoquist, Ed., C. Emerson & M. Holoquist Trans.). Austin: University of Texas Press.

Baldwin, R., & Blackburn, R. (1981). The academic career in developmental perspective. *Journal of Higher Education, 52,* 598-614.

Bandura, A. (1991). Social cognitive theory of moral thought and action. In W. M. Kurtines & J. L. Gewirtz (Eds.), *Handbook of moral behavior and development: Vol. 1. Theory* (pp. 45-103). Hillsdale, NJ: Lawrence Erlbaum.

Bateson, M. C. (1989). *Composing a life.* New York: Atlantic Monthly Press.

Baumrind, D. (1992). Leading an examined life: The moral dimension of daily conduct. In W. M. Kurtines, M. Azmitia, & J. L. Gewirtz (Eds.), *The role of values in psychology and human development* (pp. 239-280). New York: John Wiley.

Becher, T. (1989). *Academic tribes and territories: Intellectual inquiry and the cultures of the disciplines.* Milton Keynes, UK: Open University Press.

Bellah, R. N., Madsen, R., Sullivan, W. M., Swidler, A., & Tipton, S. M. (1985). *Habits of the heart: Individualism and commitment in American life.* Berkeley: University of California Press.

Bernstein, R. J. (1983). *Beyond objectivism and relativism: Science, hermeneutics, and praxis.* Philadelphia: University of Pennsylvania Press.

Bersoff, D. N. (1996). The virtue of principle ethics. *The Counseling Psychologist, 24,* 78-85.

Bhaskar, R. (1979). *The possibility of Naturalism: A critique of the contemporary human sciences.* Brighton, UK: Harvester Press.

Blasi, A. (1980). Bridging moral cognition and moral action: A critical review of the literature. *Psychological Bulletin, 88,* 1-45.

Blaug, R. (1996). New theories of discursive democracy. *Philosophy and Social Criticism, 22,* 49-80.

Bohman, J., & Kelly, T. (1996). Intelligibility, rationality, and comparison. *Philosophy and Social Criticism, 22,* 81-100.

Bromley, D. B. (1986). *The case-study method in psychology and related disciplines.* New York: John Wiley.

Brown, L. M., Tappan, M. B., Gilligan, C., Miller, B. A., & Argyris, D. E. (1989). Interpreting narratives of real-life moral conflict and choice. In M. H. Packer & R. B. Addison (Eds.), *Entering the circle: Hermeneutic investigation in psychology* (pp. 141-164). Albany: State University of New York Press.

Bruner, J. (1962). *On knowing: Essays for the left hand.* Cambridge, MA: Belknap Press of the Harvard University Press.

Bruner, J. (1983). *In search of mind: Essays in autobiography.* New York: Harper & Row.

Bruner, J. (1990). *Acts of meaning.* Cambridge, MA: Harvard University Press.

Campbell, D. T. (1975). "Degrees of freedom" and the case study. *Comparative Political Studies, 8,* 178-193.

Campbell, D. T. (1979). A tribal model of social system vehicle carrying scientific knowledge. *Knowledge: Creation, Diffusion, Utilization, 1,* 181-201.

Carlson, R. (1988). Exemplary lives: The uses of psychobiography for theory development. *Journal of Personality, 56,* 105-134.

Clark, B. R. (1987). *The academic life: Small worlds, different worlds.* Princeton, NJ: Carnegie Endowment for the Advancement of Teaching.

Cohen, D. (1995). *Psychologists on psychology* (2nd ed.). New York: Routledge.

Colby, A. (1994). Case studies of exceptional people: What can they teach us? *Journal of Narrative and Life History, 4,* 353-365.

Colby, A., & Damon, W. (1992). *Some do care: Contemporary lives of moral commitment.* New York: Free Press.

Cole, M. (1988). Cross-cultural research in the socio-historical tradition. *Human Development, 31,* 137-157.

Coupland, N., & Nussbaum, J. F. (1992). *Discourse and life-span development.* Newbury Park, CA: Sage.

Cushman, P. (1990). Why the self is empty: Toward a historically situated psychology. *American Psychologist, 45,* 599-611.

Cushman, P. (1993). Psychotherapy as moral discourse. *Journal of Theoretical and Philosophical Psychology, 13,* 103-113.

Deutsch, E. (1992). *Creative being: The crafting of person and world.* Honolulu: University of Hawaii Press.

Dokecki, P. R. (1995). *The tragicomic professional: Basic considerations for ethical reflective-generative practice.* Pittsburgh, PA: Duquesne University Press.

Eagle, M. N., & Wolitzky, D. L. (1995). Psychoanalytic theories of psychotherapy. In D. K. Freedheim (Ed.), *History of psychotherapy: A century of change.* Washington, DC: American Psychological Association.

Elms, A. C. (1994). *Uncovering lives: The uneasy alliance of biography and psychology.* New York: Oxford University Press.

Erikson, E. H. (1962). *Young man Luther: A study in psychoanalysis and history.* New York: Norton.

Erikson, E. H. (1969). *Gandhi's truth: On the origins of militant nonviolence.* New York: Norton.

Erikson, E. H. (1975). *Life history and the historical moment.* New York: Norton.

Erikson, E. H. (1980). *Identity and the life cycle.* New York: Norton.

Fowers, B. J., & Richardson, F. C. (1996). Why is multiculturalism good? *American Psychologist, 51,* 609-621.

Fox, D., & Prilleltensky, I. (Eds.). (1997). *Critical psychology.* London: Sage.

Fuller, S. (1992). Epistemology radically naturalized. In R. Giere (Ed.), *Cognitive models of science* (pp. 427-459). Minneapolis: University of Minnesota Press.

Gadamer, H. (1975). *Truth and method* (G. Barden & J. Cumming, Trans.). New York: Seabury.

Gadamer, H. G. (1976). *Philosophical hermeneutics* (D. E. Linge, Ed. and Trans.). New York: Pantheon.

Gadamer, H. G. (1987). The problem of historical consciousness. In P. Rabinow & W. M. Sullivan (Eds.), *Interpretive social science* (pp. 83-140). Berkeley: University of California Press.

Geertz, C. (1973). *The interpretation of cultures.* New York: Basic Books.

Gergen, K. J. (1991). *The saturated self: Dilemmas of identity in contemporary life.* New York: Basic Books.

Gergen, M. (1990). Finished at 40: Women's development within the patriarchy. *Psychology of Women Quarterly, 14,* 471-493.

Giddens, A. (1991). *Modernity and iaentity: Self and society in the late modern age.* Stanford, CA: Stanford University Press.

Gilligan, C. (1988). *Mapping the moral domain: A contribution of women's thinking to psychology and education.* Cambridge, MA: Harvard University Press.

Gilligan, C. (1993). *In a different voice: Psychological theory and women's development* (rev. ed.). Cambridge, MA: Harvard University Press.

Gruber, H. E. (1988). The evolving-systems approach to creative work. *Creativity Research Journal, 1,* 27-51.

Gubrium, J. F., & Holstein, J. A. (1995). Biographical work and new ethnography. In R. Josselson & A. Lieblich (Eds.), *Interpreting experience: The narrative study of lives* (Vol. 3, pp. 45-58). Thousand Oaks, CA: Sage.

Habermas, J. (1979). *Communication and the evolution of society.* Boston: Beacon.

Habermas, J. (1984). *Theory of communicative action: Vol. 1. Reason and rationality in society* (E. McCarthy, Trans.). Boston: Beacon.

Habermas, J. (1990). *Moral consciousness and communicative action.* Cambridge, MA: MIT Press.

Hare-Mustin, R. T. (1994). Uncovering clues, discovering change. In D. J. Lee (Ed.), *Life and story: Autobiographies for a narrative psychology* (pp. 143-160). Westport, CT: Praeger.

Harré, R. (1983). *Personal being.* Oxford, UK: Basil Blackwell.

Harré, R., & Krausz, M. (1996). *Varieties of relativism.* Oxford, UK: Basil Blackwell.

Harris, J. F. (1992). *Against relativism: A philosophical defense of method.* La Salle, IL: Open Court.

Heller, T. C., Sosnia, M., & Wellber, D. (1987). *Reconstructing individualism, autonomy, individuality, and the self in Western thought.* Stanford, CA: Stanford University Press.

Hermans, H.J.M. (1988). On the integration of idiographic and nomothetic research method in the study of personal meaning. *Journal of Personality, 56,* 785-812.

Hermans, H.J.M., & Hermans-Jansen, E. (1995). *Self-narratives: The construction of meaning in psychotherapy.* New York: Guilford.

Hermans, H.J.M., & Kempen, H.J.G. (1993). *The dialogical self: Meaning as movement.* San Diego, CA: Academic Press.

Hermans, H.J.M., Rijks, T. I., & Kempen, H. J. G. (1993). Imaginal dialogues in the self: Theory and method. *Journal of Personality, 61,* 207-236.

Hermans, H.J.M., & Van Gilst, W. (1991). Self-narrative and collective myth: An analysis of the Narcissus story. *Canadian Journal of Behavioral Science, 23,* 423-440.

Heshusius, L. (1994). Freeing ourselves from objectivity: Managing subjectivity or turning toward a participatory mode of consciousness? *Educational Researcher, 23,* 15-22.

Ho, D.Y.F. (1993). Toward an Asian social psychology: Relational orientation. In U. Kim & J. Berry (Eds.), *Indigenous psychologies: Research and experience in cultural context* (pp. 240-259). Newbury Park, CA: Sage.

Hogan, R., Johnson, J. A., & Emler, N. P. (1978). A socioanalytic theory of moral development. In W. Damon (Ed.), *Moral development* (pp. 1-18). San Francisco: Jossey-Bass.

Hollis, M., & Lukes, S. (Eds.). (1982). *Rationality and relativism.* Cambridge, MA: MIT Press.

Horney, K. (1950). *Neurosis and human growth.* New York: Norton.

Hoshmand, L. T. (1994). *Orientation to inquiry in a reflective professional psychology.* Albany: State University of New York Press.

Hoshmand, L. T. (1996). Cultural psychology as metatheory. *Journal of Theoretical and Philosophical Psychology, 16,* 30-48.

Hoshmand, L. T., & Ho, D.Y.F. (1995). Moral dimensions of selfhood: Chinese traditions and cultural change. *World Psychology, 1,* 47-69.

Hoshmand, L. T., & Martin, J. (1994). Naturalizing the epistemology of psychological research. *Journal of Theoretical and Philosophical Psychology, 14,* 171-189.

Hoshmand, L. T., & Martin, J. (Eds.). (1995). *Research as praxis: Lessons from programmatic research in therapeutic psychology.* New York: Teachers College Press.

Hoshmand, L. T., & Polkinghorne, D. E. (1992). Redefining the science-practice relationship and professional training. *American Psychologist, 47,* 55-66.

Howard, G. S. (1985). The role of values in the science of psychology. *American Psychologist, 40,* 255-265.

Howard, G. S. (1989). *A tale of two stories.* Notre Dame, IN: Academic Publishing.

Howard, G. S. (1996). *Understanding human nature.* Notre Dame, IN: Academic Publishing.

Howard, G. S., Maerlender, A. C., Myers, P. R., & Curtin, T. D. (1992). In stories we trust: Studies of the validity of autobiographies. *Journal of Counseling Psychology, 39,* 398-405.

Howe, M. J. (1982). Biographical evidence and the development of outstanding individuals. *American Psychologist, 37,* 1071-1081.

Jacobs, J. A. (1989). *Virtue and self-knowledge.* Englewood Cliffs, NJ: Prentice Hall.

Jameson, F. (1981). *The political unconscious: Narrative as a socially symbolic act.* Ithaca, NY: Cornell University Press.

Jay, M. (1973). *The dialectical imagination: A history of the Frankfurt school and the Institute of Social Research, 1923-1950.* Boston: Little, Brown.

Josselson, R. (1987). *Finding herself: Pathways to identity development in women.* San Francisco: Jossey-Bass.

Josselson, R. (Ed.). (1996). *Ethics and process in the narrative study of lives* (Vol. 4). Thousand Oaks, CA: Sage.

Josselson, R., & Lieblich, A. (Eds.). (1993). *Narratives and lives: New approaches to traditional issues* (Vol. 1). Thousand Oaks, CA: Sage.

Josselson, R., & Lieblich, A. (Eds.). (1995). *Interpreting experience: The narrative study of lives* (Vol. 3). Thousand Oaks, CA: Sage.

Jung, C. G. (1933). *Modern man in search of a soul.* New York: Harcourt.

Jung, C. G. (1961). *Memories, dreams, recollections.* New York: Vintage.

Keller, P. A. (Ed.). (1994). *Academic paths: Career decision and experiences of psychologists.* Hillsdale, NJ: Lawrence Erlbaum.

Kelman, H. (1963). Oriental psychological processes and creativity. *American Journal of Psycho-analysis, 23,* 67-84.

Kitchener, K. S. (1996). There is more to ethics than principles. *The Counseling Psychologist, 24,* 92-97.

Kohlberg, L. (1984). *Essays on moral development: Vol. 2. The psychology of moral development.* San Francisco: Harper & Row.

Lawrence, J., & Blackburn, R. (1985). Faculty careers: Maturation, demographic, and historical effects. *Research in Higher Education, 22,* 135-154.

Lawton, H. (1988). *The psychohistorian's handbook.* New York: Psychohistory Press.

Lee, D. J. (Ed.). (1994). *Life and story: Autobiographies for a narrative psychology.* Westport, CT: Praeger.

Lemert, C. (1986). Whole life social theory. *Theory and Society, 15,* 431-442.

Levinas, E. (1991). *The Levinas reader* (S. Hand, Ed.). Cambridge, UK: Basil Blackwell.

Levinas, E., & Kearney, R. (1986). Dialogue with Levinas. In R. A. Cohen (Ed.), *Face to face with Levinas.* Albany: State University of New York Press. (Original work published 1974)

Lieblich, A., & Josselson, R. (Eds.). (1994). *Exploring identity and gender: The narrative study of lives* (Vol. 2). Thousand Oaks, CA: Sage.

Lyons, N. (1983). Two perspectives: On self, relationship, and morality. *Harvard Educational Review, 52,* 125-145.

Lyotard, J. F. (1984). *The postmodern condition: A report on knowledge* (G. Bennington & B. Massumi, Trans.). Minneapolis: University of Minnesota Press.

MacIntyre, A. (1981). *After virtue.* London: Duckworth.

Mair, M. (1988). Psychology as storytelling. *International Journal of Personal Construct Psychology, 1,* 125-138.

Marcia, J. E. (1966). Development and validation of ego-identity status. *Journal of Personality and Social Psychology, 3,* 551-558.

Margolis, J. (1991). *The truth about relativism.* Cambridge, UK: Basil Blackwell.

Markus, H., & Kitayama, S. (1991). Culture and the self: Implications for cognition, emotion, and motivation. *Psychological Review, 98,* 224-253.

Markus, H., & Nurius, P. S. (1986). Possible selves. *American Psychologist, 41,* 954-969.

Marsella, A., DeVos, G., & Hsu, F. L. K. (Eds.). (1985). *Culture and self: Asian and Western perspectives.* New York: Tavistock.

Marx, W. (1992). *Toward a phenomenological ethics: Ethos and the life-world.* Albany: State University of New York Press.

McAdams, D. P. (1985). *Power, intimacy, and the life story: Personological inquiries into identity.* Chicago: Dorsey. (Reprinted 1988 by Guilford)

McAdams, D. P., & Ochberg, R. L. (Eds.). (1988). Psychobiography and life narratives [Special issue]. *Journal of Personality, 56*(1).

McClelland, D. C. (1961). *The achieving society.* Princeton, NJ: Van Nostrand.

McMahon, M. (1995). *Engendering motherhood: Identity and self-transformation in women's lives.* New York: Guilford.

Meara, N. M., Schmidt, L. D., & Day, J. D. (1996). Principles and virtues: A foundation for ethical decisions, policies, and character. *The Counseling Psychologist, 24,* 4-77.

Morrow, R. A., & Brown, D. D. (1994). *Critical theory and methodology.* Thousand Oaks, CA: Sage.

Much, N. C., & Harré, R. (1994). How psychologies "secrete" moralities. *New Ideas in Psychology, 12,* 291-321.

Murray, H. A. (1938). *Explorations in personality.* New York: Oxford University Press.

Myerson, G. (1994). *Rhetoric, reason, and society: Rationality as dialogue.* Thousand Oaks, CA: Sage.

Neimeyer, G. J. (Ed.). (1993). *Casebook of constructivist assessment.* Newbury Park, CA: Sage.

Neimeyer, R., & Mahoney, M. (Eds.). (1995). *Constructivism in psychotherapy.* Washington, DC: American Psychological Association Books.

Newbrough, J. R. (1993). The post-modern professional: Reflective and generative practice. *Interamerican Journal of Psychology, 27,* 1-22.

O'Connell, A., & Russo, N. (1983). *Models of achievement: Reflections of eminent women in psychology.* New York: Columbia University Press.

Ochberg, R. L. (1988). Life stories and the psychosocial construction of careers. *Journal of Personality, 56,* 173-204.

Packer, M. J. (1992). The role of values in psychology and human development. In W. M. Kurtines, M. Azmitia, & J. L. Gewirtz (Eds.), *The role of values in psychology and human development* (pp. 256-280). New York: Wiley.

Parry, A., & Doan, R. E. (1994). *Story re-visions: Narrative therapy in the postmodern world.* New York: Guilford.

Pepper, S. (1942). *World hypotheses.* Berkeley: University of California Press.

Piaget, J. (1970). *Psychology and epistemology: Toward a theory of knowledge.* New York: Viking.

Pletsch, C. (1985). Subjectivity and biography. In S. H. Baron & C. Pletsch (Eds.), *Introspection in biography: The biographer's quest for self-awareness* (pp. 355-360). Hillsdale, NJ: Analytic Press.

Polkinghorne, D. E. (1988). *Narrative knowing and the human sciences.* Albany: State University of New York Press.

Prilleltensky, I. (1994). *The morals and politics of psychology: Psychological discourse and the status quo.* Albany: State University of New York Press.

Prilleltensky, I., & Walsh-Bowers, R. (1993). Psychology and the moral imperative. *Journal of Theoretical and Philosophical Psychology, 13,* 310-319.

Rabinow, P., & Sullivan, W. M. (Eds.). (1987). *Interpretive social science.* Berkeley: University of California Press.

Renza, L. A. (1980). The veto of imagination: A theory of autobiography. In J. Olney (Ed.), *Autobiography: Essays theoretical and critical.* Princeton, NJ: Princeton University Press.

Ricoeur, P. (1980). Existence and hermeneutics (K. McLaughlin, Trans.). In J. Bleicher (Ed.), *Contemporary hermeneutics: Hermeneutics as method, philosophy, and critique* (p. 107). London: Routledge & Kegan Paul.

Ricoeur, P. (1984). *Time and narrative* (Vol. 1). Chicago: University of Chicago Press.

Riegel, K. F. (1976). The dialectic of human development. *American Psychologist, 31,* 689-700.

Rogoff, B. (1990). *Apprenticeship in thinking: Cognitive development in social context.* New York: Oxford University Press.

Rorty, R. (1982). *Consequences of pragmatism.* Minneapolis: University of Minnesota Press.

Rosenwald, G. (1988). A theory of multiple-case research. *Journal of Personality, 56,* 239-264.

Runyun, W. M. (1983). Idiographic goals and methods in the study of lives. *Journal of Personality, 51,* 413-437.

Runyun, W. M. (1988). Progress in psychobiography. *Journal of Personality, 56,* 295-326.

Runyun, W. M. (1996). Psychobiography: Understanding one life at a time. *Contemporary Psychology, 41,* 984-987.

Sampson, E. (1988). The debate on individualism: Indigenous psychologies of the individual and their role in personal and societal functioning. *American Psychologist, 43,* 15-22.

Sampson, E. (1989). The challenge of social change for psychology: Globalization and psychology's theory of the person. *American Psychologist, 44,* 914-921.

Sampson, E. (1993). Identity politics: Challenges to psychology's understanding. *American Psychologist, 48,* 1219-1230.

Sarason, S. B. (1986). And what is the public interest? *American Psychologist, 41,* 899-905.

Sarason, S. B. (1988). *The making of an American psychologist: An autobiography.* San Francisco: Jossey-Bass.

Sarason, S. B. (1993). American psychology, and the needs for transcendence and community. *American Journal of Community Psychology, 21,* 185-202.

Sarbin, T. R. (Ed.). (1986). *Narrative psychology: The storied nature of human conduct.* New York: Praeger.

Schutz, A. (1966). *Studies in phenomenological philosophy.* The Hague, The Netherlands: Martinus Nijhoff.

Selznick, P. (1992). *The moral commonwealth.* Berkeley: University of California Press.

Shotter, J. (1984). *Social accountability and selfhood.* New York: Basil Blackwell.

Shotter, J., & Gergen, K. J. (Eds.). (1989). *Texts of identity.* London: Sage.

Shweder, R., Mahaputra, I., & Miller, J. G. (1987). Culture and moral development. In J. Kagan & S. Lamb (Eds.), *The emergence of morality in young children* (pp. 1-83). Chicago: University of Chicago Press.

Spence, D. P. (1982). *Narrative truth and historical truth.* New York: Norton.

Sternberg, R. J., & Lubart, T. I. (1996). Investing in creativity. *American Psychologist, 51,* 677-688.

Strozier, C. B. (Ed.). (1985). *Self psychology and the humanities: Reflections on a new psychoanalytic approach.* New York: Norton.

Tappan, M. B., & Brown, L. M. (1992). Hermeneutics and developmental psychology: Toward an ethic of interpretation. In W. M. Kurtines, M. Azmitia, & J. L. Gewirtz (Eds.), *The role of values in psychology and human development* (pp. 105-130). New York: John Wiley.

Taylor, C. (1989). *Sources of the self: The making of the modern identity.* Cambridge, MA: Harvard University Press.

Tierney, N. L. (1994). *Imagination and ethical ideals: Prospects for a unified philosophical and psychological understanding.* Albany: State University of New York Press.

Trainer, T. (1991). *The nature of morality: An introduction to the subjectivist perspective.* Brookfield, VT: Gower.

Vygotsky, L. (1978). *Mind in society* (M. Cole, Ed.). Cambridge, MA: Harvard University Press.

Wallace, D. B., & Gruber, H. E. (Eds.). (1989). *Creative people at work: Twelve cognitive case studies.* New York: Oxford University Press.

Wallach, M. A., & Wallach, L. (1990). *Rethinking goodness.* Albany: State University of New York Press.

Weiland, S. (1994). Writing the academic life: Faculty careers in narrative perspective. *Review of Higher Education, 17,* 395-422.

Weiland, S. (1995). Life history and academic work: The career of Professor G. In R. Josselson & A. Lieblich (Eds.), *Interpreting experience: The narrative study of lives* (Vol. 3, pp. 59-99). Thousand Oaks, CA: Sage.

Wertsch, J. V. (1991). *Voices of the mind: A sociocultural approach to mediated action.* New York: Cambridge University Press.

White, M., & Epston, D. (1990). *Narrative means to therapeutic ends.* New York: Norton.

Winter, D. G. (1973). *The power motive.* New York: Free Press.

Index

Action, 12, 17, 37, 38, 119-120, 195,
    202, 205. *See also* Moral
    models of, 10
    theories of, 12
Agency, 6, 11, 14, 16, 159, 197, 199. *See
    also* Ethics; Moral
Arasteh, A., 5
Arasteh, J., 5
Aristotle, 11-12
Autobiographical:
    account, 179, 196, 199
    life line, 20-21, 176, 178
    methodology, 25, 175-176, 184
    See also Biographical
Autonomy, 17, 184, 194, 198

Bandura, A., 10
Biographical, 4, 176. *See also*
    Autobiographical
Blaug, R., 204
Bromley, D., 23
Bruner, J., 4, 19, 22

Campbell, D., 18-19, 23
Cohen, D., 18

Colby A., 17
Collective, 11, 13, 190, 194-197. *See
    also* Communitarianism;
    Community
Commitment, 4, 200. *See also* Moral
Communitarianism, 198-199, 203, 207
Community, 7-8, 11, 194-195, 202, 203
    in contemporary life, 7
    psychological sense of, 7
    social, 7, 197-198
    symbolic, 21, 208
Consciousness:
    collective, 13, 192
    participatory mode of, 7, 191
    state of, 7, 184, 208
Constructionism, 15, 17, 201. *See also*
    Creativity; Identity; Narrative;
    Social
Contextualism, 24, 176, 202
Creativity, 5, 19, 176, 192-195. *See also*
    Constructionism; Identity;
    Narrative; Social
    conditions of, 4, 194, 198
    process of, 18, 194
    cultural forms of, 4, 194
    cultural roots of, 5
    theory and research of, 5

About the Authors

Elizabeth M. Altmaier was born 1952 in New York City. A fellow of the Division of Counseling Psychology of the American Psychological Association and the American Psychological Society, she is the author of 3 books, 10 book chapters, 9 book reviews, and more than 70 articles. She was recognized by the American Psychological Association with the Distinguished Contributions to Education and Training in Psychology Award in 1994. She has been the principal investigator in research projects in health psychology that have received major grant awards from the National Institutes of Health.

Leo Goldman was born 1920 in Kingston, New York. He is the author of 2 books, 4 book chapters, 50 articles, 15 book reviews, and various research and development products. He has given more than 40 presentations at professional meetings. A Fellow and former president of the Division of Counseling Psychology of the American Psychological Association as well as trustee/diplomate of the American Board of Examiners in professional psychology, he has held many offices and provided leadership in the profession, especially in counselor education.

Lisa Tsoi Hoshmand was born in 1947 in Hong Kong. She is the author or coauthor/coeditor of 3 books, 2 book chapters, 5 book reviews, and 26 journal articles, and has given presentations at more than 20 professional meetings. She is associate editor of the *Journal of Theoretical and Philosophical Psychology* and has served on several editorial boards, including those of *Contemporary Psychology, Journal of Community Psychology, Journal of Constructivist Psychology, Journal of Counseling Psychology,* and *The Counseling Psychologist.*

Barbara K. Keogh was born 1925 in Glendale, California. The editor of five volumes in the series Advances in Special Education, she is the author of 5 coauthored or coedited books and more than 150 journal articles. She has provided leadership on the Council for Exceptional Children and for the UCLA-U.S. Office of Education Training Program in Special Education. In her work on learning disabilities and special education, she had been the recipient of a number of major awards and distinctions.

Donald Peterson was born 1923 in Pillager, Minnesota. A Fellow of the Division of Clinical Psychology of the American Psychological Association, he is the author or coauthor of 5 books, 50 journal articles, and more than 20 book chapters. He was the recipient of the APA Award for Distinguished Professional Contributions to Applied Psychology as a Professional Practice (1983). His leadership in developing the PsyD model and standards of professional training was recognized by the APA Award for Distinguished Career Contribution to Education and Training in Psychology (1989).

Jill N. Reich was born 1945 in Lowell, Massachusetts. She is the author or coauthor of 1 book, 4 book chapters, more than 30 journal articles, and numerous conference papers and technical reports. An educator, researcher, administrator, and consultant, and the recipient of several major grants and awards, she has been recognized by the American Psychological Association with the Centennial Award for Early Career Contributions to Education and Training (1992) and the Distinguished Contributions to Education in Psychology Award (1993).

Derald Wing Sue was born 1942 in Portland, Oregon. Cited as one of the most influential researchers in the area of multicultural counseling, he is the author of 7 books, 15 book chapters, and 38 journal articles. He has six media productions to his credit and has given numerous professional presentations and workshops. A Fellow of Divisions 1, 17, and 45 of the American Psychological Association, the American Psychological Society, and the American Association of Applied and Preventive Psychology, he has been the recipient of awards for distinguished contributions to cross-cultural theory and practice from the Third World Counselors Association, the Asian American Psychological Association, the Society for the Psychological Study of Ethnic Minority Issues, the Association of Multicultural Counseling and Development, and various universities.

Roland G. Tharp was born 1930 in La Marque, Texas. He is the author or coauthor of 4 books, 21 book chapters, 70 journal articles, and more than 100 conference papers and technical reports. A diplomate of the American Board of Examiners in Professional Psychology, he has maintained a multifaceted career, with contributions to psychology, education, literature, and the arts. He was the recipient of the Grawemeyer Award in Education in 1993 and has received other honors for scholarly achievement and excellence in teaching. His literary contributions include a book of poems and 47 poems, short fiction, and essays. He was the recipient of a number of literary awards, including the Grand Prize in the Atlantic Monthly National Contest for Essay in 1956, the Robert Frost Fellowship in Poetry in 1960, and the Arizona Quarterly Prize for Fiction in 1964. He also has been the producer, writer, and director of 6 films, video, and photography-poetry and poetry-drama. He received the Silver Monitor Award from the International Television Association in 1985 and the American Film Magazine Award in the Hawaii International Film Festival in 1990.